The VOCABULARY GUIDE *to* BIBLICAL HEBREW

Also by Miles Van Pelt and Gary Pratico

Basics of Biblical Hebrew Grammar
Basics of Biblical Hebrew Workbook

The

VOCABULARY
GUIDE
to
BIBLICAL
HEBREW

MILES V.
VAN PELT
and
GARY D.
PRATICO

ZONDERVAN™

GRAND RAPIDS, MICHIGAN 49530 USA

ZONDERVAN™

The Vocabulary Guide to Biblical Hebrew
Copyright © 2003 by Miles Van Pelt and Gary Pratico

Requests for information should be addressed to:
Zondervan, *Grand Rapids, Michigan 49530*

Library of Congress Cataloging-in-Publication Data

Van Pelt, Miles V., 1969–
 The vocabulary guide to biblical Hebrew / Miles V. Van Pelt, Gary D. Pratico.
  p. cm.
 Includes bibliographical references and index.
 ISBN 0-310-25072-2
  1. Hebrew language—Glossaries, vocabularies, etc. 2. Hebrew language—Word frequency.
 3. Hebrew language—Grammar. 3. Bible. O.T.—Language, style. I. Practico, Gary Davis.
 II. Title.
 PJ4845.V36 2003
 492.4'82421—dc21

                     2003008438
                      CIP

Interior design by Miles Van Pelt

Printed in the United States of America

---

03 04 05 06 07 08 09 /❖ ML/ 10 9 8 7 6 5 4 3 2

To Laurie

רַבּוֹת בָּנוֹת עָשׂוּ חָיִל וְאַתְּ עָלִית עַל־כֻּלָּנָה

Prov 31:29

To Mary

Prov 5:18b

וּשְׂמַח מֵאֵשֶׁת נְעוּרֶךָ

"I do"

Prov 5:19b

בְּאַהֲבָתָהּ תִּשְׁגֶּה תָמִיד

"I am"

כּוֹשֵׁל יְקִימוּן מִלֶּיךָ

Job 4:4a

TABLE OF CONTENTS

PREFACE

One of the essential tasks in learning any language is the memorization of vocabulary. Regardless of the language, vocabulary memorization is required of the beginning, intermediate, and advanced student. Ideally, the study of vocabulary should focus on high frequency words but, in the setting of most language courses, it is not always possible for a student to learn only frequency vocabulary. Nevertheless, the gradual mastery of the most common words in Hebrew is an essential part in becoming proficient with this biblical language. *The Vocabulary Guide to Biblical Hebrew* was written for this purpose. This volume presents, in a number of different ways, all of the Hebrew vocabulary of the Old Testament that occurs ten or more times.

In the preparation of this volume, we utilized a number of excellent resources. For the creation of initial lists and the calculation of frequency statistics, we used the computer software *Accordance* with the *GRAMCORD Hebrew MT* (Groves-Wheeler Westminster Hebrew Morphology) database. It is distributed by Oaktree Software, Inc. At this point, it will be appropriate to note that minor discrepancies in frequency numbers are observable throughout the various lexical sources. Except for occasional and minor adjustments for the sake of consistency, we have followed those frequency numbers derived from *Accordance* – which is, in our opinion, the best resource of its kind. In addition to *Accordance*, the lexical resources commonly referred to as BDB, *HALOT* (or KB), and *NIDOTTE* were used in our shaping and presentation of a Hebrew word's range of meaning. Full bibliographic information for these lexical resources is provided at the end of this section, following the introduction.

We are indebted to a number of individuals and institutions. We would like to thank Zondervan for their support in the preparation of this volume – especially Verlyn Verbrugge and Jack Kragt. We also recognize Bob Buller and Lee Fields for their editorial work and Paul Sumner for his preparation of the index. Special thanks are due to Jonathan Kline for his expert work in numerous aspects of the preparation of this volume for print. Finally, we are indebted to our families, and especially our wives, whose encouragement, support and love have sustained us in our work.

Miles V. Van Pelt
Gary D. Pratico
April, 2003

INTRODUCTION

We all recognize that vocabulary memorization can be one of the most painful aspects of language acquisition. Most students who complete their first year of Hebrew language instruction resonate with the words of Job 19:2, "How long will you torment me and crush me with *words*?" Nevertheless, few things will hinder a student's proficiency and enjoyment of a language more than an inadequate stock of basic vocabulary. In fact, those who would minimize the issue of vocabulary memorization will almost certainly struggle with proficiency in the language and find it difficult to fully realize the benefits of studying and reading Hebrew. Stated plainly, vocabulary memorization is vitally important.

Let the student be encouraged, however. A little vocabulary can go a long way in providing a good measure of competence with reading Hebrew. By memorizing only the first fifty words in the frequency vocabulary list, students will be equipped to recognize almost 55% of the total words that occur in the Hebrew Old Testament (419,687). Students who master the 641 words that occur fifty or more times will be able to recognize over 80% of all words. Finally, those who are brave enough to master all 1,903 words in the frequency vocabulary list will be equipped to recognize almost 90% of all words that occur in the Hebrew Old Testament. In other words, memorization of only 22% of the total stock of Hebrew vocabulary (1903 out of 8679 total lexical items) will enable a student to recognize 90% of all words appearing in the Hebrew Bible. The remaining 6,776 lexical items occur only 49,914 total times, a figure significantly less than the number of occurrences of the Hebrew conjunction וֹ (and).

A glance at the table of contents will reveal that this volume is composed of a number of different vocabulary lists. The first list is the most important. Entitled *Hebrew Words Arranged by Frequency*, this list contains all of the Hebrew words that occur ten or more times in the Old Testament (excluding proper nouns which are located in list 3a). This list is arranged by frequency, beginning with the most frequent Hebrew words and progressing to those that occur only ten times. The entries in this list are sequentially numbered from 1-1903. These numbers are a helpful point of reference and provide a convenient system for breaking the words into discrete groups for memorization. Please note that this is the only list in the book that contains all of the Hebrew words (excluding proper nouns) that occur ten or more times. All subsequent lists contain only parts of this list, arranged in various ways in order to provide a number of venues for memorization, review, and reference.

The format of each entry in the vocabulary lists is arranged as follows. The Hebrew word appears in the left column. In the larger, right-hand column, lexical and other related information is provided. There is sometimes an abbreviation that appears in parentheses, identifying the part of speech or another point of grammatical information, such as gender and/or number. Note that not all entries have been identified by part of speech. Verbs will be easy to recognize because each verbal entry begins with an abbreviation that identifies the verbal stem, such as Q (Qal) or Ni (Niphal). Following any initial abbreviations, the student will find a brief selection of translation values that will provide a sense of the word's "semantic range" or "semantic field." The selection of translation values is based largely on frequency of occurrence. With verbal entries, it is especially important to observe that we have not included definitions for derived stems that occur fewer than ten times with a particular verbal root. It is also worthy of note that a Qal stem definition may be provided as a point of reference even if the Qal stem is not attested more than ten times with the verbal root.

Following the selection of translation values, we have oftentimes provided the spelling of various inflected forms or grammatical constructions. In each case, these forms have been provided because of the frequency with which a particular form or construction appears in the Hebrew Old Testament. We have been careful to provide the spellings of irregular plural (see entries #22 and #23) and irregular construct (see entry #25) forms. Additionally, nouns, prepositions, and others words are sometimes shown with pronominal suffixes (see entry #16). We have also included, in selected instances, defective spellings (see entry #97), full or *plene* spellings (see entry #12), and occasionally, special or significant uses of a particular word (see entries #107 and #132). At times, we will also designate the frequency with which an alternative spelling occurs (see entries #54 and #72) in order to provide the student with a sense of the distribution and significance of that particular spelling. Finally, entries conclude with a number in parentheses that identifies how many times a word occurs in the Old Testament. Occasionally, other information may follow, such as a reference to a related or cognate form (see entries #50, #51 and #52).

DISTINGUISHING BETWEEN IDENTICAL ROOTS

While verbal entries are quite straightforward in the format of their presentation, the reader must be alerted to how we have handled the numerous instances of verbal roots that are spelled the same. Traditionally, standard lexicons and vocabulary guides have designated verbal roots having identical spelling with Roman numerals such as I שָׁבַר (to smash, shatter) and II שָׁבַר (to buy grain). In this volume, we have opted not to designate identical roots in this way. The rationale for departure from this widely-practiced system of designation was based, in large measure, on the frequent inconsistencies between and within standard lexicons with respect to the assignment of Roman numerals. Additionally, most Hebrew students and, even a few instructors, give little attention to the memorization of the Roman numeral designations that are assigned to identical roots. With a view to simplicity of presentation, notably for the beginning student, identical verbal roots and other words that appear in the "frequency" list have been cross-referenced (see entries #280 and #1238). Additionally, we have provided a catalogue of all "identical" Hebrew words that occur more than ten times (see word list 5).

UNDERSTANDING AND USING THE DIFFERENT LISTS

In any number of configurations, students can utilize the first major list of frequency vocabulary to complement their Hebrew language studies. For the beginning student, an appropriate level of vocabulary mastery for a single academic year would be those words that occur fifty times or more. The 642 words that fall into this category could be spread throughout an academic year. In an academic year with ten weeks in each of the two semesters, a mere 32 words per week would equip a student with this level of vocabulary. In those institutions with a greater number of weeks in each semester, fewer words per week would be required to reach this modest goal. Some will prefer a less rigorous course of study and others will want to be more aggressive. Either way, a simple calculation of the number of words to memorize in the time allotted for memorization will accommodate any academic schedule or personal aspiration.

The second major list in this volume is an alphabetical listing of words that share a common root. This type of list is sometimes called a "cognate" list. In language study, the term "cognate" refers to words that are related by derivation. For example, the verb מָלַךְ means "to reign" or "to be(come) king." Understanding the idea of a verbal root as a grammatical abstraction, we can say that there are a number of forms that derive from the root מלך, such as מֶלֶךְ (king), מַלְכָּה (queen) and מַלְכוּת (kingdom). The essential nuances of "being king," "reigning" or "exercising royal authority" are inherent in the meanings of each of these derived or cognate forms. They are etymologically related to one another and to the triconsonantal root מלך. Recognizing and understanding these types of relationships are of great benefit for building vocabulary. Please note that this list, together with all of the following lists, do not contain all of the Hebrew words that occur more than ten times. Only the "frequency" list has all 1,903 words that fall into this category. All other lists (except the list of proper nouns) contain only portions of the frequency list, organized and presented in various ways.

Following the listing of words by their common root, there are six smaller lists that relate to non-verbal forms. In these lists, we have grouped certain categories of words to facilitate review, reference, and testing. Those lists that contain nouns with common gender and endingless feminine singular nouns will provide students with an opportunity to focus on specific word categories that are often troublesome for the beginning student.

There are twelve lists that are devoted to the organization and presentation of verbs. We have provided an alphabetical listing of all Hebrew verbs that occur more than ten times. We have also provided a list that presents information related to the appearance of certain verbal roots in the derived stems. Additionally, there are ten lists that catalogue (alphabetically) the most common weak verb classes.

Our final list includes words that are spelled the same but have different meanings. These words are a perennial source of confusion to students and we hope that this list will provide a good starting point for overcoming this difficult aspect of language study.

The appendices organize and present selected statistics that relate to the verbal system and should be instructive to anyone who works with this language.

ADDITIONAL RESOURCES

In addition to this vocabulary guide, the authors are producing boxed sets of vocabulary cards that will include all 1,903 words (excluding proper nouns) that occur ten or more times in the Hebrew Bible. These vocabulary cards will be available for sale through the authors' website at *www.basicsofbiblicalhebrew.com*.

We will also be offering an electronic version of the vocabulary guide. With it, students will be able to hear, sort, practice, and review their vocabulary on the computer in an interactive environment. This resource will also be available through our website at *www.basicsofbiblicalhebrew.com*.

BIBLIOGRAPHY
OF WORKS CONSULTED

Andersen, F. I., and A. D. Forbes. *The Vocabulary of the Old Testament.* Rome: Pontifical Biblical Institute, 1992.

_____ . *Spelling in the Hebrew Bible.* Rome: Pontifical Biblical Institute, 1986.

Brown, F., S. R. Driver, and C. A. Briggs. *The New Brown-Driver-Briggs-Gesenius Hebrew and English Lexicon.* Peabody: Hendrickson, 1979.

Holladay, W. L. *A Concise Hebrew and Aramaic Lexicon of the Old Testament.* Grand Rapids: Eerdmans, 1988.

Köhler, L., W. Baumgartner, and J. Stamm. *The Hebrew and Aramaic Lexicon of the Old Testament.* Study Edition. 2 vols. Translated and edited by M. E. J. Richardson. Leiden: E. J. Brill, 2001.

Landes, G. M. *Building Your Hebrew Vocabulary: Learning Words by Frequency and Cognate.* Atlanta: Society of Biblical Literature, 2001.

Mitchel, L. A. *A Student's Vocabulary for Biblical Hebrew and Aramaic.* Grand Rapids: Zondervan, 1984.

VanGemeren, W. A., ed. *The New International Dictionary of Old Testament Theology and Exegesis.* Grand Rapids: Zondervan, 1997.

Accordance Bible Software with the GRAMCORD Hebrew MT (Groves-Wheeler Westminster Hebrew Morphology) database. Distributed by Oaktree Software, Inc. (www.oaksoft.com)

ABBREVIATIONS AND SYMBOLS

Adjective	adj		Negative	neg
Adverb	adv		Niphal	Ni
Collective	coll		Noun	n
Common	c		Participle	Ptc
Conjunction	conj		Passive	pass
Construct	cstr		Personal	pers
Demonstrative	dmstr		Piel	Pi
Dual	d		Plural	p
Feminine	f		Prefix	pref
Hiphil	Hi		Preposition	prep
Hithpael	Hith		Pronoun	pron
Hophal	Hoph		Pual	Pu
Idiomatically	idiom		Qal	Q
Interrogative	interrog		Relative	rel
Infinitive	Inf		Singular	s
Literally	lit		Suffix	suff
Masculine	m			

\# preceeding a number (#718), identifies an entry in the frequency list

x following a number (816x), indicates the number of times a particular inflected form occurs

˘ located over a Hebrew letter (אֶ֫רֶץ), identifies Hebrew words with penultimate stress (next-to-last syllable)

WORD LIST 1

HEBREW WORDS
ARRANGED BY FREQUENCY

The following list contains all Hebrew words, except proper nouns, that occur ten times or more in the Hebrew Old Testament. Words are arranged by frequency – from the most to the least frequent. There are 1,903 words. In this list, for the sake of convenience and reference, each word is numbered sequentially.

1	וְ	(conj) and, but, also, even, then (50,524)
2	הַ ·	(definite article) the (24,058)
3	לְ	(prep) to, toward, for (20,321)
4	בְּ	(prep) in, at, with, by, against (15,559)
5	אֵת	(definite direct object marker) not translated; also spelled אֶת־; (with 3ms suff) אֹתוֹ (10,978); compare with אֵת (#50)
6	מִן	(prep) from, out of; (with 3ms suff) מִמֶּנּוּ; (prefixed to a word) · מִ (7,592)
7	עַל	(prep) on, upon, on account of, according to (5,777)
8	אֶל־	(prep) to, toward, in, into; (with 3ms suff) אֵלָיו (5,518)
9	אֲשֶׁר	(rel pron) who, that, which (5,503)
10	כֹּל	all, each, every; (cstr) כָּל־ (5,415)
11	אָמַר	(Q) to say, mention, think; (Ni) be said, be called; (Hi) declare, proclaim (5,316)
12	לֹא	(neg particle) no, not; also spelled לוֹא (5,189)
13	בֵּן	son; (ms cstr) בֶּן־; (mp) בָּנִים; (mp cstr) בְּנֵי (4,941)
14	כִּי	that, because; (adversative) but, except; (emphatic) indeed, truly (4,487); כִּי־אִם but, except, only
15	הָיָה	(Q) to be, become, take place, happen, occur; (Ni) be done, be brought about, come to pass, occur (3,576)
16	כְּ	(prep) as, like, according to; (with 2ms suff) כָּמוֹךָ (3,053)
17	עָשָׂה	(Q) to do, make, create, acquire, prepare, carry out; (Ni) be done, be made (2,632)
18	אֱלֹהִים	God, gods (2,602)
19	בּוֹא	(Q) to go in, enter, come to, come upon, arrive; (Hi) bring (in), come (in); (Hoph) be brought (2,592)
20	מֶלֶךְ	king, ruler (2,530)

21	אֶרֶץ	(fs) land, earth, ground (2,505)
22	יוֹם	day; (mp) יָמִים (2,301)
23	אִישׁ	man, husband, each; (mp) אֲנָשִׁים (2,188)
24	פָּנִים	(cp) face, front; (cp cstr with prep לְ) לִפְנֵי (1102x) before, in front of (2,126)
25	בַּיִת	(ms) house, household; (ms cstr) בֵּית (1,497x); (mp) בָּתִּים (2,047)
26	נָתַן	(Q) to give, put, set; (Ni) be given (2,014)
27	עַם	people; (mp) עַמִּים (1,869)
28	יָד	(fs) hand; (metaphorically) side, power (1,627)
29	הָלַךְ	(Q) to go, walk (metaphorically, behave), die, pass away; (Pi) go, walk; (Hith) walk about, move to and fro (1,554)
30	דָּבָר	word, matter, thing (1,454)
31	הוּא	(3ms pers pron) he, it; (ms dmstr pron and adj) that (1,398)
32	רָאָה	(Q) to see, perceive, understand; (Ni) appear, become visible; (Pu) be seen; (Hi) let or cause someone to see (something), show someone (something) (1,311)
33	עַד	(prep) until, as far as, during (1,263); compare with עֹד (#678)
34	אָב	father, ancestor; (ms cstr) אֲבִי; (mp) אָבוֹת (1,210)
35	זֶה	(ms dmstr pron and adj) this (1,178)
36	שָׁמַע	(Q) to hear, listen to, understand, obey; (Ni) be heard; (Hi) cause to hear, proclaim (1,165)
37	דָּבַר	(Q) to speak (rare in Q); (Pi) speak to, with or about (someone or something) (1,136)
38	יָשַׁב	(Q) to sit (down), remain, dwell, inhabit; (Hi) cause to sit or dwell, settle (a city) (1,088)
39	עִיר	(fs) city, town; (fp) עָרִים (1,088)

40   יָצָא   (Q) to go out, go forth, come out, come forth; (Hi)
             cause to go out or come out, lead out, bring forth
             (1,076)

41   שׁוּב   (Q) to turn back, return, go back, come back, turn
             away from; (Hi) cause to return, bring back, lead
             back, give back, restore; (Polel) bring back, restore
             (1,075)

42   אִם   if (1,070); כִּי־אִם but, except, only

43   הִנֵּה   behold, look; (with 1cs suff) הִנְנִי (1,061)

44   עִם   (prep) with, together with; (with 3ms suff) עִמּוֹ
             (1,048)

45   אֶחָד   one; (fs) אַחַת (976)

46   לָקַח   (Q) to take, grasp, capture, seize, lay hold of, accept,
             receive; (Ni) be captured, be taken away; (Pu) be
             taken (away) (967)

47   יָדַע   (Q) to know, have understanding, notice, observe,
             be(come) acquainted with, know sexually (have
             intercourse with); (Ni) be(come) known, reveal
             oneself; (Hi) make known (something to someone),
             inform (956)

48   עַיִן   (cs) eye, spring; (cs cstr) עֵין; (cd cstr) עֵינֵי (900)

49   עָלָה   (Q) to go up, ascend; (Ni) be taken up; (Hi) bring or
             lead up or out, offer up (sacrifice) (894)

50   אֵת   (prep) with, beside; also spelled אֶת־; (with 3ms suff)
             אִתּוֹ (890); compare with אֵת (#5)

51   שָׁנָה   year; (fp) שָׁנִים (878); compare with שָׁנָה (#1534)

52   אֲנִי   (1cs pers pron) I (874); compare with אָנֹכִי (#136)

53   שֵׁם   name, reputation (864)

54   לֵב   heart, mind, will; (mp) לִבּוֹת; (ms) also spelled (252x)
             לֵבָב (854)

55   שָׁלַח   (Q) to send, stretch out; (Pi) send, stretch out, send
             away, expel, let go free; (Pu) be sent away (off) (847)

56	מוּת	(Q) to die; (Hi) kill, put to death; (Hoph) be killed, suffer death (845)
57	שָׁם	there, then, at that time (835)
58	אָכַל	(Q) to eat, consume; (Ni) be eaten, be consumed; (Hi) feed, cause to eat (820)
59	עֶבֶד	slave, servant (803)
60	אַיִן	(particle of nonexistence) is not, are not; most often spelled (747x) אֵין nothing (790); compare with אַיִן (#1361)
61	אִשָּׁה	woman, wife; (fs cstr) אֵשֶׁת; (fp) נָשִׁים (781)
62	אָדוֹן	lord, master; (of God 439x) אֲדֹנָי Lord (774)
63	גַּם	also, even (769)
64	שְׁנַיִם	(md) two; (fd) שְׁתַּיִם (769)
65	נֶפֶשׁ	(fs) soul, life, person, neck, throat (757)
66	כֹּהֵן	priest; (mp) כֹּהֲנִים (750)
67	אַתָּה	(2ms pers pron) you (749)
68	אֵלֶּה	(cp dmstr pron and adj) these (744)
69	כֵּן	so, thus (741); compare with כֵּן (#1122, #1783)
70	קָרָא	(Q) to call, summon, proclaim, announce, shout, read aloud, give a name to; (Ni) be called, be summoned, be proclaimed (739); compare with קָרָא (#301)
71	אַל	(neg particle) no, not (729)
72	אַחֲרֵי	(prep) after, behind; also spelled (97x) אַחַר (718)
73	דֶּרֶךְ	(cs) way, road, journey (712)
74	הֲ	(interrog particle) prefixed to the first word of a question (664)
75	נָשָׂא	(Q) to lift, carry, raise, bear (load or burden), take (away); (Ni) be carried, be lifted up, be exalted; (Pi) lift up, exalt; (Hith) lift oneself up, exalt oneself (659)
76	אָח	brother; (ms cstr) אֲחִי; (mp) אַחִים (629)

77	קוּם	(Q) to rise, arise, get up, stand (up); (Hi) set up, erect, put up, cause to arise, establish (627)
78	שָׁלֹשׁ	(ms) three; (fs) שְׁלֹשָׁה; (mp) שְׁלֹשִׁים thirty (606)
79	זֹאת	(fs dmstr pron and adj) this (605)
80	רֹאשׁ	head, top, chief; (mp) רָאשִׁים (600); compare with רֹאשׁ (#1735)
81	שִׂים	(Q) to set (up), put, place, lay (upon), set in place, establish, confirm; also spelled שׂוּם (588)
82	בַּת	daughter; (fp) בָּנוֹת (587); compare with בַּת (#1616)
83	מֵאָה	hundred; (fp) מֵאוֹת; (fd) מָאתַיִם two hundred (583)
84	מַיִם	water; (md cstr) מֵי (585)
85	כֹּה	thus, here (577)
86	מָה	(interrog pron) what? also spelled מַה and מֶה (571)
87	גּוֹי	nation, people; (mp) גּוֹיִם (567)
88	הֵם	(3mp pers pron) they; (mp dmstr) those; also spelled הֵמָּה (565)
89	הַר	mountain, hill, hill country; (mp) הָרִים (558)
90	עָבַר	(Q) to pass over, pass through, pass by, cross; (Hi) cause to pass over, bring over, cause or allow to pass (through), cause to pass through fire, sacrifice (553)
91	אָדָם	man, mankind (546)
92	טוֹב	(adj) good, pleasant (530); compare with טוֹב (#714)
93	גָּדוֹל	(adj) great, big, large (527)
94	עָמַד	(Q) to stand (up), take one's stand, stand still; (Hi) station, set up, set in position, appoint, designate (524)
95	תַּחַת	(prep) under, below, instead of (510)
96	חָמֵשׁ	five; (fs) חֲמִשָּׁה; (mp) חֲמִשִּׁים fifty (508)
97	קוֹל	voice, sound, noise; also spelled קֹל (505)

98	נָכָה	(Hi) to strike, smite, beat, strike dead, destroy, injure; (Hoph) be struck down dead, be beaten (501)
99	יָלַד	(Q) to bear (children), give birth, bring forth, beget; (Ni) be born; (Pi) help at birth, serve as midwife; (Pu) be born; (Hi) beget, become the father of (499)
100	פֶּה	(ms) mouth, opening; (ms cstr) פִּי (498)
101	אֶלֶף	thousand; (md) אַלְפַּיִם two thousand (496); compare with אֶלֶף (#1749)
102	צָוָה	(Pi) to command, give an order, charge; (Pu) be ordered, be told, receive a command (496)
103	עֶשֶׂר	ten; (fs) עֲשָׂרָה; (mp) עֶשְׂרִים twenty, twentieth (492)
104	הִיא	(3fs pers pron) she, it; (fs dmstr pron and adj) that; also spelled הוּא in the Pentateuch (491)
105	עוֹד	again, still, as long as (491)
106	שֶׁבַע	(ms) seven; (fs) שִׁבְעָה; (mp) שִׁבְעִים seventy (490)
107	צָבָא	(cs) host, army, war, service; (cp) צְבָאוֹת (487); יְהוָה צְבָאוֹת "Lord of Hosts;" compare with צָבָא (#1589)
108	קֹדֶשׁ	holiness, something that is holy; (mp) קָדָשִׁים (470)
109	שָׁמַר	(Q) to watch (over), guard, keep, observe, preserve, protect, take care of; (Ni) to be kept, be protected, be on one's guard (469)
110	מָצָא	(Q) to find (out), reach, obtain, achieve; (Ni) be found, be found sufficient (457)
111	אַרְבַּע	four; (fs) אַרְבָּעָה; (mp) אַרְבָּעִים forty (455)
112	עוֹלָם	forever, everlasting, ancient; also spelled עֹלָם (439)
113	נָפַל	(Q) to fall, fall prostrate, fall upon; (Hi) cause to fall, bring to ruin (435)
114	עַתָּה	now, after all, at last, then (435)
115	מִשְׁפָּט	judgment, decision, ordinance, law, custom, manner (425)
116	מִי	(interrog pron) who? (424)

117	שַׂר	chief official, ruler, prince (421)
118	שָׁמַיִם	heaven, sky (421)
119	רַב	(adj) great, many; (mp) רַבִּים (419); compare with רֹב (#974)
120	חֶרֶב	(fs) sword (413)
121	בֵּין	(prep) between (409)
122	נָא	(emphatic particle) please, now, surely (405)
123	כֶּסֶף	silver, money (403)
124	מִזְבֵּחַ	altar; (mp) מִזְבְּחוֹת (403)
125	מָקוֹם	place, location; (mp) מְקֹמוֹת (401)
126	יָם	sea; (mp) יַמִּים (396)
127	זָהָב	gold (392)
128	יָרַד	(Q) to go down, come down, descend; (Hi) bring down, lead down (382)
129	רוּחַ	(cs) spirit, wind, breath; (cp) רוּחוֹת (378)
130	בָּנָה	(Q) to build (up), rebuild, build (establish) a family; (Ni) be built, get a child from (with מִן) (377)
131	אֵשׁ	(cs) fire (376)
132	נְאֻם	utterance, announcement, revelation (376); נְאֻם־יְהוָה "says (declares) the Lord"
133	שַׁעַר	gate (373)
134	נָגַד	(Hi) to tell, announce, report, declare, inform; (Hoph) be told, be announced, be reported (371)
135	דָּם	blood; (mp) דָּמִים bloodshed (361)
136	אָנֹכִי	(1cs pers pron) I (359); compare with אֲנִי (#52)
137	רָעָה	evil, wickedness, calamity, disaster (354); compare with רַע (#153), רָעָה (#255), and רֹעַ (#1310)
138	מָלַךְ	(Q) to be(come) king or queen, reign, rule; (Hi) make someone king or queen, install someone as king or queen (350)

139	אֹהֶל	tent (348)
140	לֶחֶם	bread, food (340)
141	סָבִיב	around, about; (substantive) surroundings, circuit; (fp) סְבִיבוֹת (338)
142	עָשָׂר	ten; (fs) עֶשְׂרֵה; used in constructions to express numerals eleven to nineteen; אַחַד עָשָׂר eleven, etc. (337)
143	עֵץ	tree, wood (330)
144	שָׂדֶה	(ms) field, pasture land (329)
145	בָּרַךְ	(Q Pass Ptc) blessed, praised, adored; (Pi) bless, praise (327)
146	כְּלִי	vessel, implement, weapon; (mp) כֵּלִים; (mp cstr) כְּלֵי (325)
147	אוֹ	(conj) or (321)
148	בְּתוֹךְ	(prep) in the midst (middle) of, inside (319); combination of (prep) בְּ and (n) תָּוֶךְ (middle, center); also מִתּוֹךְ (68x) and אֶל־תּוֹךְ (22x)
149	מִלְחָמָה	war, battle, struggle (319)
150	יָרֵא	(Q) to fear, be afraid, be in awe of, reverence, hold in deference; (Ni) be feared, be held in honor (317); compare with יְרֵא (#539)
151	נָבִיא	prophet (317)
152	עָנָה	(Q) to answer, respond, reply, testify; (Ni) be answered, receive answer (316); compare with עָנָה (#449, #1467)
153	רַע	(adj) bad, evil, wicked, of little worth; also spelled רָע (312); compare with רָעָה (#137)
154	מִשְׁפָּחָה	family, clan (304)
155	פָּקַד	(Q) to attend, attend to, pay attention to, take care of, miss (someone), muster, number, appoint, visit; (Ni) be missed, be visited, be appointed; (Hi) appoint, entrust (304)

156   מְאֹד   very, exceedingly (300)

157   חַטָּאת   sin, sin offering; (fs cstr) חַטַּאת; (fp cstr) חַטֹּאות and חַטֹּאת (298)

158   סוּר   (Q) to turn aside, turn off, leave (off), desist; (Hi) remove, take away, get rid of (298)

159   עֵת   (cs) time, point of time; (cp) עִתִּים and עִתּוֹת (296)

160   חָזַק   (Q) to be(come) strong, grow firm, have courage; (Pi) make firm, make strong, strengthen; (Hi) strengthen, seize, grasp, take hold of; (Hith) strengthen oneself, show oneself as strong or courageous (290)

161   כָּרַת   (Q) to cut off, cut down, make a covenant (with בְּרִית); (Ni) be cut off (down); (Hi) cut off, eliminate, destroy, exterminate (289)

162   עָבַד   (Q) to work, serve, toil, till, cultivate (289)

163   בְּרִית   covenant (287)

164   עֹלָה   whole burnt offering (sacrifice that is completely burned); also spelled עוֹלָה (286)

165   אֹיֵב   enemy; also spelled אוֹיֵב (285)

166   אַתֶּם   (2mp pers pron) you (283)

167   חֹדֶשׁ   month, new moon; (mp) חֳדָשִׁים (283)

168   חָיָה   (Q) to live, be alive, stay alive, revive, restore to life; (Pi) preserve alive, let live, give life; (Hi) preserve, keep alive, revive, restore to life (283)

169   קָרַב   (Q) to approach, draw near, come near, make a sexual advance; (Hi) bring (near), present, offer a sacrifice or offering (280)

170   אַף   nostril, nose; (metaphorically) anger; (md) אַפַּיִם (277); compare with אַף (#309)

171   אֶבֶן   (fs) stone; (fp) אֲבָנִים (276)

172   צֹאן   (cs) flock(s), flock of sheep and goats (274)

173   שֵׁשׁ   six; (fs) שִׁשָּׁה; (fs cstr) שֵׁשֶׁת; (mp) שִׁשִּׁים sixty (274); compare with שֵׁשׁ (#800)

174	לְמַ֫עַן	(prep) on account of, for the sake of (272)
175	בָּשָׂר	flesh, meat, skin (270)
176	מִדְבָּר	wilderness, desert, pasture (269)
177	רָשָׁע	(adj) wicked, guilty; (mp) רְשָׁעִים (264)
178	חַי	(adj) living, alive; (mp) חַיִּים (254)
179	מַטֶּה	(ms) staff, rod, tribe; (mp) מַטּוֹת (252)
180	מָלֵא	(Q) to be full, fill (up); (Ni) be filled (with); (Pi) fill, perform, carry out, consecrate as priest (252); compare with מָלֵא (#554)
181	גְּבוּל	border, boundary, territory; (fs) גְּבוּלָה (10x) (251)
182	רֶ֫גֶל	(fs) foot (251)
183	אַמָּה	cubit (distance between elbow and tip of middle finger), forearm (249)
184	חֶ֫סֶד	loyalty, faithfulness, steadfast love, lovingkindness (249)
185	חַ֫יִל	strength, wealth, army (246)
186	חָטָא	(Q) to miss (a goal or mark), sin, commit a sin; (Pi) make a sin offering; (Hi) induce or cause to sin (240)
187	נַ֫עַר	boy, youth, servant (240)
188	אֵל	God, god (237)
189	שָׁלוֹם	peace, welfare, wholeness, deliverance (237)
190	זָכַר	(Q) to remember, recall, call to mind, mention; (Ni) be remembered, be thought of; (Hi) cause to be remembered, remind, mention (235)
191	מַעֲשֶׂה	(ms) work, deed, act (235)
192	לַ֫יְלָה	(ms) night; (mp) לֵילוֹת (234)
193	עָוֹן	transgression, iniquity, guilt, punishment (of sin); (mp) עֲוֹנוֹת (233)
194	יָרַשׁ	(Q) to inherit, take possession of, dispossess, take away someone's property; (Hi) cause to possess or inherit, dispossess, impoverish (232)

195	זֶרַע	seed, offspring, descendants (229)
196	רָבָה	(Q) to be(come) numerous, be(come) great, increase; (Hi) make many, make great, multiply, increase (229)
197	קֶרֶב	inner part(s), organ(s), body; (prep) בְּקֶרֶב (155x) in the middle of, among (227)
198	בָּקַשׁ	(Pi) to seek, seek to find, seek to obtain, search for, look for, discover, demand, require; (Pu) be sought (225)
199	כָּתַב	(Q) to write (upon), register, record; (Ni) be written (225)
200	מוֹעֵד	appointed time (of feast), meeting place, assembly (223)
201	תּוֹרָה	law, instruction, teaching, custom (223)
202	אֲדָמָה	ground, land, earth (222)
203	נַחֲלָה	inheritance, property, possession (222)
204	אֵם	(fs) mother; (with 3ms suff) אִמּוֹ (220)
205	כּוּן	(Ni) to be established, stand firm, be steadfast, be ready, be arranged; (Hi) establish, set up, prepare, make ready, make firm; (Polel) set up, establish (219)
206	אָהַב	(Q) to love (of human and divine love); (Pi Ptc) lover (217)
207	שָׁתָה	(Q) to drink (217)
208	בֶּגֶד	clothes, garment, covering (216)
209	נָטָה	(Q) to spread out, stretch out, extend, pitch (a tent), turn, bend; (Hi) turn, incline, stretch out, spread out (216)
210	מַחֲנֶה	(cs) camp, army; (cp) מַחֲנוֹת and מַחֲנִים (215)
211	עָזַב	(Q) to leave, leave behind, forsake, abandon, set free, let go (214)
212	בֹּקֶר	morning (213)
213	יָסַף	(Q) to add, continue (do something more or again); (Hi) add, increase, do again or more (213)

214	מַלְאָךְ	messenger, angel (213)
215	נָצַל	(Ni) to be rescued, be delivered, be saved, save oneself; (Hi) tear from, snatch away, take away, deliver from (213)
216	שָׁכַב	(Q) to lie down, have sexual intercourse (with) (213)
217	מִנְחָה	gift, offering, tribute (211)
218	כָּלָה	(Q) to (be) complete, be finished, be at an end, come to an end, be accomplished, be spent, be exhausted; (Pi) complete, finish, bring to an end (207); compare with כָּלָה (#1184)
219	צַדִּיק	(adj) righteous, just, innocent (206)
220	יָשַׁע	(Ni) to be delivered, be victorious, receive help; (Hi) help, save, deliver, rescue, come to the aid of (205)
221	שָׁפַט	(Q) to judge, make a judgment, decide (between), settle (a dispute or controversy); (Ni) go to court, plead, dispute (204)
222	אָרוֹן	(cs) ark, chest, coffin (202); אֲרוֹן הַבְּרִית "the ark of the covenant"
223	אָסַף	(Q) to gather (in), take in, take away, destroy; (Ni) be gathered, assemble, be taken away (200)
224	כָּבוֹד	glory, splendor, honor, abundance (200); כְּבוֹד יְהוָה "the glory of the Lord"
225	רוּם	(Q) to be high, be exalted, rise, arise; (Hi) raise, lift up, exalt, take away; (Hoph) be exalted; (Polel) exalt, bring up, extol, raise (children) (197)
226	כַּף	(fs) hand, palm, sole of the foot; (fp) כַּפּוֹת (195)
227	יָכֹל	(Q) to be able, be capable of, endure, prevail, be victorious (193)
228	שֶׁמֶן	oil, fat (193)
229	חָצֵר	(cs) courtyard, village, settlement; (cp) חֲצֵרִים and חֲצֵרוֹת (192)
230	סֵפֶר	book, scroll, document (191); סֵפֶר הַתּוֹרָה "the book of the law"

231	בְּהֵמָה	animal(s), beast(s), cattle (190)
232	שֵׁבֶט	rod, staff, scepter, tribe (190); שִׁבְטֵי יִשְׂרָאֵל "the tribes of Israel"
233	אֹזֶן	(fs) ear; (fd cstr) אָזְנֵי (188)
234	רֵעַ	friend, companion, neighbor (188)
235	גָּלָה	(Q) to uncover, reveal, disclose; (Ni) uncover (reveal) oneself, be revealed, be exposed; (Pi) uncover, reveal, disclose; (Hi) take (carry away) into exile (187)
236	שָׁבַע	(Ni) to swear, swear (take) an oath, adjure; (Hi) cause to take an oath, adjure, plead with someone (186)
237	אָבַד	(Q) to perish, vanish, be(come) lost, go astray; (Pi) cause to perish, destroy; (Hi) exterminate (185)
238	מִצְוָה	commandment; (fp) מִצְוֹת (184); מִצְוֹת יְהוָה "the commandments of the Lord"
239	בָּקָר	cattle, herd (183)
240	רִאשׁוֹן	(adj) first, former; (fs) רִאשֹׁנָה; (mp) רִאשֹׁנִים (182)
241	זָקֵן	(adj) old; (n) elder (180); compare with זָקָן (#1055)
242	לָמָה	why? also spelled לָמֶה (178)
243	שָׂפָה	lip, language, edge, shore; (fs cstr) שְׂפַת (178)
244	שָׁאַל	(Q) to ask (of), inquire (of), request, demand (176)
245	חָוָה	(Hishtaphel) to bow down, worship (173)
246	בָּחַר	(Q) to choose, test, examine (172)
247	אַיִל	ram, ruler; (adj) mighty (171); compare with אֱיָל (#1173)
248	בִּין	(Q) to understand, perceive, consider, give heed to; (Ni) be discerning, have understanding; (Hi) understand, make understand, teach; (Hith) show oneself perceptive, behave intelligently (171)
249	לָחַם	(Q, Ni) to fight, do battle with (rare in Q) (171)
250	עֵדָה	congregation, assembly (171)

251   קָדַשׁ   (Q) to be holy, set apart or consecrated; (Ni) show oneself holy (of God), be honored or treated as holy; (Pi) set apart, consecrate or dedicate as holy, observe as holy; (Hi) consecrate, dedicate or declare as holy; (Hith) show or keep oneself holy (171)

252   דּוֹר   generation; also spelled דֹּר; (mp) דֹּרוֹת and דֹּרֹת (167)

253   הָרַג   (Q) to kill, slay (167)

254   מְלָאכָה   work, occupation, service (167)

255   רָעָה   (Q) to pasture, tend (flocks), graze, shepherd, feed (167); compare with רָעָה (#137)

256   אַחֵר   (adj) other, another, foreign; (fs) אַחֶרֶת; (mp) אֲחֵרִים (166)

257   דָּרַשׁ   (Q) to seek, inquire (of or about), investigate, ask for, require, demand (165)

258   חוּץ   outside, street; (mp) חוּצוֹת; (prefixed with prep מִן) מִחוּץ from outside, outside (164)

259   פֶּתַח   opening, entrance, doorway (164)

260   סָבַב   (Q) to turn (about), go around, march around, surround; (Ni) turn; (Hi) cause to go around, lead around; (Polel) encompass with protection (163)

261   זֶבַח   sacrifice (162)

262   טָמֵא   (Q) to be(come) unclean; (Ni) defile oneself; (Pi) defile, pronounce or declare unclean; (Hith) defile oneself, become unclean (162); compare with טָמֵא (#417)

263   אַךְ   only, surely, nevertheless (161)

264   בַּעַל   owner, master, husband, (divine title) Baal (161)

265   לְבַד   alone, by oneself; (with 3ms suff) לְבַדּוֹ (161)

266   גִּבּוֹר   (adj) mighty, valiant, heroic; (n) hero (160)

267   נוּס   (Q) to flee, escape (160)

268   צְדָקָה   righteousness, righteous act, justice (159)

269	שָׂמַח	(Q) to rejoice, be joyful, be glad; (Pi) cause to rejoice, gladden, make someone happy (156)
270	שֵׁנִי	(adj) second; (fs) שֵׁנִית (156)
271	חָכְמָה	wisdom, skill (153)
272	כָּסָה	(Q) to cover, conceal, hide; (Pi) cover (up), conceal, clothe (153)
273	מָוֶת	death, dying; (ms cstr) מוֹת (153)
274	צָפוֹן	(fs) north, northern (153)
275	שָׁחַת	(Pi, Hi) to ruin, destroy, spoil, annihilate (152)
276	נֶגֶד	(prep) opposite, in front of (151)
277	נָגַע	(Q) to touch, strike, reach; (Hi) touch, reach, throw, arrive (150)
278	רֹב	multitude, abundance, greatness (150)
279	שָׂנֵא	(Q) to hate; (Pi Ptc) enemy, (lit) the one who hates (148)
280	שָׁבַר	(Q) to break (up), break in pieces, smash, shatter; (Ni) be smashed, broken, shattered or destroyed; (Pi) shatter, smash, break (148); compare with שָׁבַר (#1238)
281	שְׁמֹנֶה	eight; (fs) שְׁמֹנָה; (mp) שְׁמֹנִים eighty (147)
282	הָלַל	(Pi) to praise, sing hallelujah; (Pu) be praised, be praiseworthy; (Hith) boast (146); compare with הָלַל (#1501)
283	נָסַע	(Q) to pull (out or up), set out, start out, depart, journey, march (on) (146)
284	עֲבֹדָה	work, labor, service, worship; also spelled עֲבוֹדָה (145)
285	רָדַף	(Q) to pursue, follow after, chase, persecute (144)
286	חָנָה	(Q) to decline, camp, encamp, pitch camp, lay seige to (143)
287	שֶׁ	(prefixed rel pron) who, which, that (143); synonym of אֲשֶׁר

288	אָז	then, since, before (141)
289	יַיִן	wine; (ms cstr) יֵין (141)
290	יָמִין	(fs) right hand, south (141); cf. בִּנְיָמִין (Benjamin) "son of the right hand"
291	חַיִּים	life, lifetime (140)
292	מַעַל	above, upward, on top of (140); compare with מַעַל (#992)
293	נוּחַ	(Q) to rest, settle down, repose; (Hi) cause to rest, secure rest, set, lay, leave (behind, untouched) (140)
294	מִשְׁכָּן	dwelling place, tabernacle; (mp) מִשְׁכָּנוֹת (139)
295	נְחֹשֶׁת	copper, bronze (139)
296	חָכָם	(adj) wise, skillful, experienced (138)
297	יֵשׁ	(particle of existence) there is, there are (138)
298	סוּס	horse (138)
299	נַחַל	stream, brook, wadi (137)
300	פָּתַח	(Q) to open (up); (Ni) be opened, be loosened, be set free; (Pi) let loose, loosen, free, unsaddle (136)
301	קָרָא	(Q) to meet, encounter, befall, happen; Inf Cstr with prep לְ (לִקְרַאת) toward, against, opposite (136); compare with קָרָא (#70) and קָרָה (#1198)
302	חָלַל	(Ni) to be defiled, be profaned, defile oneself; (Pi) profane, pollute, defile, dishonor, violate; (Hi) let something be profaned, begin (135)
303	כִּסֵּא	seat, chair, throne (135)
304	זָבַח	(Q) to slaughter (for sacrifice), sacrifice; (Pi) offer sacrifice, sacrifice (134)
305	מִסְפָּר	number (134)
306	עֶרֶב	evening, sunset (134)
307	פָּנָה	(Q) to turn (toward, from, to the side, away) (134)
308	שֶׁמֶשׁ	(cs) sun (134)

309   אַף   (conj) also, indeed, even (133); compare with אַף (#170)

310   חוֹמָה   wall (133)

311   פֶּן־   lest, otherwise (133)

312   פַּר   bull, ox, steer (133)

313   קָבַר   (Q) to bury; (Ni) be buried (133)

314   שָׁאַר   (Ni) to remain, be left over, survive; (Hi) leave (someone or something) remaining, spare (133)

315   חֹק   statute, appointed time, portion; (mp) חֻקִּים (131); compare with חֻקָּה (#373)

316   נָשִׂיא   chief, leader, prince (130)

317   שָׁכַן   (Q) to settle (down), abide, reside, dwell, inhabit; (Pi) abide, dwell (130)

318   אֱמֶת   truth, fidelity; (with 2ms suff) אֲמִתֶּךָ (127)

319   קָבַץ   (Q) to collect, gather, assemble; (Ni) be gathered, be assembled; (Pi) gather together, assemble (127)

320   כֹּחַ   strength, power (126)

321   עֶצֶם   (fs) bone, skeleton; (fp) עֲצָמוֹת (126)

322   בּוֹשׁ   (Q) to be ashamed; (Hi) put to shame, be ashamed (125)

323   חֵמָה   wrath, heat, poison; (with 1cs suff) חֲמָתִי (125)

324   חֲצִי   half, middle (125)

325   נָגַשׁ   (Q) to draw near, come near, approach; (Ni) draw near; (Hi) bring (near), offer (sacrifice) (125)

326   שָׁלַךְ   (Hi) to send, throw (down, into or away), cast; (Hoph) be thrown, be cast (125)

327   חָשַׁב   (Q) to think, consider, devise, plan, value, esteem, reckon; (Ni) be reckoned, be accounted, be esteemed, be considered (as); (Pi) think, consider, devise, plan (124)

328   צֶדֶק   righteousness, equity (123)

329	קָהָל	assembly, community, crowd (123)
330	אֲנַחְנוּ	(1cp pers pron) we (121)
331	לָכַד	(Q) to take, capture, catch, seize; (Ni) be caught, be captured (121)
332	אוֹר	(cs) light, daylight, sunshine (120); compare with אוֹר (#707)
333	בְּכוֹר	firstborn, oldest offspring; also spelled בְּכֹר (120)
334	רֶכֶב	chariot, (coll) chariots or chariot riders, upper millstone (120)
335	אָחוֹת	sister, relative, loved one (119)
336	יָשָׁר	(adj) upright, just, level, straight (119)
337	נָהָר	river, stream; (mp) נְהָרוֹת and נְהָרִים (119)
338	פְּרִי	fruit, offspring (119)
339	בָּטַח	(Q) to trust, be confident, rely (upon) (118)
340	פַּעַם	(fs) foot, pace, time; (fp) פְּעָמִים (118)
341	תּוֹעֵבָה	abomination, abhorrence, offensive thing (118)
342	גָּדַל	(Q) to grow up, be(come) great, become strong, wealthy or important; (Pi) bring up (children), make great, extol; (Hi) make great, magnify, do great things (117)
343	יָטַב	(Q) to be well with, go well with, be pleasing (to); (Hi) make things go well for, do good to, deal well with, treat kindly (117); compare with טוֹב (#714)
344	לָשׁוֹן	(cs) tongue, language (117)
345	מַמְלָכָה	kingdom, dominion, reign (117)
346	קָדוֹשׁ	(adj) holy, set apart (117)
347	שָׂרַף	(Q) to burn (completely), destroy; (Ni) be burned (117)
348	שָׁפַךְ	(Q) to pour (out), spill, shed (blood) (117)

349	שָׁלֵם	(Q) to be complete, be finished; (Pi) complete, finish, make whole, restore, repay, requite, recompense, reward, perform (a vow); (Hi) bring to completion, consummate, make peace (116); compare with שָׁלֵם (#1024)
350	נָבָא	(Ni) to prophesy, be in a state of prophetic ecstasy; (Hith) speak or behave as a prophet, be in a state of prophetic ecstasy (115)
351	קָטַר	(Pi) to make a sacrifice go up in smoke, offer (a sacrifice) by burning; (Hi) cause a sacrifice to go up in smoke (115)
352	בָּכָה	(Q) to weep (in grief or joy), weep for (114)
353	כָּבֵד	(Q) to be heavy, be weighty, be honored; (Ni) be honored; (Pi) make insensitive, honor; (Hi) make heavy, dull or insensitive, harden (heart), cause to be honored (114); compare with כָּבֵד (#773, #1563)
354	מִגְרָשׁ	open land, pasture (114)
355	שֶׁקֶר	lie, deception, falsehood (113)
356	בִּלְתִּי	(negates Inf Cstr) not, except; also spelled לְבִלְתִּי (86x) with prep לְ (112)
357	לָבַשׁ	(Q) to put on a garment, clothe, be clothed; (Hi) clothe (112)
358	עַמּוּד	pillar, column, tent pole (112)
359	יָדָה	(Hi) to thank, praise, confess; (Hith) confess (111)
360	כָּנָף	(fs) wing, edge, extremity; (fd) כְּנָפַיִם (111)
361	שַׁבָּת	(cs) Sabbath, period of rest; (cp) שַׁבָּתוֹת (111)
362	עָפָר	dust, dry earth (110)
363	רַק	only, still, but, however (109)
364	נָחַם	(Ni) to be sorry, regret, console oneself, comfort oneself, have compassion; (Pi) comfort, console (108)
365	שְׁלִישִׁי	(adj) third; (fs) שְׁלִשִׁית and שְׁלִישִׁיָּה (108)
366	הֵן	behold, if (107)

367　כֶּבֶשׂ　lamb, sheep; (mp) כְּבָשִׂים (107)

368　סָפַר　(Q) to count; (Pi) count, recount, relate, make known, proclaim, report, tell (107)

369　בָּמָה　(cultic) high place, hill; (fp) בָּמוֹת (106)

370　יָתַר　(Ni) to be left over, remain; (Hi) leave (over), have (something) left over or remaining (106)

371　בַּעַד　(prep) behind, through (104)

372　גָּאַל　(Q) to redeem, deliver, act as kinsman (perform the responsibilities of the next-of-kin), avenge (104); compare with גָּאַל (#1756)

373　חֻקָּה　statute, ordinance (104); compare with חֹק (#315)

374　רוּץ　(Q) to run (104)

375　תָּמִיד　continually (104)

376　מַרְאֶה　(ms) vision, sight, appearance (103)

377　כָּפַר　(Pi) to cover (over), atone (for), make atonement (102)

378　שָׁכַח　(Q) to forget; (Ni) be forgotten (102)

379　מְעַט　(adj) little, few (101)

380　רֹחַב　width, breadth, expanse (101)

381　רָעָב　famine, hunger (101)

382　יַעַן　on account of (100)

383　עוֹר　skin, hide, leather; (mp cstr) עֹרֹת (99)

384　רָעַע　(Q) to be bad, evil or displeasing; (Hi) do evil, do wickedly, do injury, harm, treat badly (98)

385　שְׁבִיעִי　(adj) seventh; (fs) שְׁבִיעִת (98)

386　שָׁרַת　(Pi) to minister, serve, attend to the service of God (98)

387　אָמַן　(Ni) to (prove to) be reliable, faithful or trustworthy; (Hi) believe (in), trust, have trust in, put trust in (97)

388　יֶתֶר　rest, remainder, excess (97)

389	שָׂבַע	(Q) to be satisfied or satiated, have one's fill (of), eat or drink one's fill; (Hi) satisfy (97)
390	חַיָּה	animal, beast; (fs cstr) חַיַּת (96); compare with חַיָּה (#1768)
391	חֲמוֹר	donkey; also spelled חֲמֹר (96)
392	טָהוֹר	(adj) clean, pure; also spelled טָהֹר (96)
393	יַחְדָּו	together, at the same time (96)
394	אֹרֶךְ	length; (with 3ms suff) אָרְכּוֹ (95)
395	הָפַךְ	(Q) to turn, overturn, overthrow, destroy; (Ni) be destroyed, be turned into, be changed (95)
396	חָלָל	(adj) pierced, slain, defiled; (mp) חֲלָלִים; (mp cstr) חַלְלֵי (94)
397	טָהֵר	(Q) to be clean (ceremonially), be pure (morally); (Pi) cleanse, purify, pronounce clean; (Hith) purify or cleanse oneself (94)
398	כֶּרֶם	vineyard; (mp) כְּרָמִים (94)
399	מָלַט	(Ni) to escape, flee to safety, slip away; (Pi) let someone escape, save someone, leave undisturbed (94)
400	שִׂמְחָה	joy, gladness (94)
401	חָרָה	(Q) to be(come) hot, burn with anger, become angry (93)
402	פֶּשַׁע	transgression, rebellion, crime; (mp cstr) פִּשְׁעֵי (93)
403	גֵּר	stranger, sojourner, alien (92)
404	חֵלֶב	fat; (metaphorically) best, choice part (92)
405	עֵבֶר	beyond, other side, edge, bank (92)
406	קָצֶה	(ms) end, border, outskirts; (ms cstr) קְצֵה (92)
407	שָׁמֵם	(Q) to be deserted, be uninhabited, be desolated, be appalled; (Ni) be made uninhabited, desolate or deserted; (Hi) cause to be deserted or desolated (92)

408	זְרוֹעַ	(fs) arm, forearm; (metaphorically) strength or power; (fp) זְרֹעוֹת (91)
409	כְּרוּב	cherub; (mp) כְּרוּבִים cherubim (91)
410	מַלְכוּת	kingdom, dominion, royal power (91)
411	סָגַר	(Q) to shut (in), close; (Hi) deliver (up), hand over, surrender, give up (91)
412	תָּמִים	(adj) blameless, perfect, honest, devout; (mp) תְּמִימִם and תְּמִימִים (91)
413	שָׁמַד	(Ni) to be exterminated, destroyed or annihilated; (Hi) exterminate, annihilate, destroy (90)
414	יֶלֶד	child, boy, youth (89)
415	דֶּלֶת	door; (fp cstr) דַּלְתוֹת (88)
416	דַּעַת	knowledge, understanding, ability (88)
417	טָמֵא	(adj) unclean; (fs) טְמֵאָה (88); compare with טָמֵא (#262)
418	שִׁיר	(Q) to sing (of); (Q and Polel Ptc) singer (88); compare with שִׁיר (#455) and שִׁירָה (#1675)
419	שֶׁקֶל	measurement of weight, shekel (88)
420	לָמַד	(Q) to learn; (Pi) teach (87)
421	עָנָן	(coll) clouds, cloud mass (87)
422	עֵצָה	counsel, plan, advice; (fs cstr) עֲצַת (87)
423	שֶׁלֶם	peace offering; (mp) שְׁלָמִים (87)
424	פֵּאָה	corner, side, edge; (fs cstr) פְּאַת (86)
425	שִׁית	(Q) to set, put, place, lay (hand upon), set one's mind to (86)
426	הָמוֹן	multitude, crowd, sound, roar (85)
427	קָנָה	(Q) to get, acquire, buy (85)
428	פָּלַל	(Hith) to pray, make intercession (84)
429	רָחוֹק	(adj) distant, remote, far away; also spelled רָחֹק (84)

430	גּוּר	(Q) to sojourn, dwell (stay) as a foreigner or alien, dwell as a newcomer for a definite or indefinite time (82); compare with גּוּר (#1839)
431	זָכָר	male, man (82)
432	סָתַר	(Ni) to be hidden, hide oneself; (Hi) hide (82)
433	עָזַר	(Q) to help, assist, come to the aid of (82)
434	פֹּה	here, at this place; also spelled פוֹ (82)
435	קָלַל	(Q) to be small, be insignificant, be of little account, be swift; (Ni, Pi) declare cursed; (Hi) lighten, make lighter, treat with contempt (82)
436	אָוֶן	iniquity, wickedness, evildoer (81)
437	מָהַר	(Pi) to hasten, hurry, go or come quickly; Inf often used as an adverb with the sense of "hastily" (81)
438	מָשַׁל	(Q) to rule, reign, govern, have dominion (81); compare with מָשַׁל (#1389)
439	שָׁחַט	(Q) to slaughter (esp. animals for sacrifice) (81)
440	הֵיכָל	temple, palace (80)
441	חֹשֶׁךְ	darkness (80)
442	יָעַץ	(Q) to advise, counsel, plan, decide; (Ni) consult (take counsel) together (80)
443	מָכַר	(Q) to sell, hand over; (Ni) be sold, sell oneself (80)
444	עוּר	(Q) to be awake, stir up; (Hi) arouse, rouse, wake up, stir up; (Polel) arouse, disturb, awaken (80)
445	עָנִי	(adj) poor, humble, afflicted; (mp) עֲנִיִּים (80); compare with עָנִי (#853)
446	קָרְבָּן	gift, offering (80)
447	אוֹצָר	treasure, treasury, storehouse; (mp cstr) אֹצְרוֹת (79)
448	אוֹת	(cs) sign, mark, pledge; (cp) אֹתוֹת (79)
449	עָנָה	(Q) to be afflicted, be humbled, become low; (Pi) afflict, oppress, humiliate, violate (79); compare with עָנָה (#152, #1467)

450	שׁוֹר	ox, bull, cow (79)
451	יְשׁוּעָה	salvation, help, deliverance; (with 1cs suff) יְשׁוּעָתִי (78)
452	מִשְׁמֶרֶת	watch, guard, responsibility (78)
453	נֶגַע	mark, plague, affliction (78)
454	רָכַב	(Q) to mount and ride, ride; (Hi) cause or make to ride (78)
455	שִׁיר	song (78); compare with שִׁיר (#418) and שִׁירָה (#1675)
456	תֵּשַׁע	nine; (fs) תִּשְׁעָה; (mp) תִּשְׁעִים ninety (78)
457	גּוֹרָל	lot, portion, allotment; (mp) גּוֹרָלוֹת (77)
458	חָנַן	(Q) to be gracious to, show favor to, favor; (Hith) plead for grace, implore favor or compassion (77)
459	תְּפִלָּה	prayer; (with 1cs suff) תְּפִלָּתִי (77)
460	בַּרְזֶל	iron (76)
461	מִקְנֶה	(ms) cattle, livestock, property (76)
462	נַעֲרָה	young girl, newly married woman, maidservant (76)
463	עֹז	strength, power, might; (with 3ms suff) עֻזּוֹ (76); compare with עֹז (#1399)
464	קֶרֶן	(fs) horn; (fp cstr) קַרְנוֹת (76)
465	קֶשֶׁת	bow, weapon (76)
466	תְּרוּמָה	offering, contribution, tribute (76)
467	חָלָה	(Q) to be(come) weak or tired, be(come) sick; (Ni) be exhausted, be made sick; (Pi) appease, flatter (75)
468	מִקְדָּשׁ	sanctuary (75); 31x in Ezek
469	עָרַךְ	(Q) to lay out, set in rows, arrange, set in order, stack (wood), draw up a battle formation (75)
470	קָרוֹב	(adj) near, close; also spelled קָרֹב (75)
471	חָפֵץ	(Q) to delight in, take pleasure in, desire, be willing (74); compare with חָפֵץ (#1632)

472	מָאַס	(Q) to refuse, reject, despise (74)
473	מִזְרָח	east, sunrise (74)
474	נָצַב	(Ni) to stand (firm), take one's stand, station oneself, be positioned; (Hi) station, set (up), place, establish (74)
475	סֶלָה	technical poetic notation of uncertain meaning; occurs in Pss and 3x in Habakkuk (74)
476	עֵז	(fs) goat, goat's hair; (fp) עִזִּים (74)
477	קָטֹן	(adj) small, young, insignificant; (fs) קְטַנָּה (74); compare with קָטָן (#1048)
478	שָׁלָל	plunder, spoil, loot (74)
479	אָסַר	(Q) to tie, bind, fetter, imprison (73)
480	אֶרֶז	cedar; (mp) אֲרָזִים (73)
481	בַּל	(poetic) no, never (73); 69x in Isa, Pss, Prov
482	הֶבֶל	vanity, futility, breath (73); 38x in Eccl
483	זָעַק	(Q) to cry (out), call for help, summon (73)
484	חֶרְפָּה	reproach, disgrace, shame (73)
485	צוּר	rock, boulder (73); compare with צוּר (#956)
486	קִיר	wall; (mp) קִירוֹת (73)
487	בֶּטֶן	(fs) belly, stomach, womb (72)
488	גִּבְעָה	hill (72)
489	מַדּוּעַ	why? (72)
490	צַר	adversary, enemy; (mp cstr) צָרֵי (72); compare with צַר (#1047)
491	רָחַץ	(Q) to wash (with water), wash (off or away), bathe, bathe oneself (72)
492	רִיב	(Q) to strive, contend, quarrel, dispute, conduct a legal case (72); compare with רִיב (#547)
493	שׁוֹפָר	trumpet, ram's horn; (mp) שׁוֹפָרוֹת (72)

494	בְּרָכָה	blessing, gift (71)
495	לִין	(Q) to remain overnight, spend the night, stay, dwell (71)
496	עוֹף	(coll) flying creatures, birds, insects (71)
497	פָּלָא	(Ni) to be extraordinary, be wonderful, be too difficult; (Hi) do something wonderful (71)
498	שָׁבַת	(Q) to stop, cease, rest; (Hi) put an end to, bring to a stop, remove, put away (71)
499	שֻׁלְחָן	table; (mp) שֻׁלְחָנוֹת (71)
500	זָר	(adj) foreign, strange; (mp) זָרִים (70)
501	כְּסִיל	fool, shameless person (70)
502	מָשַׁח	(Q) to smear (with a liquid, oil or dye), anoint (70)
503	נָבַט	(Hi) to look (at or out), gaze, behold (70)
504	עֵמֶק	valley, plain (70)
505	צָרָה	distress, anxiety, trouble (70)
506	תָּקַע	(Q) to drive or thrust (weapon into a person), pitch (tent), blow (trumpet), clap one's hands (70)
507	חֵן	favor, grace, charm (69)
508	עֵד	witness; (mp) עֵדִים (69)
509	קָדִים	east, eastern, east wind (69); compare with קֶדֶם (#556)
510	רָפָא	(Q) to heal; (Ni) be healed, become whole; (Pi) heal, make healthy (69)
511	כִּכָּר	(fs) something round, talent (weight), valley; (fp) כִּכָּרִים (68)
512	אַתְּ	(2fs pers pron) you (67)
513	בּוֹר	pit, cistern, well (67)
514	כָּתֵף	(fs) side, shoulder; (fp) כְּתֵפוֹת (67)
515	פָּרַשׂ	(Q) to spread out (as with wings or hands in prayer), stretch (out or over) (67)

516	קֶבֶר	grave, burial site; (mp) קְבָרִים and קְבָרוֹת (67)
517	קֵץ	end, border, limit (67)
518	אֲחֻזָּה	property, possession; (with 3ms suff) אֲחֻזָּתוֹ (66)
519	גֶּבֶר	strong man, young man, hero (66)
520	חֵלֶק	portion, share (66)
521	שְׁאֵרִית	remnant, remainder (66); 37x in Isa, Jer, Ezek; compare with שְׁאָר (#1077)
522	אִשֶּׁה	(ms) offering by fire (65)
523	חֲלוֹם	dream (65)
524	כָּשַׁל	(Q) to stumble, totter, stagger; (Ni) be caused to stumble, stumble (65)
525	נָצַח	(Pi) to supervise, oversee or inspect works and activities related to the temple; מְנַצֵּחַ (Ptc) used as title (superscription) in 55 psalms (65)
526	פּוּץ	(Q) to be spread, be dispersed, be scattered, overflow; (Ni) be scattered, be dispersed; (Hi) scatter, disperse (65)
527	צָלַח	(Q) to succeed, prosper, be successful; (Hi) be successful, succeed, cause to succeed or prosper (65)
528	שְׁאוֹל	(cs) underworld, Sheol (65)
529	שָׁכַם	(Hi) to get up early, rise early, do (something) early (65)
530	תָּפַשׂ	(Q) to lay (take) hold of, seize, capture, grasp; (Ni) be seized, be caught, be captured, be conquered (65)
531	גַּיְא	(cs) valley; (cp) גֵּאָיוֹת; also spelled גַּיְא (64)
532	יְאֹר	stream, river, Nile (64)
533	תָּמַם	(Q) to be(come) complete or finished, come to an end, cease, be consumed, be spent, be burned out (64)
534	אָחַז	(Q) to seize, grasp, take hold (of), hold fast (63)
535	אָרַר	(Q) to curse (63)

536	בָּרַח	(Q) to run away, flee, go (pass) through (63)
537	דָּרַךְ	(Q) to tread (also in the sense of pressing for wine or oil), march, bend (draw) the bow; (Hi) cause to tread, march or walk (63)
538	יָצַר	(Q) to form, fashion, shape, create (63)
539	יָרֵא	(adj) fearful, afraid of (63); compare with יָרֵא (#150)
540	נָצַר	(Q) to keep watch, watch over, guard, protect, preserve (63)
541	קָרַע	(Q) to tear, rend, cut up, tear away (63)
542	שִׁפְחָה	female slave, slave girl, maidservant (63)
543	אֵצֶל	(prep) beside, near (62)
544	גְּבוּרָה	power, strength; (fp) גְּבוּרוֹת mighty deeds (62)
545	חַג	feast, festival, procession; also spelled חָג; (mp) חַגִּים (62)
546	קָנֶה	(ms) reed (62)
547	רִיב	dispute, quarrel, lawsuit (62); compare with רִיב (#492)
548	שָׁקָה	(Hi) to give drink to, provide drink for, irrigate (62)
549	אֶבְיוֹן	(adj) poor, needy (61)
550	אַחֲרִית	end, extremity, last (61)
551	אֵיךְ	how? (61)
552	אוּלָם	porch; also spelled אֵילָם (61); compare with אוּלָם (#1273)
553	דּוֹד	beloved, uncle (61); 39x in Song
554	מָלֵא	(adj) full, filled (61); compare with מָלֵא (#180)
555	עֵדוּת	witness, testimony; also spelled עֵדֻת; (fp) עֵדוֹת (61)
556	קֶדֶם	east, ancient times (61); compare with קָדִים (#509)
557	אַלּוּף	tribal chief, leader (60)
558	בָּעַר	(Q) to burn (up), consume; (Pi) kindle, burn (60); compare with בָּעַר (#1030)

559   זָנָה   (Q) to commit fornication, be a harlot (prostitute), be unfaithful (60)

560   חָמָס   violence, wrong (60)

561   מָגֵן   (cs) shield; (cp) מָגִנִּים (60)

562   נֶדֶר   vow; also spelled נֵדֶר (60)

563   נֶסֶךְ   drink offering; also spelled נֵסֶךְ (60)

564   עֲרָבָה   desert plain, Arabah (60)

565   פָּדָה   (Q) to ransom, redeem, buy out (60)

566   קְטֹרֶת   incense, smoke (60)

567   שָׂכַל   (Hi) to understand, comprehend, have insight, make wise, have success (60)

568   אֹרַח   (cs) road, path, way; (cp cstr) אָרְחוֹת (59)

569   בְּלִי   without, nothing (59)

570   הֵנָּה   here (59); compare with הֵנָּה (#982)

571   יָבֵשׁ   (Q) to dry up, be(come) dry, wither; (Hi) make dry (up), make wither (59)

572   יָכַח   (Hi) to reprove, rebuke, reproach, chasten, punish, decide, mediate, arbitrate (59)

573   נָחַל   (Q) to take (as a) possession, obtain (receive) property, give as an inheritance; (Hi) give (leave) as an inheritance (59)

574   נָטַע   (Q) to plant (59)

575   סֶלַע   rock, stone, cliff (59)

576   רָחַק   (Q) to be(come) far or distant, keep far from; (Hi) remove, put (keep) far away, keep at a distance (59)

577   שָׁדַד   (Q) to devastate, ruin, deal violently with, violently destroy; (Pu) be devastated (59)

578   אֱלוֹהַּ   God, god (58)

579   פָּעַל   (Q) to do, make, perform, practice (58)

580   רֵיחַ   smell, odor, scent (58)

581	תְּהִלָּה	praise, song of praise (58)
582	אֶדֶן	base, pedestal; (mp) אֲדָנִים; (mp cstr) אַדְנֵי (57)
583	חָזָק	(adj) strong, mighty, hard (57)
584	יַעַר	forest, woods, thicket (57)
585	מִזְמוֹר	psalm, song (57); all in Pss
586	פָּרָשׁ	horseman, horse; (mp) פָּרָשִׁים (57)
587	אָמָה	female servant, handmaid, maidservant (56)
588	זָרַע	(Q) to sow, scatter seed (56)
589	טֶרֶם	before, not yet; also spelled בְּטֶרֶם (39x) with prep בְּ (56)
590	מַחֲשָׁבָה	thought, plan, scheme (56)
591	רָצוֹן	pleasure, acceptance, favor (56)
592	שְׁמָמָה	desolation, waste, ruin (56)
593	אַלְמָנָה	widow (55)
594	גֶּפֶן	(cs) vine, grapevine (55)
595	דָּבַק	(Q) to cling, cleave to, stick to; (Hi) cause to cling, cleave or stick to, pursue closely (55)
596	חָדַל	(Q) to cease, end, stop, refrain (from), desist, discontinue (55)
597	חָזָה	(Q) to see, behold, perceive (55)
598	חָלַק	(Q) to divide, share (with), share (in), apportion, distribute; (Pi) divide (in pieces), apportion, scatter (55)
599	חֵץ	arrow; (mp) חִצִּים (55)
600	חָתַת	(Q) to be shattered, be dismayed, be filled with terror (55)
601	כָּעַס	(Q) to be angry, be vexed; (Hi) vex, provoke, provoke to anger (God) (55)
602	מִדָּה	measure, measurement (55)

603	צָעַק	(Q) to shout, cry (out), call for help; (Ni) be called together, be summoned (55)
604	רְבִיעִי	(adj) fourth; (fs) רְבִיעִית (55)
605	שֵׁן	(cs) tooth, ivory; (cd cstr) שִׁנֵּי (55)
606	אָבָה	(Q) to be willing, consent, yield to, accede to, want something (54)
607	גָּמָל	camel; (mp) גְּמַלִּים (54); 44x in Exod
608	דְּבַשׁ	honey (54)
609	יְרִיעָה	tent curtain (54)
610	מָרוֹם	height, elevation, pride (54)
611	סֹפֵר	scribe, secretary; also spelled סוֹפֵר (54)
612	עָמָל	trouble, labor, toil (54)
613	עֶרְוָה	nakedness (54)
614	שְׂמֹאל	left, left side, north; also spelled שְׂמֹאול (54)
615	שָׁוְא	worthlessness, vanity, emptiness (54)
616	חָדָשׁ	(adj) new, fresh; (fs) חֲדָשָׁה (53)
617	יוֹמָם	by day, daily, in the daytime (53)
618	יָצַק	(Q) to pour, pour out (liquid), cast (metal), flow (into); (Hoph) be cast, be poured out, be emptied out (53)
619	מְדִינָה	province, district (53)
620	מַצָּה	unleavened bread; (fp) מַצּוֹת (53)
621	סֹלֶת	flour (53)
622	עֶלְיוֹן	(adj) upper; (divine title) Most High (53)
623	צֵל	shadow, shade, protection; (with 3ms suff) צִלּוֹ (53)
624	רָנַן	(Q) to call or cry aloud, shout with joy; (Pi) cry out (with joy), exult (53)
625	אַיֵּה	where? (52)

626	מָדַד	(Q) to measure, measure off (distance or expanse), measure out (grain) (52)
627	מָחָר	tomorrow (52); compare with מָחֳרָת (#927)
628	שָׂעִיר	male goat (52)
629	אַחֲרוֹן	(adj) last, behind, west (51)
630	בָּקַע	(Q) to cleave, split, breach, break open; (Ni) be cleft, be split (open); (Pi) split, rip open (51)
631	הוֹי	woe! oh! ha! (51)
632	כָּבַס	(Pi) to clean, cleanse, wash away guilt (51)
633	נָדַח	(Ni) to be scattered, be banished, be driven away, be thrust out; (Hi) scatter, drive away, disperse, thrust out, tempt, seduce (51)
634	קֶרֶשׁ	board, plank (51); 48x in Exod
635	רֵאשִׁית	beginning, first (51)
636	תָּעָה	(Q) to err, wander (about), stagger, go astray (animal); (Hi) lead astray, cause to err (51)
637	בְּתוּלָה	virgin (50)
638	חָרַם	(Hi) to devote to the ban, dedicate for destruction, exterminate (50)
639	טַבַּעַת	ring, signet ring; (fp) טַבָּעֹת (50)
640	מוּסָר	discipline, correction, instruction (50); 41x in Exod
641	נָכַר	(Hi) to recognize, know, investigate, be acquainted with, acknowledge (50)
642	נָשַׂג	(Hi) to reach, overtake (50)
643	אֱמוּנָה	faithfulness, reliability (49)
644	אֵפֹד	ephod, priestly garment; also spelled אֵפוֹד (49)
645	בָּגַד	(Q) to act or deal treacherously, faithlessly or deceitfully with (49)
646	בַּעֲבוּר	on account of, in order that (49)
647	גָּאוֹן	majesty, exaltation, pride (49)

648 מַעֲלָה   ascent, step, stairs; (fp) מַעֲלוֹת (49); compare with
                מַעֲלָה (#1188)

649 מִשְׁקָל   weight (49)

650 נָגַף   (Q) to smite, strike, injure; (Ni) be smitten, be struck
                (with) (49)

651 פַּחַד   trembling, terror, dread (49)

652 פֶּסַח   Passover (49)

653 קָצִיר   harvest (49)

654 תְּכֵלֶת   blue or purple material (49)

655 תִּפְאֶרֶת beauty, glory, splendor (49)

656 אֵמֶר   word, saying, speech; (mp cstr) אִמְרֵי (48)

657 בָּרָא   (Q) to create (only with God as subject); (Ni) be
                created (48)

658 גִּלּוּלִים   (mp) idols (48)

659 דַּל   (adj) poor, weak, needy; (mp) דַּלִּים (48)

660 חֶבֶל   rope, cord, field, region (48)

661 חִיל   (Q) to writhe, travail, be in labor, tremble; also
                spelled חוּל (48); compare with חוּל (#1845)

662 חֲנִית   spear (48)

663 יָצַב   (Hith) to take one's stand, stand firm, station oneself,
                present oneself before, resist (48)

664 לִשְׁכָּה   room, chamber, hall; (fp) לִשְׁכוֹת (48)

665 מַכָּה   wound, injury, defeat (48)

666 נְבֵלָה   carcass, corpse (48)

667 סָמַךְ   (Q) to support, uphold, sustain, help, lean or lay
                (hand upon); (Ni) lean (on or against), support
                oneself (48)

668 רָצָה   (Q) to be pleased with, be favorable to, be well
                disposed toward, accept (with pleasure), become
                friends with (48)

669	שַׂק	sack, sackcloth; (mp) שַׂקִּים (48)
670	שְׁבִי	captivity, captives (48)
671	שַׁדַּי	(divine title) Almighty, Shaddai (48); אֵל־שַׁדַּי (uncertain etymology) "God Almighty"
672	אַרְיֵה	(ms) lion (47); compare with אֲרִי (#861)
673	גִּיל	(Q) to shout with joy, rejoice (47)
674	חָרַשׁ	(Q) to be silent, be deaf; (Hi) be(come) silent, be deaf, keep still (47); compare with חָרַשׁ (#1032)
675	יָרָה	(Hi) to instruct, teach (47); compare with יָרָה (#1008)
676	מָתְנַיִם	(md) hips, waist, loins (47)
677	סָלַח	(Q) to pardon, forgive; (Ni) be forgiven (47)
678	עַד	forever, eternal; spelled וְעַד with conjunction וְ (47); compare with עַד (#33)
679	פָּרַר	(Hi) to break (out), destroy, put an end to, frustrate, make ineffectual (47)
680	צָפָה	(Pi) to overlay, plate (with gold) (47); compare with צָפָה (#834)
681	צָרַר	(Q: transitive) to wrap (up), tie up, bind, shut away; (Q: intransitive) be cramped, be restricted, be hampered, be depressed; (Hi) oppress, harass, afflict (47); compare with צָרַר (#1070)
682	קָוָה	(Pi) to wait (for), wait with eagerness, hope (47)
683	רָחַם	(Pi) to show love for, have compassion, take pity on someone, greet (meet) someone with love (47)
684	רָצַח	(Q) to kill, murder, slay (47)
685	שֶׂה	(ms) sheep, lamb (47)
686	שָׁבָה	(Q) to take captive, deport (47)
687	אָשָׁם	guilt, guilt offering (46); 27x in Lev
688	דֶּבֶר	plague, pestilence (46)
689	יַחַד	together, along with (46)

690	מִשְׁכָּב	bed, couch (46)
691	מִשְׁתֶּה	(ms) feast, banquet (46); 20x in Esther
692	נָכְרִי	(adj) foreign, strange; (fs) נָכְרִיָּה (46)
693	נְעוּרִים	youth (46)
694	עָצַר	(Q) to hold back, restrain, hinder, imprison; (Ni) be restrained, be shut up, be brought to a halt, be detained (46)
695	פָּגַע	(Q) to meet, encounter, fall upon, attack, assail, reach (46)
696	פָּרַץ	(Q) to break through, break (out or into), make a breach, burst open, spread out (46)
697	קוֹמָה	height; (with 3ms suff) קוֹמָתוֹ (46)
698	קָשַׁב	(Hi) give (pay) attention, listen carefully or attentively (46)
699	רָפָה	(Q) to sink, drop, relax, grow slack; (Hi) abandon, forsake, desert, leave (someone) alone (46)
700	אוּלַי	perhaps, maybe (45)
701	גָּרַשׁ	(Q) to drive out, banish; (Pi) drive out (away) (45)
702	זָמַר	(Pi) to sing, praise, make music, play an instrument (45)
703	חֲמִישִׁי	(adj) fifth; (fs) חֲמִישִׁית (45)
704	מִגְדָּל	tower; (mp) מִגְדָּלִים and מִגְדָּלוֹת (45)
705	סָרִיס	official, eunuch (45)
706	עִמָּד	(prep) with; (with 1cs suff) עִמָּדִי (45)
707	אוֹר	(Hi) to give light, shine, illuminate, light up (44); compare with אוֹר (#332)
708	אַשְׁרֵי	blessed, happy (44); 26x in Pss
709	בָּחוּר	young man; (mp) בַּחוּרִים (44)
710	בָּלַל	(Q) to mix (up), confuse or confound (languages), mingle (44)

711	חָגַר	(Q) to gird (on), gird (oneself or someone), get ready (44)
712	חָלָב	milk (44)
713	חָלַץ	(Q) to draw (off), draw out, take off, withdraw, be girded (ready for battle); (Pi) rescue, deliver (44)
714	טוֹב	(Q) to be good, be pleasing, be pleasant, be joyful, be well with (44); compare with טוֹב (#92) and יָטַב (#343)
715	יִרְאָה	fear; (fs cstr) יִרְאַת (44); יִרְאַת יְהוָה "the fear of the Lord"
716	מוֹשָׁב	dwelling, settlement, seat; (mp) מוֹשָׁבוֹת (44)
717	מָרָה	(Q) to be rebellious, obstinate or contentious; (Hi) behave rebelliously or obstinately (44)
718	מֶרְכָּבָה	chariot (44)
719	מַשָּׂא	load, burden (44); compare with מַשָּׂא (#1254)
720	נָגִיד	leader, ruler (44); 21x in 1 and 2 Chron
721	נָקָה	(Ni) to be free (of), be without guilt (innocent), be exempt from (punishment), be emptied; (Pi) leave unpunished, hold innocent (44)
722	נֵר	lamp, light; (mp) נֵרוֹת (44)
723	קָשַׁר	(Q) to bind, be in league together, conspire (against) (44)
724	רוּעַ	(Hi) to shout, cry (out), shout a war cry (alarm of battle), sound a signal for war, cheer, shout in triumph (44)
725	שֶׁבֶר	break, fracture, collapse (44)
726	אֶפֶס	end, nothing (43)
727	בָּזַז	(Q) to plunder, spoil (43)
728	הָרָה	(Q) to conceive, be(come) pregnant (43); compare with הָרָה (#1502)
729	הָרַס	(Q) to tear down, demolish, destroy, throw down, overthrow, break through; (Ni) be ruined (43)

730   לוּחַ   tablet, board, plank; (mp) לֻחֹת (43)

731   מָתַי   when? (43)

732   נִיחֹחַ   soothing or pleasing scent; also spelled נִיחוֹחַ (43); 35x in Lev, Num

733   נֶצַח   forever, everlasting; also spelled לָנֶצַח with prep לְ (43)

734   נָקִי   (adj) blameless, innocent; (mp) נְקִיִּם (43)

735   פָּשַׁט   (Q) to take off (clothes), strip off, rush out, dash out, make a raid; (Hi) take off (clothes or armor), strip off (skin), flay (43)

736   קִנְאָה   jealousy, zeal (43)

737   רְחוֹב   (fs) public square, street; (fp) רְחֹבוֹת (43)

738   תְּבוּאָה   produce, harvest (43)

739   אָנָה   where? עַד־אָנָה how long? also spelled אָן (42)

740   אֱנוֹשׁ   man, humankind (42); 31x in Pss, Job

741   בָּדַל   (Ni) to separate oneself, withdraw; (Hi) divide, separate, set apart, make a distinction (between), single out (42)

742   בָּזָה   (Q) to despise, regard with contempt (42)

743   בֶּטַח   security, safety (42)

744   בָּלַע   (Q, Pi) to swallow (up), engulf (42)

745   גּוֹלָה   captivity, exiles (42)

746   זוּב   (Q) to flow (away), suffer a discharge (42)

747   חָרְבָּה   desolation, ruin; (fp) חֲרָבוֹת (42)

748   יָחַל   (Pi, Hi) to wait (for), hope for (42)

749   יָפֶה   (adj) beautiful; (fs) יָפָה (42)

750   יָתוֹם   orphan (42)

751   כִּנּוֹר   lyre, harp; (mp) כִּנֹּרוֹת (42)

752   מַחֲלֹקֶת   division, portion; (fp cstr) מַחְלְקוֹת (42)

753	מְנוֹרָה	lampstand; also spelled מְנֹרָה (42); 20x in Exod
754	מַעֲלָל	deed, act (42); 18x in Jer
755	נוּעַ	(Q) to tremble, shake, totter, wave (of trees); (Hi) make unstable or unsteady, shake (up), disturb (42)
756	נָתַץ	(Q) to tear down, pull down, break down, demolish (42)
757	שָׁנִי	scarlet, crimson (42); 26x in Exod
758	שָׁקַט	(Q) to be quiet, be peaceful, be at peace, be at rest; (Hi) give (keep) peace (42)
759	תְּבוּנָה	understanding, skill (42); 19x in Prov
760	אָזַן	(Hi) to give ear (to), listen (to), hear, heed (41)
761	אָחוֹר	back, behind (41)
762	אָמֵץ	(Q) to be strong, be bold; (Pi) make firm, strengthen, harden someone's heart (41)
763	אָרַב	(Q) to lie in ambush, lie in wait, ambush (41)
764	בְּרִיחַ	bar (41)
765	בֹּשֶׁת	shame, disgrace (41)
766	גָּבֹהַּ	(adj) high, exalted; (fs) גְּבֹהָה (41)
767	גַּן	(cs) garden; (cp) גַּנִּים (41)
768	חָמַל	(Q) to have compassion (for), have pity (for), spare (41)
769	חָרוֹן	anger, fury, burning (41)
770	טַף	children; (with 2mp suff) טַפְּכֶם (41)
771	יָסַד	(Q) to found, establish, appoint, destine, allocate; (Pi) found, appoint, establish (41)
772	יָסַר	(Pi) to teach, discipline, correct, chastise, rebuke (41)
773	כָּבֵד	(adj) heavy, severe (41); compare with כָּבֵד (#353, #1563)
774	מָאֵן	(Pi) to refuse (41)

775   מְעָרָה   cave (41)

776   פָּשַׁע   (Q) to revolt, rebel (against), transgress, break with, break away from, behave as a criminal (41)

777   צָדַק   (Q) to be in the right, have a just cause, be just (justified), be righteous; (Hi) declare righteous, just or innocent, justify (41)

778   צַוָּאר   neck (41)

779   רָגַז   (Q) to shake, quake, tremble, be agitated, be perturbed, be excited, be upset (41)

780   אֵיפָה   a dry measurement of corn or wheat, ephah (40)

781   אֲשֵׁרָה   Asherah (pagan goddess), cultic pole; (fp) אֲשֵׁרִים and אֲשֵׁרוֹת (40)

782   בַּד   carrying pole, gate bar; (mp) בַּדִּים (40); compare with בַּד (#1136)

783   גָּנַב   (Q) to steal, deceive (40)

784   דָּגָן   grain, corn (40)

785   מָשָׁל   proverb, wisdom saying (40)

786   נָטַשׁ   (Q) to leave, forsake, abandon, give up (something); (Ni) be forsaken (40)

787   עוּד   (Hi) to warn, admonish, witness, be a witness, call as witness, testify (40)

788   עֹל   yoke; (with 3ms suff) עֻלּוֹ (40)

789   צֵלָע   (fs) rib, side; (fp) צְלָעוֹת (40)

790   צִפּוֹר   (cs) bird; also spelled צִפֹּר; (cp) צִפֳּרִים (40)

791   רַחֲמִים   compassion, mercy (40)

792   בָּהַל   (Ni) to be terrified, be horrified, be dismayed, be disturbed, make haste, be hasty; (Pi) terrify, make haste, act hastily (39)

793   דַּי   sufficiency, enough; (ms cstr) דֵּי (39)

794   חָרַד   (Q) to tremble, do something with trembling, shudder, quake; (Hi) startle (39)

795	מוֹט	(Q) to totter, shake, waver, sway, stagger; (Ni) be made to stagger, stumble or totter (39)
796	מִרְמָה	deceit, deception (39)
797	נָחָה	(Q) to lead; (Hi) lead, guide, conduct (39)
798	קָהַל	(Ni) to assemble, meet together (intransitive); (Hi) assemble (transitive), summon (39)
799	שַׁמָּה	desolation, horror (39)
800	שֵׁשׁ	linen (39); 33x in Exod; compare with שֵׁשׁ (173)
801	תְּאֵנָה	fig tree, fig; (fp) תְּאֵנִים (39)
802	תּוֹלֵדוֹת	(fp) generations, descendants; (fp cstr) תּוֹלְדֹת and תֹּלְדוֹת (39)
803	תּוֹלַעַת	worm (39); 27x in Exod
804	אֹכֶל	food (38)
805	אַרְגָּמָן	purple (38); 26x in Exod
806	בִּינָה	understanding, insight (38)
807	זַיִת	olive tree, olive; (mp) זֵיתִים (38)
808	זָרָה	(Q) to scatter; (Pi) scatter, disperse, spread (38)
809	חֶדֶר	room, chamber (38)
810	חֵיק	bosom, lap (38)
811	חֵפֶץ	delight, desire, pleasure, joy (38)
812	חָרַף	(Q) to taunt, reproach; (Pi) taunt, reproach, revile (38)
813	כּוּל	(Q) to comprehend; (Pilpel) contain, sustain, provide, support; (Hi) contain, hold (in), sustain, endure (38)
814	כָּלַם	(Ni) to be hurt, be humiliated, be ashamed, be disgraced, be dishonored, be confounded; (Hi) put to shame, humiliate, disgrace, harm (38)
815	מָטָר	rain (38)
816	מְלֹא	that which fills, fullness, abundance; also spelled מְלוֹא (38)

817   מִלָּה   word, speech; (fp) מִלִּים and מִלִּין (38); 34x in Job

818   מַר   (adj) bitter; (n) bitterness (38)

819   מָשִׁיחַ   (adj) anointed; (n) anointed one, Messiah (38)

820   עֵדֶר   flock, herd (38)

821   תִּירוֹשׁ   new wine (38)

822   בְּאֵר   (fs) well, pit (37)

823   גָּמַל   (Q) to complete, finish, wean, ripen, render, do (to);
                 recompense, requite (37)

824   גֹּרֶן   (fs) threshing floor (37)

825   חָסָה   (Q) to seek or take refuge (37)

826   כּוֹכָב   star; (mp) כּוֹכָבִים (37)

827   כָּכָה   thus, so (37)

828   לָקַט   (Q) to gather (together), glean; (Pi) gather (up),
                 collect (37)

829   מִבְצָר   fortress, stronghold (37)

830   מָעוֹז   refuge, stronghold; (mp) מָעֻזִּים (37)

831   עָשַׁק   (Q) to oppress, exploit, wrong (someone) (37)

832   עֹשֶׁר   wealth, riches (37)

833   פִּילֶגֶשׁ   (fs) concubine; also spelled פִּלֶּגֶשׁ; (fp) פִּילַגְשִׁים (37)

834   צָפָה   (Q) to keep watch, watch attentively, spy (37);
                 compare with צָפָה (#680)

835   שָׂחַק   (Q) to laugh, play; (Pi) play, entertain, amuse (37)

836   שׁוֹעֵר   gatekeeper; (mp) שֹׁעֲרִים (37)

837   אָבַל   (Q) to mourn, lament; (Hith) observe mourning rites
                 (36)

838   אִי   coastland, island; (mp) אִיִּים (36); 30x in Isa, Jer, Ezek

839   אִמְרָה   word, saying; (with 1cs suff) אִמְרָתִי (36)

840   חָרֵב   (Q) to dry up (intransitive), lie in ruins; (Hi) cause to
                 dry up, lay waste, reduce to ruins, make desolate
                 (36); compare with חָרַב (#1850)

841	חָרָשׁ	craftsman; (mp) חָרָשִׁים (36)
842	טֻמְאָה	uncleanness, impurity; (with 3ms suff) טֻמְאָתוֹ (36)
843	יָקָר	(adj) precious, valuable; (fs) יְקָרָה (36)
844	יֵשַׁע	salvation, deliverance, help; (with 1cs suff) יִשְׁעִי (36)
845	כָּנַע	(Ni) be subdued, be humbled, humble oneself; (Hi) humble or subdue someone (36)
846	כָּרַע	(Q) to bow (down), kneel (down), fall to one's knees (36)
847	מוּל	(prep) in front of, opposite (36); compare with מוּל (#925)
848	מוֹפֵת	wonder, sign, miracle (36)
849	מָעַל	(Q) to be unfaithful, act unfaithfully or treacherously, act counter to one's duty or legal obligations (36)
850	מָשַׁךְ	(Q) to draw, pull, drag, draw out, prolong, stretch (36)
851	נֵכָר	foreigner, stranger (36)
852	נָסָה	(Pi) to test, put someone to the test, try, tempt (36)
853	עֳנִי	poverty, affliction, misery (36); compare with עָנִי (#445)
854	פֹּעַל	work, deed; (with 3ms suff) פָּעֳלוֹ (36)
855	קָצַר	(Q) to gather in, reap, harvest (36); compare with קָצַר (#1598)
856	קָשֶׁה	(adj) difficult, hard, severe; (fs) קָשָׁה (36)
857	תֵּבֵל	(fs) world (36)
858	תְּהוֹם	(cs) primeval ocean, deep, depth; (cp) תְּהֹמוֹת (36)
859	תְּרוּעָה	shout, alarm, signal (36)
860	אוֹפַן	wheel; (mp) אוֹפַנִּים (35)
861	אֲרִי	lion; (mp) אֲרָיוֹת (35); compare with אַרְיֵה (#672)
862	אָשַׁם	(Q) to be(come) guilty, commit an offense, do a wrong (35)

863	גֶּשֶׁם	rain, showers (35)
864	חָזוֹן	vision, revelation (35)
865	מַלְכָּה	queen (35)
866	מִשְׁנֶה	(ms) double, second (35)
867	נָקַם	(Q) to avenge, take vengeance, take revenge; (Ni) avenge oneself, take revenge (35)
868	סֵתֶר	hiding place, secret place, shelter (35)
869	עֵגֶל	calf, young bull (35)
870	עָרֵל	(adj) uncircumcised; (mp) עֲרֵלִים (35)
871	צָרַעַת	leprosy, skin disease (35)
872	קָצֶה	end, edge, tip; (fp cstr) קְצוֹת (35)
873	רָשַׁע	(Hi) to condemn, declare or pronounce guilty (35)
874	אָלָה	oath, curse (34)
875	אָרַךְ	(Hi) to make long, lengthen, extend (34)
876	אָתוֹן	(fs) female donkey; (fp) אֲתֹנוֹת (34)
877	גָּבַהּ	(Q) to be high, be tall, be lofty, be exalted, be haughty; (Hi) make high, exalt (34)
878	הָמָה	(Q) to make (a) noise, make a sound, roar, growl, moan, groan, be boisterous (34)
879	זוֹנָה	prostitute, harlot; also spelled זֹנָה (34)
880	זָרַק	(Q) to toss, throw, scatter, sprinkle (34)
881	חָבָא	(Ni) to hide (oneself), be hidden; (Hith) keep oneself hidden (34)
882	חֵטְא	sin (34)
883	חָסִיד	(adj) godly, faithful, pious (34)
884	יָרֵךְ	(fs) thigh, loin, side (34)
885	כַּלָּה	daughter-in-law, bride (34)
886	מָחָה	(Q) to wipe, wipe out, destroy, annihilate (34)

887	נוּף	(Hi) to move back and forth, wave, brandish, wield (34)
888	עֶבְרָה	wrath, anger, fury (34)
889	עַוְלָה	iniquity, injustice, wickedness (34)
890	פָּרַח	(Q) to bud, sprout, bloom, shoot, break out, break open (34)
891	צָפַן	(Q) to hide, store (up), treasure (up), keep, save up (34)
892	צָרַף	(Q) to smelt (metal), refine (by smelting), test (34)
893	קָנָא	(Pi) to envy, be envious of, be jealous, be zealous for (34)
894	קָצַף	(Q) to be(come) angry or furious (34)
895	שְׂעֹרָה	barley; (fp) שְׂעֹרִים (34)
896	תְּשׁוּעָה	salvation, deliverance, victory (34)
897	אֵי	where? (33)
898	חָבַשׁ	(Q) to saddle, bind, bind on, buckle on, bind up (wound), wrap, twist (rope), imprison (33)
899	יְהַב	(Q) to give, come (33)
900	יוֹנָה	dove; (fp) יוֹנִים (33)
901	יְמָנִית	(fs adj) right, southern; (ms) יְמָנִי (33)
902	יָנַק	(Q) to suck; (Hi) suckle, nurse (33)
903	מַצֵּבָה	sacred stone, pillar (33)
904	עֵרֶךְ	value, assessment; (with 2ms suff) עֶרְכְּךָ (33)
905	עֹרֶף	(back of) neck (33)
906	עֵשֶׂב	green plant, grass (33)
907	עִשָּׂרוֹן	tenth part; (mp) עֶשְׂרֹנִים (33)
908	צַד	side; (mp) צְדִּים (33)
909	צָמַח	(Q) to sprout, spring up, grow; (Hi) make grow or sprout (33)

910	קְלָלָה	curse (33)
911	רִמּוֹן	pomegranate, pomegranate tree (33)
912	רִנָּה	shout of joy, shout of lament (33)
913	שֹׁרֶשׁ	root; (mp with 3ms suff) שָׁרָשָׁיו (33)
914	אַהֲבָה	love (32)
915	אֳנִיָּה	ship, boat; (fp) אֳנִיּוֹת (32)
916	אַרְמוֹן	palace, stronghold (32)
917	חַלּוֹן	(cs) window; (cp) חַלּוֹנוֹת and חַלּוֹנִים (32)
918	חִנָּם	without cause, without compensation, for nothing (32)
919	טַבָּח	guard, cook; (mp) טַבָּחִים (32)
920	טוּב	goodness, well-being, happiness (32)
921	כָּחַד	(Ni) to be hidden, effaced; (Pi) hide, conceal (32)
922	כֶּלֶב	dog, male temple prostitute (32)
923	לְבוּשׁ	clothing, garment (32)
924	מְאוּמָה	(ms) something, anything (32)
925	מוּל	(Q) to circumcise; (Ni) be circumcised (32); compare with מוּל (#847)
926	מִזְרָק	bowl; (mp) מִזְרָקוֹת (32)
927	מָחֳרָת	the next day (32); compare with מָחָר (#627)
928	מֵעֶה	(ms) stomach, womb, entrails; (mp with 2ms suff) מֵעֶיךָ (32)
929	מַעֲשֵׂר	tithe, tenth (32)
930	נָוֶה	(ms) pasture, dwelling (32); compare with נָוָה (#1516)
931	נָשַׁק	(Q) to kiss (32)
932	לְעֻמַּת	(prep) beside, alongside, corresponding to; combination of prep לְ and עֻמָּה (32)
933	פְּנִימִי	(adj) inner; (fs) פְּנִימִית (32)

934	פְּקֻדָּה	appointment, service, watch, punishment (32)
935	תּוֹדָה	thanksgiving, thank offering, song of thanksgiving (32)
936	תִּקְוָה	hope, expectation (32)
937	אֶצְבַּע	(fs) finger, toe; (fp cstr) אֶצְבְּעֹת (31)
938	גָּג	roof; (mp) גַּגּוֹת (31)
939	גְּדוּד	band of raiders, military troops (31)
940	טַל	dew, light rain (31)
941	טָמַן	(Q) to hide (31)
942	יָלַל	(Hi) to howl, lament, wail (31)
943	כּוֹס	(fs) cup (31)
944	כָּזָב	lie, deception, falsehood (31)
945	כְּלָיוֹת	(fp) kidneys, place of thought or emotion; also spelled כְּלָיֹת (31)
946	כְּפִיר	young lion (31)
947	לְאֹם	people, nation; (mp) לְאֻמִּים (31)
948	מִין	kind, type, species (31)
949	נָאַף	(Q) to commit adultery; (metaphorically) commit idolatry; (Pi) commit adultery (31)
950	נָדַר	(Q) to make (perform) a vow, keep (make) a promise (31)
951	נָחָשׁ	serpent, snake (31)
952	סֻכָּה	booth, tabernacle; (fp) סֻכּוֹת (31)
953	עָב	cloud, clouds (31)
954	עָצוּם	(adj) mighty, numerous (31)
955	פֶּסֶל	idol, carved image (31)
956	צוּר	(Q) to tie up, bind, shut in, shut up, enclose, encircle, besiege (31); compare with צוּר (#485)

957	שִׂמְלָה	garment, clothing (31); compare with שַׂלְמָה (#1482)
958	שָׁטַף	(Q) to flood (over), overflow, rinse, wash (away) (31)
959	שְׁמִינִי	(adj) eighth; (fs) שְׁמִינִית (31)
960	אָוָה	(Pi) to wish, desire, want; (Hith) crave, wish for, long for (30)
961	אָמֵן	amen, surely (30)
962	בְּכִי	weeping (30)
963	בֹּשֶׂם	spice, perfume; (mp) בְּשָׂמִים (30)
964	גָּזַל	(Q) to tear off, tear away, seize, rob, take away by force (30)
965	דָּמָה	(Q) to be like, resemble; (Pi) liken, compare, imagine, ponder, devise (30); compare with דָּמָה (#1690)
966	הָדָר	majesty, glory, splendor (30); 20x in Isa, Pss
967	חִטָּה	wheat; (fp) חִטִּים (30)
968	יְרֵכָה	side, hip, far end, remote part; (fd cstr) יַרְכְּתֵי (30)
969	כְּלִמָּה	insult, disgrace, humiliation (30)
970	מַאֲכָל	food (30)
971	נָהַג	(Q) to drive (flocks), lead, guide; (Pi) lead (people), lead away, drive away (30)
972	סָפַד	(Q) to lament, wail, bewail, mourn for someone (30)
973	פִּנָּה	corner, cornerstone (30)
974	רַב	chief, captain, ruler (30); compare with רַב (#119)
975	רָבַץ	(Q) to lie down, couch (of animals), rest, stretch out (30)
976	רֶשַׁע	evil, wickedness, offense, injustice (30)
977	שְׁבוּעָה	oath; also spelled שְׁבֻעָה (30)
978	שָׁפֵל	(Q) to be(come) low, be(come) humble, humiliated or abased; (Hi) bring down, overthrow, abase, humiliate (30)

979	תְּנוּפָה	wave offering, waving (30)
980	בָּחַן	(Q) to test, put to the test, try, examine (29)
981	בָּרָד	hail (29)
982	הֵנָּה	(3fp pers pron) they; (fp dmstr pron and adj) those (29); compare with הֵנָּה (#570)
983	זִמָּה	evil plan, shameful behavior (29)
984	חָלַם	(Q) to dream (29)
985	חֲצֹצְרָה	trumpet; (fp) חֲצֹצְרוֹת (29)
986	חֵרֶם	something set apart for destruction, something banned, devoted thing (29)
987	יָעַד	(Q) to designate, appoint; (Ni) make or have an appointment, meet by appointment, gather or assemble by appointment (29)
988	כֻּתֹּנֶת	tunic, garment, robe; also spelled כְּתֹנֶת (29)
989	לָבָן	(adj) white (29)
990	מִטָּה	couch, bed (29)
991	מָנַע	(Q) to withhold, hold back, retain, refuse, restrain (29)
992	מַעַל	unfaithfulness, infidelity (29); compare with מַעַל (#292)
993	נֶגֶב	south, Negev (29)
994	נִדָּה	menstrual flow, impurity, defilement (29)
995	סִיר	(cs) basin, pot, tub (29)
996	עֲשִׂירִי	(adj) tenth; (fs) עֲשִׂירִית (29)
997	עַתּוּד	male goat, leader; (mp) עַתּוּדִים and עַתֻּדִים (29)
998	פָּרָה	(Q) to bear fruit, be fruitful (29); compare with פָּרָה (#1068)
999	קִרְיָה	city, town (29)
1000	רָעַשׁ	(Q) to quake, shake (29)

1001	שָׂרִיד	survivor (29)
1002	שְׁבוּת	captivity, exile, imprisonment (29)
1003	תָּלָה	(Q) to hang (up) (29)
1004	בָּשַׁל	(Q) to boil; (Pi) boil, cook, roast (28)
1005	חָבַר	(Q) to unite, ally oneself (with), be joined, join forces (28)
1006	חָכַם	(Q) to be(come) wise, act wisely (28)
1007	חָשַׂךְ	(Q) to withhold, keep back, refrain, spare, save, restrain (28)
1008	יָרָה	(Q) to throw, shoot, cast (lots); (Hi) throw, shoot, cast (28); compare with יָרָה (#675)
1009	לִיץ	(Q) to boast (28)
1010	מָנָה	(Q) to count, number, reckon, assign, appoint (28); compare with מָנָה (#1711)
1011	מְעִיל	robe, cloak (28)
1012	נֵבֶל	stringed instrument, harp; (mp) נְבָלִים (28); compare with נֶבֶל (#1869)
1013	נָדַד	(Q) to flee, wander (about), depart, move, flutter (of wings) (28)
1014	סוּף	reed, (coll) reeds; יַם־סוּף "Red Sea" (or "Sea of Reeds") (28)
1015	עָלַם	(Ni) to be concealed, be hidden; (Hi) conceal, hide, cover up; (Hith) hide oneself (28)
1016	פֶּחָה	governor; (mp) פַּחוֹת (28)
1017	פְּלֵיטָה	survivor, escape, deliverance (28)
1018	קֶצֶף	wrath, anger (28)
1019	קָשָׁה	(Q) to be heavy, hard or difficult; (Hi) make hard, harden, make stubborn or obstinate (28)
1020	רְכוּשׁ	goods, property, equipment (28)
1021	שָׂכָר	wages, payment, reward (28)
1022	שֵׂעָר	hair, hairiness (28)

1023	שִׁטָּה	acacia; (fp) עֲצֵי שִׁטִּים ;שִׁטִּים "acacia wood" (28)
1024	שָׁלֵם	(adj) whole, complete, safe (28); compare with שָׁלֵם (#349)
1025	שִׁקּוּץ	abomination, detestable thing (28)
1026	שִׁשִּׁי	(adj) sixth; (fs) שִׁשִּׁית (28)
1027	תֵּבָה	ark, basket, box (28); 26x in Gen 6-9
1028	אַדִּיר	(adj) noble, majestic, mighty (27)
1029	בְּלִיַּעַל	(adj) useless, worthless; (n) worthlessness (27)
1030	בָּעַר	(Pi) to graze, sweep away, remove, get rid of, purge (27); compare with בָּעַר (#558)
1031	חָקַר	(Q) to explore, search, spy out (27)
1032	חָרַשׁ	(Q) to plow, engrave, devise, plan (27); compare with חָרַשׁ (#674)
1033	חָתַם	(Q) to seal (up), affix a seal (27)
1034	יוֹבֵל	ram's horn, trumpet, (year of) jubilee; also spelled יֹבֵל (27)
1035	יָצַת	(Q) to kindle, burn; (Hi) set on fire, set fire to (27)
1036	יָרֵחַ	moon (27)
1037	יָשַׁר	(Q) to be straight, be upright, be right, please, go straight (27)
1038	כַּפֹּרֶת	mercy seat, place of atonement, lid (27); 25x in Exod–Lev
1039	מוֹצָא	act of going forth, exit, source, spring (27)
1040	מוֹקֵשׁ	snare, trap (27)
1041	מְסִלָּה	highway, main road (27)
1042	נְקָמָה	vengeance, revenge (27)
1043	נָתַק	(Q) to pull off, tear away; (Ni) be drawn out or away, be torn apart, be separated; (Pi) tear up (out), tear apart, tear to pieces (27)
1044	עוּף	(Q) to fly (27)

1045	פָּלַט	(Pi) to bring out, bring forth, bring to safety, save (27)
1046	פָּתָה	(Q) to be simple, be inexperienced, be gullible; (Pi) fool, deceive, persuade, seduce (27)
1047	צַר	(adj) narrow; (n) anxiety, distress (27); compare with צַר (#490)
1048	קָטָן	(adj) small, young; (mp) קְטַנִּים (27); compare with קָטֹן (#477)
1049	שׂוּשׂ	(Q) to rejoice; also spelled שִׂישׂ (27)
1050	שְׁמוּעָה	message, report, news (27)
1051	אֱוִיל	fool, idiot (26); 19x in Prov; compare with אִוֶּלֶת (#1079)
1052	בָּצוּר	(adj) fortified, inaccessible; (fp) בְּצֻרוֹת (26)
1053	בֶּרֶךְ	(fs) knee; (fd) בִּרְכַּיִם (26)
1054	הוֹן	wealth, possessions (26)
1055	זָקֵן	(Q) to be(come) old, grow old (26); compare with זָקֵן (#241)
1056	חָלַף	(Q) to pass on or away (quickly), pass by, vanish; (Hi) change, replace, substitute (26)
1057	טוּר	row, course (26); 23x in Exod, 1 Kgs
1058	יָגַע	(Q) to toil, labor, struggle, grow or be weary (26)
1059	מָבוֹא	entrance, setting (of the sun), west (26)
1060	מַגֵּפָה	plague, slaughter (26)
1061	מַסֵּכָה	molten (metal) image, idol (26)
1062	נְדָבָה	freewill offering, voluntary gift (26)
1063	נָדִיב	(adj) noble, willing, generous (26)
1064	נֶשֶׁר	eagle, vulture (26)
1065	עִוֵּר	(adj) blind; (mp) עִוְרִים (26)
1066	עֶזְרָה	help, assistance, support; (with 1cs suff) עֶזְרָתִי (26)

1067	פָּרַד	(Ni) to divide, separate (intransitive), be scattered, be separated (26)
1068	פָּרָה	cow; (fp) פָּרוֹת (26); compare with פָּרָה (#998)
1069	צוֹם	fast, (period of) fasting (26)
1070	צָרַר	(Q) to be hostile (toward), treat with hostility, attack (26); compare with צָרַר (#681)
1071	קָדַם	(Pi) to be in front, confront, meet, go before, walk at the head, do something early or for the first time (26)
1072	קֵדְמָה	eastward, toward the east (26); קֶדֶם plus directional ה
1073	רָגַל	(Pi) to spy (out), scout (26)
1074	רָחַב	(Q) to open wide; (Hi) make wide (large), enlarge, extend (26)
1075	רֶחֶם	womb (26)
1076	שָׂטָן	adversary, accuser, Satan (26)
1077	שְׁאָר	remnant, remainder (26); compare with שְׁאֵרִית (#521)
1078	תַּאֲוָה	desire, longing (26)
1079	אִוֶּלֶת	folly, foolishness (25); 23x in Prov; compare with אֱוִיל (#1051)
1080	אָפָה	(Q) to bake (25)
1081	בַּז	plunder, spoil (25)
1082	גָּבַר	(Q) to be strong, be mighty, be superior, excel, achieve, accomplish, prevail (25)
1083	דְּמוּת	likeness, form, image (25)
1084	הָגָה	(Q) to utter a sound, growl, moan, groan, coo (of a dove), speak, proclaim (25)
1085	חִיצוֹן	(adj) outer, external; (fs) חִיצוֹנָה (25)
1086	חֹשֶׁן	breastplate (of the high priest) (25); 23x in Exod
1087	טָרַף	(Q) to tear (in pieces), rend (25)
1088	מְכוֹנָה	stand, base, support; (fp) מְכוֹנוֹת (25); 15x in 1 Kgs

1089   מָסָךְ   cover, curtain (25)

1090   מָרַד   (Q) to rebel, revolt (25)

1091   נוּד   (Q) to move to and fro, sway, wander, be(come) aimless or homeless, express grief or sympathy (by shaking the head) (25)

1092   נֵזֶר   consecration, dedication, crown; (with 3ms suff) נִזְרוֹ (25)

1093   נֹכַח   (prep) in front of, opposite (25)

1094   נָסַךְ   (Q) to pour out, pour (cast) a metal image or statue; (Hi) pour out libations, offer a drink offering (25)

1095   סַף   threshold, doorframe; (mp) סִפִּים (25)

1096   עֲגָלָה   cart, wagon (25)

1097   עָנָו   (adj) afflicted, oppressed, humble, meek; (mp) עֲנָוִים (25)

1098   עָשָׁן   smoke (25)

1099   פַּח   snare, trap, net (25)

1100   פָּחַד   (Q) to tremble, shiver, be startled, be in dread, be in awe (25)

1101   פָּרֹכֶת   curtain (25)

1102   פִּתְאֹם   suddenly, unexpectedly (25)

1103   שֹׁד   violence, destruction (25)

1104   שׁוֹטֵר   officer, official; (mp) שֹׁטְרִים (25)

1105   שָׁלַף   (Q) to draw out (sword), pull out, take out, pull off (25)

1106   שִׁלְשׁוֹם   day before yesterday, previously (25); תְּמוֹל שִׁלְשֹׁם "yesterday and the day before"

1107   תּוֹצָאוֹת   end, limit, outermost area (25)

1108   תְּחִנָּה   plea, petition (for favor) (25)

1109   אֵבֶל   mourning, funeral ceremony (24)

1110   אוֹי   woe! alas! (24)

1111	אֵיד	disaster, calamity (24)
1112	אַרְבֶּה	(ms) locust (24)
1113	בָּשַׂר	(Pi) to bring good news, tell, announce (24)
1114	גָּוַע	(Q) to die, expire, pass away, perish (24)
1115	דִּין	(Q) to judge, minister or execute judgment, plead one's cause, contend with (24); compare with דִּין (#1279)
1116	הוֹד	splendor, majesty (24)
1117	זִכָּרוֹן	memorial, remembrance (24)
1118	חוּס	(Q) to pity, look upon with compassion, spare (24)
1119	חֳלִי	illness, sickness (24)
1120	יָתֵד	(fs) tent peg, stake, pin; (fp) יְתֵדֹת (24)
1121	כָּבָה	(Q) to go out, be quenched, be extinguished; (Pi) put out, quench, extinguish (24)
1122	כֵּן	(adj) honest, correct, right (24); compare with כֵּן (#69, #1783)
1123	כֹּתֶרֶת	capital (top) of a pillar (24); 15x in 1 Kgs
1124	מְלוּכָה	kingship, royalty (24)
1125	נָאַץ	(Q) to spurn, despise; (Pi) treat disrespectfully or with irreverence (24)
1126	נָזָה	(Q) to spatter (blood); (Hi) sprinkle (24)
1127	נְשָׁמָה	breath (24)
1128	סוּג	(Q) to backslide, be disloyal; (Ni) turn back, withdraw, become disloyal (24)
1129	עֲלִילָה	deed, action; (fp) עֲלִילוֹת (24)
1130	פִּקּוּדִים	precepts, directions, instructions; (with 2ms suff) פִּקּוּדֶיךָ (24); all in Pss, 21x in Ps 119
1131	רוּשׁ	(Q) to be poor (24)
1132	שָׁכַל	(Q) to become childless; (Pi) make someone childless, deprive of children, cause a miscarriage (24)

1133	תּוֹכַ֫חַת	rebuke, correction (24)
1134	תּוּר	(Q) to spy out, reconnoiter, explore, investigate (24)
1135	תֵּימָן	(fs) south; (with directional ה) תֵּימָ֫נָה "southward" (24)
1136	בַּד	linen cloth; (mp) בַּדִּים (23); compare with בַּד (#782)
1137	בֶּ֫צַע	unjust gain (23)
1138	גָּלַח	(Pi) to shave (23)
1139	דִּמְעָה	(coll) tears (23)
1140	זֵ֫כֶר	memory, remembrance; (with 3ms suff) זִכְרוֹ (23)
1141	חֶלְקָה	piece (of land), portion (23)
1142	חָמַם	(Q) to be(come) warm, grow warm (23)
1143	חָפַר	(Q) to dig, track, search (for), scout out, spy out (23); compare with חָפַר (#1372)
1144	חָפַשׂ	(Q) to search (out), examine; (Pi) search thoroughly, track down; (Hith) disguise oneself (23)
1145	יָעַל	(Hi) to profit, gain profit, benefit (23)
1146	יִצְהָר	olive oil (23)
1147	כָּהַן	(Pi) to perform the duties of a priest, minister as a priest (23)
1148	כִּיּוֹר	wash basin, cooking pot; also spelled כִּיֹּר (23)
1149	לוּ	if only, oh that (23)
1150	מִישׁוֹר	plain, level ground, fairness; also spelled מִישֹׁר (23)
1151	מֶ֫לַח	salt (23)
1152	מַס	forced labor (23)
1153	מַעְיָן	spring, fountain (23)
1154	מִקְרָא	summons, assembly (23); 20x in Exod–Num
1155	מְרִי	rebellion (23); 16x in Ezek
1156	נָגַשׂ	(Q) to oppress, press, force to work, be a slave driver or taskmaster, exact (contributions), collect (offerings) (23)

1157	עַז	(adj) strong, mighty; (mp) עַזִּים (23)
1158	עֲטָרָה	crown, wreath; (fs cstr) עֲטֶרֶת (23)
1159	עָשִׁיר	(adj) rich, wealthy (23)
1160	פְּסִיל	idol, cultic statue (23)
1161	צָהֳרַיִם	noon, midday (23)
1162	צָעִיר	(adj) little, small, young (23)
1163	רָבַב	(Q) to be(come) many, numerous or great (23)
1164	שֹׁחַד	bribe, gift (23)
1165	שַׁחַר	dawn, daybreak (23)
1166	שַׁחַת	pit, grave (23)
1167	שֵׁכָר	intoxicating drink, beer (23)
1168	שֵׁנָה	sleep (23)
1169	שָׁקַל	(Q) to weigh (out) (23)
1170	תְּחִלָּה	beginning (23)
1171	תֹּם	integrity, innocence, perfection; (with 3ms suff) תֻּמּוֹ (23)
1172	תְּמוֹל	yesterday, previously (23); תְּמוֹל שִׁלְשׁוֹם "yesterday and the day before"
1173	אַיִל	pillar, doorpost; (ms cstr) אֵיל (22); 21x in Ezek; compare with אַיִל (#247)
1174	אֵפֶר	ashes, dust (22)
1175	גָּדַע	(Q) to cut off, cut down; (Ni) be cut off, be cut down, be cut into pieces; (Pi) cut down (through, off), cut to pieces (22)
1176	דָּת	law, decree (22); 20x in Esther
1177	הִין	liquid measurement, hin (22); 16x in Exod–Num
1178	זָהַר	(Hi) to warn (about), admonish, caution (22)
1179	זַעַם	anger, indignation, curse (22)

1180   חוֹל   sand (22)

1181   חָסֵר   (Q) to diminish, decrease, lack, be lacking (22); compare with חָסֵר (#1371)

1182   טֶרֶף   prey, food (22)

1183   כָּחַשׁ   (Pi) to deny, delude, deceive, lie, act deceptively, feign submission or obedience (22)

1184   כָּלָה   complete destruction, annihilation (22); compare with כָּלָה (#218)

1185   מוֹלֶדֶת   relatives, offspring, native (land) (22)

1186   מַחְתָּה   fire pan, censer (22); 18x in Exod–Num

1187   מָעַט   (Q) to be(come) few, be too small; (Hi) make small or few, diminish, reduce, collect or gather little (22)

1188   מַעֲלָה   ascent, stairs, rise; (ms cstr) מַעֲלֵה (22); compare with מַעֲלָה (#648)

1189   מִשְׁמָר   prison, guard(ing), custody, watch (22)

1190   מְתִים   (mp) men, few; (mp cstr) מְתֵי (22)

1191   נַעַל   (fs) sandal, shoe (22)

1192   נְקֵבָה   female, woman (22)

1193   סָקַל   (Q) to stone, put to death by stoning; (Ni) be stoned (to death) (22)

1194   פֶּגֶר   corpse, carcass; (mp cstr) פִּגְרֵי (22)

1195   פָּשָׂה   (Q) to spread (the symptoms of disease) (22)

1196   קִיץ   (Hi) to awake, wake up (22)

1197   קָסַם   (Q) to practice divination, consult a spirit of the dead, predict (22)

1198   קָרָה   (Q) to encounter, meet, befall, happen to (22); compare with קָרָא (#301)

1199   רֶגַע   moment, instant (22)

1200   רָדָה   (Q) to rule (over), have dominion over, govern (with the nuance of oppression), tread (in) the winepress (22)

1201   רֶשֶׁת   net, trap (22)

1202	שָׂשׂוֹן	joy, exultation (22)
1203	שְׁכֶם	shoulder; (with 3ms suff) שִׁכְמוֹ (22)
1204	שָׁעַן	(Ni) to lean (on or against), support oneself on, depend on (22)
1205	שָׁקַף	(Ni) to look down on (from above); (Hi) look down from above (22)
1206	תַּזְנוּת	prostitution, fornication (22); all in Ezek 16 and 23
1207	תָּעַב	(Pi) to abhor, loathe, make an abomination (22)
1208	אֱלִיל	worthlessness, idol (21)
1209	אָתָה	(Q) to come; (Hi) bring (21)
1210	בָּרָק	lightning (21)
1211	גָּרַע	(Q) to shave, trim (a beard), diminish, restrain, withdraw, take (away) (21)
1212	חָלִיל	far be it! never! (21); חָלִילָה לִּי "far be it from me!"
1213	חָמַד	(Q) to desire, take pleasure (delight) in, crave, covet (21)
1214	חֹתֵן	father-in-law (21)
1215	כַּעַס	anger, vexation (21)
1216	לְבוֹנָה	frankincense; also spelled לְבֹנָה (21)
1217	לְחִי	(fs) jaw, cheek, chin (21)
1218	מְגִלָּה	scroll (21)
1219	מוּם	defect, blemish (21); 16x in Lev–Deut
1220	מוּשׁ	(Q) to withdraw (from a place), cease from, leave off, depart (21)
1221	מְנוּחָה	rest, resting place (21)
1222	מָסַס	(Ni) to melt (away), dissolve, become weak (21)
1223	מִשְׁחָה	anointing (21)
1224	נֵס	flag, banner (21); 15x in Isa, Jer

1225	נְתִיבָה	path, way; (fp) נְתִיבוֹת (21)
1226	נָתַךְ	(Q) to gush forth, pour out, be poured out; (Ni) gush forth, be poured (out or forth) (21)
1227	נָתַשׁ	(Q) to uproot, pull out, extract, pull up, remove, drive out (nations) (21)
1228	סוֹד	confidential conversation, circle of confidants (21)
1229	סָחַר	(Q) to pass through (of shepherds), travel about (conducting business); (Q Ptc) trader, merchant (21)
1230	סֶרֶן	ruler, lord; (mp cstr) סַרְנֵי (21); 19x in Judg, 1 Sam
1231	עָוֶל	iniquity, injustice, wrong (21)
1232	פָּקַח	(Q) to open (the) eyes (21)
1233	פַּרְסָה	hoof (21)
1234	צוּם	(Q) to fast, abstain from food and drink (21)
1235	צְעָקָה	outcry, yelling (21)
1236	שָׂמֵחַ	(adj) joyful, glad, happy; (mp) שְׂמֵחִים (21)
1237	שָׁאַג	(Q) to roar (21)
1238	שָׁבַר	(Q) to buy grain (for food) (21); compare with שָׁבַר (#280)
1239	שָׁגָה	(Q) to stray (of sheep), go astray (morally), err, do or go wrong (unintentionally), stagger, reel (21)
1240	שַׁד	breast; (md) שָׁדַיִם (21)
1241	שָׁוַע	(Pi) to cry (call) for help (21)
1242	שָׁזַר	(Hoph Ptc) twisted; always spelled מָשְׁזָר (21); all in Exod 26–39
1243	שַׁחַק	layer of dust, cloud of dust, cloud; (mp) שְׁחָקִים (21)
1244	תָּמַךְ	(Q) to grasp, take hold of, hold, support (21)
1245	בְּרוֹשׁ	pine tree, juniper; (mp) בְּרוֹשִׁים (20)
1246	חֶרֶשׂ	earthenware, potsherd (20)
1247	חָתָן	bridegroom, son-in-law (20)

1248	יָחַשׂ	(Hith) to have oneself (to be) registered in a genealogical table, be enrolled in a genealogical list; (Hith Inf as noun) genealogy, registration (20)
1249	יְסוֹד	foundation wall, base (20)
1250	מְהֵרָה	quickly, at once (20)
1251	מַחְסֶה	(ms) refuge, shelter (20)
1252	מָצוֹר	distress, siege, affliction (20)
1253	מִקְלָט	refuge, asylum (20)
1254	מַשָּׂא	oracle, pronouncement (20); compare with מַשָּׂא (#719)
1255	נָבֵל	(Q) to fade, wither, decay, crumble away, wear out (20)
1256	עֲלִיָּה	upper room, roof chamber (20)
1257	עָרִיץ	(adj) ruthless, fierce, violent; (mp) עָרִיצִים (20)
1258	עָתַר	(Q) to pray, plead, entreat; (Ni) be pleaded with, be entreated; (Hi) pray, plead (20)
1259	צִנָּה	large shield (20)
1260	צָרַע	(Q) to be afflicted with a skin disease (traditionally leprosy); (Pu) be struck with a skin disease (20)
1261	קַיִץ	summer, summer fruit (20)
1262	רָחָב	(adj) wide, spacious; (fp) רְחָבָה (20)
1263	רָעֵב	(adj) hungry; (mp) רְעֵבִים (20); compare with רָעֵב (#1670)
1264	שָׂגַב	(Ni) to be high, be exalted, be inaccessible; (Pi) make high, make inaccessible, protect (20)
1265	שִׂיחַ	(Q) to consider, meditate, complain, lament, praise (20); compare with שִׂיחַ (#1603)
1266	שָׂכַר	(Q) to hire (for wages) (20)
1267	שָׁבוּעַ	week, (period of) seven; (mp) שָׁבֻעִים and שָׁבֻעוֹת (20)
1268	שֶׁלֶג	snow (20)

1269   שְׁפֵלָה   foothills, Shephelah (20)

1270   תַּבְנִית   pattern, form (20)

1271   תֹּהוּ   emptiness, wasteland, formlessness (20)

1272   תְּמֹרָה   palm tree ornament; (fp) תִּמֹרִים and תִּמֹרוֹת (20); 14x in Ezek

1273   אוּלָם   but, however (19); compare with אוּלָם (#552)

1274   אַשְׁמָה   guilt, blame (19)

1275   בִּקְעָה   valley, plain (19)

1276   גַּאֲוָה   pride, arrogance (19)

1277   גְּמוּל   recompense, requital (19)

1278   דָּג   fish (19); compare with (fs) דָּגָה (#1499)

1279   דִּין   judgment, legal claim (19); compare with דִּין (#1115)

1280   דָּמַם   (Q) to be silent, keep quiet, be still, be motionless, stand still, be (struck) dumb (19)

1281   זָנַח   (Q) to reject, spurn, exclude from (19)

1282   זְעָקָה   outcry, call for help (19)

1283   זָקָן   (cs) beard (19)

1284   חַטָּא   (adj) sinful; (n) sinner; (mp) חַטָּאִים (19)

1285   חָקַק   (Q) to hew out or carve out (a grave), inscribe, engrave, enact, decree (19)

1286   יָנָה   (Q, Hi) to oppress, mistreat (19)

1287   יְפִי   beauty; (with 2fs suff) יָפְיֵךְ (19); porch in Ezek

1288   לָאָה   (Q) to be(come) tired or weary; (Ni) tire (oneself) out, weary oneself, be tired of something; (Hi) make weary (19)

1289   לֶהָבָה   flame (19)

1290   לָחַץ   (Q) to squeeze, crowd, press, oppress, torment (19)

1291   מְזוּזָה   doorpost, doorframe (19)

1292	מְזִמָּה	purpose, plan, deliberation; (fp) מְזִמּוֹת (19)
1293	מַטָּה	downward, beneath, below (19)
1294	מֵישָׁרִים	level path, uprightness, fairness (19)
1295	מַעֲרָכָה	row, battle line (19)
1296	מַשְׁקֶה	(ms) cupbearer, drink; (mp) מַשְׁקִים (19)
1297	נֹגַהּ	brightness, radiance (19)
1298	נָפַץ	(Q) to shatter, smash to pieces; (Pi) smash (19)
1299	נָקַב	(Q) to pierce, bore (through), stipulate, specify, designate, curse, slander (19)
1300	סָפָה	(Q) to take, sweep, snatch or carry away; (Ni) be carried, swept or snatched away (19)
1301	עֲבֹת	(cs) cord, rope; (cp) עֲבֹתֹת and עֲבֹתִים (19)
1302	עָלֶה	(ms) leaf, foliage (19)
1303	עָלַל	(Poel) to deal (act) severely with, treat violently, glean (19)
1304	עֵנָב	grape; (mp) עֲנָבִים (19)
1305	עַשְׁתֵּי	eleven, eleventh (19); always in the construction עַשְׁתֵּי־עָשָׂר or עַשְׁתֵּי־עֶשְׂרֵה
1306	פָּלִיט	fugitive, survivor (19)
1307	פֶּרֶץ	breach, gap (19)
1308	רִיק	(Hi) to empty out, pour out (19); compare with רִיק (#1738) and רֵיק (#1601)
1309	רָמַס	(Q) to trample (down, out), tread (potter's clay, grapes), crush to pieces (19)
1310	רֹעַ	corruption, evil (19)
1311	רַעֲנָן	(adj) green, fresh, luxuriant (19)
1312	רָצַץ	(Q) to crush, oppress, mistreat (19)
1313	שֵׂיבָה	gray hair, old age (19)
1314	שָׁאַב	(Q) to draw water (19)

1315	שְׁגָגָה	error, accident (19)
1316	שׁוֹק	(fs) thigh, leg (19)
1317	שָׁכֵן	neighbor, resident (19)
1318	תַּחְתִּית	(fs adj) lower; (fp) תַּחְתִּיּוֹת (19)
1319	אָחַר	(Pi) to delay, cause one to delay, detain, hesitate, linger (18)
1320	אָכְלָה	food, nourishment (18)
1321	אָפִיק	river, channel, stream bed; (mp cstr) אֲפִיקֵי (18)
1322	בָּאַשׁ	(Q) to stink, have a bad smell; (Hi) make odious, become hated (18)
1323	בִּירָה	citadel, fortress (18)
1324	גַּחֶלֶת	coal, burning charcoal; (fp) גֶּחָלִים (18)
1325	גַּל	heap, pile; (mp) גַּלִּים (18); compare with גַּל (1440)
1326	גָּלַל	(Q) to roll (away) (18)
1327	דָּכָא	(Pi) to crush, beat to pieces (18)
1328	זָרַח	(Q) to rise (sun), shine, come out (leprosy), appear, break out (18)
1329	חוּשׁ	(Q) to hurry, make haste (18)
1330	חֵךְ	roof of the mouth, palate; (with 1cs suff) חִכִּי (18)
1331	יָאַל	(Hi) to be intent (keen) on something, be determined, be resolved, show willingness (undertake) to do something, agree to (18)
1332	יָבַל	(Hi) to bring (as gift or tribute), lead; (Hoph) be brought, be led (18)
1333	כַּד	(fs) jar, pitcher; (fp) כַּדִּים (18)
1334	כַּפְתֹּר	decorative knob of a lampstand; also spelled כַּפְתּוֹר (18); 16x in Exod 25 and 37
1335	לָעַג	(Q, Hi) to mock, ridicule, deride (18)
1336	מָאוֹר	light, luminary, light-bearer (18); 15x in Gen–Num

1337 מִסְגֶּרֶת rim (of table), border, prison; (fp) מִסְגְּרוֹת (18)

1338 מְצוּדָה (mountain) stronghold, fortress (18); compare with מְצָד (#1713)

1339 מָקוֹר spring, fountain (18)

1340 מַקֵּל (cs) rod, staff, branch; (cp) מַקְלוֹת (18)

1341 מֶרְחָק distance, distant place (18)

1342 נָבָל (adj) foolish, good-for-nothing; (n) fool (18)

1343 נָטַף (Q) to drop, drip, secrete; (Hi) cause to drip, cause to flow (metaphorically, of prophetic speech), drivel (18)

1344 נָשָׁה (Q) to forget (18)

1345 סוּת (Hi) to incite (against), stir up, provoke, instigate, seduce, mislead, lead astray (18)

1346 סְעָרָה windstorm, tempest, gale (18)

1347 צְבִי ornament, something beautiful, splendor (18); compare with צְבִי (#1730)

1348 צַלְמָוֶת (ms) shadow of death, deep darkness, gloom (18)

1349 קִינָה lament, funeral song, dirge (18); 10x in Ezek

1350 רְבָבָה ten thousand, great multitude, immense number (18)

1351 שָׂכִיר (adj) hired (worker); (n) day-laborer (18)

1352 שָׁחַח (Q) to cower, crouch, bow down (18)

1353 שָׁכַר (Q) to be(come) drunk; (Pi, Hi) make (someone) drunk (18)

1354 תַּחֲנוּן plea for mercy, supplication (for favor) (18)

1355 תָּכַן (Q) to examine, consider, weigh; (Ni) be examined, be in order (18)

1356 תְּשִׁיעִי (adj) ninth; (fs) תְּשִׁיעִית (18)

1357 אַבִּיר (adj) mighty, strong, powerful; (mp) אַבִּירִים (17)

1358 אֶזְרָח native, citizen (17)

1359	אֵיכָה	how? where? (17)
1360	אֵימָה	terror, fright, horror (17)
1361	אַיִן	where (from)? whence? (17); compare with אַיִן (#60)
1362	אָכֵן	surely, however (17)
1363	בִּכּוּרִים	firstfruits, early harvest (17)
1364	בִּלְעֲדֵי	(prep) apart from, except for, without (17)
1365	בְּרֵכָה	pool, pond, reservoir (17)
1366	גֹּבַהּ	(ms) height, pride (17)
1367	גַּנָּב	thief, kidnapper (17); 13x in Ezek
1368	דָּרוֹם	south, south wind (17)
1369	חִידָה	riddle, difficult question (17)
1370	חֹמֶר	mud, clay, mortar (17); compare with חֹמֶר (#1629)
1371	חָסֵר	(adj) lacking, wanting; (ms cstr) חֲסַר (17); compare with חָסֵר (#1181)
1372	חָפַר	(Q) to be ashamed (17); compare with חָפַר (#1143)
1373	חָפְשִׁי	(adj) free, exempt; (mp) חָפְשִׁים (17)
1374	חָצִיר	grass (17)
1375	חָשַׁךְ	(Q) to be(come) dark, grow dim (eyes) (17)
1376	יָצַג	(Hi) to set, place, establish, take one's stand (17)
1377	יְקָר	precious thing, something valuable, honor, respect (17)
1378	כָּלָא	(Q) to shut up, restrain, withhold, keep back (17)
1379	כְּתָב	writing, something written, document, register (17)
1380	כָּתַת	(Q) to beat, crush fine, hammer (into pieces); (Pi) beat, hammer, crush to pieces (17)
1381	לוּן	(Ni, Hi) to murmur (against), grumble (17)
1382	מָדוֹן	strife, dispute, quarrel (17)
1383	מוּג	(Q) to waver, melt; (Ni) wave, sway back and forth, undulate (17)

1384	מָטַר	(Hi) to make (let) rain fall, send rain (17)
1385	מָכוֹן	place, site, foundation, support (17)
1386	מֶמְשָׁלָה	rule, dominion, authority (17)
1387	מָעוֹן	dwelling place, habitation, refuge (17)
1388	מִשְׂגָּב	high point, fortress, refuge (17)
1389	מָשַׁל	(Q) to use a proverb, speak in parables or sentences of poetry; (Ni) be(come) like, similar or the same (17); compare with מָשַׁל (#438)
1390	מַתָּנָה	gift, present (17)
1391	נָדַב	(Q) to incite, instigate; (Hith) volunteer, make a voluntary decision, enlist as a volunteer, offer voluntarily, give a freewill offering (17)
1392	נֶזֶם	earring, nose-ring (17)
1393	נָקָם	vengeance, revenge (17)
1394	נָקַף	(Hi) to surround, go around, encircle, encompass, enclose, complete a circuit (17)
1395	נָתִין	temple servant; (mp) נְתִינִים (17)
1396	סָגָן	official, ruler; (mp) סְגָנִים (17)
1397	סָרַר	(Q) to be stubborn or rebellious (17)
1398	עָוָה	(Q) to do wrong; (Ni) be disturbed, be irritated; (Hi) twist, pervert, do wrong (17)
1399	עֹז	refuge, protection; (with 1cs suff) עֻזִּי (17); compare with עֹז (#463)
1400	עֵזֶר	help, assistance (17)
1401	עָיֵף	(adj) tired, exhausted, weary; (fs) עֲיֵפָה (17)
1402	עָלַז	(Q) to exult, triumph (17)
1403	עָמֹק	(adj) deep, unfathomable, mysterious; (fs) עֲמֻקָּה (17)
1404	עָצָב	idol, image, false god; (always mp) עֲצַבִּים (17)
1405	עָצַם	(Q) to be vast, mighty, powerful or numerous (17)

1406	עָרַב	(Q) to stand (as) surety for, pledge oneself (as surety for debts), be responsible for someone, conduct trade, barter (17)
1407	עָשַׁר	(Q) to be(come) rich; (Hi) make rich, gain riches (17)
1408	פֶּרַח	blossom, bud, flower (17)
1409	פֶּתִי	naïve person, simpleton; (mp) פְּתָאיִם (17); 13x in Prov
1410	צוּד	(Q) to hunt (for) (17)
1411	צָמָא	thirst (17); compare with צָמֵא (#1889)
1412	קָדַר	(Q) to be(come) dark or dirty, be untidy, be dressed in the clothes of a mourner (17)
1413	קָלוֹן	shame, dishonor (17)
1414	קְעָרָה	dish, bowl, platter; (fs cstr) קַעֲרַת (17)
1415	רָכַל	(Q Ptc) to go about as a trader (tradesman), merchant (17)
1416	רָמַשׂ	(Q) to crawl, creep, swarm, teem (17)
1417	רֶמֶשׂ	creeping thing, animal that creeps upon the earth (17); 10x in Gen
1418	רַעַשׁ	earthquake, clatter, commotion (17)
1419	רָקִיעַ	expanse, firmament (17)
1420	שְׂבָכָה	network, lattice, grid (17)
1421	שִׂנְאָה	hatred, enmity, malice (17)
1422	שָׁאוֹן	noise, uproar, tumult (17)
1423	שׁוּשַׁן	lily, lotus flower; also spelled (ms) שׁוֹשָׁן; (mp) שׁוֹשַׁנִּים (17)
1424	שָׁלִישׁ	officer, third man in a chariot; (mp) שָׁלִישִׁים (17)
1425	שֵׁמַע	report, news, rumor (17)
1426	שָׁפָל	(adj) low, lowly, humble, deep; (fs) שְׁפָלָה (17)
1427	תָּא	chamber, guardroom (17); 15x in Ezek

1428	תֶּבֶן	straw, chaff (17)
1429	תֹּף	tambourine, hand drum; (mp) תֻּפִּים (17)
1430	אוֹב	medium, necromancer, ghost; (mp) אֹבוֹת (16)
1431	אוֹן	strength, vigor, manhood, wealth (16)
1432	אָזַר	(Q) to gird (on), equip (16)
1433	בֹּהֶן	thumb, big toe (16)
1434	בָּלָה	(Q) to be(come) worn out, used up or exhausted (16)
1435	בָּעַל	(Q) to rule over, be lord (husband), marry, own (take someone into possession as betrothed) (16)
1436	בָּעַת	(Pi) to terrify, frighten, startle (16)
1437	בָּצַע	(Q) to cut off, sever, break off (away), make profit (16)
1438	בָּרַר	(Q) to purify, purge out, sort, choose, select (16)
1439	גְּדִי	young goat, kid (16)
1440	גַּל	wave; (mp with 3ms suff) גַּלָּיו (16); compare with גַּל (1325)
1441	דְּבִיר	inner sanctuary, most holy place (16); 11x in 1 Kgs
1442	דּוּשׁ	(Q) to tread on, trample down (out), thresh, exterminate, destroy; also spelled דִּישׁ (16)
1443	הָלְאָה	beyond, far away, out there (16)
1444	זוּלָה	except, only; (with 1cs suff) זוּלָתִי (16)
1445	חָגַג	(Q) to stagger, reel, celebrate a pilgrimage festival (16)
1446	חֹזֶה	(ms) seer (16)
1447	חֶמְדָּה	something desirable, precious or valuable (16)
1448	חָצַב	(Q) to quarry, hew (out), dig, dress (stones) (16)
1449	חֹרֶב	dryness, drought, heat, waste (16)
1450	חָשָׁה	(Q) to be silent; (Hi) be silent, order (someone) to be silent, hesitate, delay (16)

1451	טָבַל	(Q) to dip (something into), dip into (16)
1452	יְגִיעַ	labor, work, product of labor, gain (16)
1453	יֶקֶב	wine vat, winepress (16)
1454	יָשֵׁן	(Q) to sleep, go to sleep, be asleep (16)
1455	כָּזַב	(Pi) to lie, deceive (16)
1456	מַחֲצִית	half, middle (16)
1457	מַטָּרָה	guard, prison, (archery) target (16)
1458	מַכְאוֹב	pain, suffering; also spelled מַכְאֹב (16)
1459	מִכְסֶה	(ms) cover, covering (16)
1460	מִסְפֵּד	wailing, mourning, funeral ceremony (16)
1461	מָרַר	(Q) to be bitter (of taste, experience or attitude), be desperate; (Hi) embitter, cause bitterness or grief (16)
1462	מָשׂוֹשׂ	joy, delight (16)
1463	נָזִיר	one who is devoted, consecrated one, a Nazirite (16)
1464	נָזַל	(Q) to trickle, drip down, flow (16)
1465	סָכַךְ	(Q) to overshadow, cover (protectively), protect (16)
1466	סַם	perfume, spices; (mp) סַמִּים (16)
1467	עָנָה	(Q) to sing (16); compare with עָנָה (#152, #449)
1468	עָרוֹם	(adj) naked; (mp) עֲרוּמִּים (16)
1469	עָרְלָה	foreskin (16)
1470	עָשׂוֹר	ten, tenth (day) (16)
1471	פָּרַע	(Q) to let go, loose or free (i.e., remove restraint from), let the hair of the head hang loose, allow to run wild, leave unattended, neglect (16)
1472	פֵּשֶׁת	linen, flax; (fp) פִּשְׁתִּים (16)
1473	צִיָּה	desert, dry land (16)
1474	צֶמֶר	wool (16)
1475	קֶלַע	curtain; (mp) קְלָעִים (16)

1476	קַשׁ	stubble, chaff (16)
1477	קֶשֶׁר	alliance, conspiracy, treason (16)
1478	רָגַם	(Q) to stone, kill by stoning (16)
1479	רֵיקָם	empty-handed, without success (16)
1480	רַךְ	(adj) tender, frail, weak, soft; (fs) רַכָּה (16)
1481	שֵׂכֶל	insight, understanding, success; also spelled שֶׂכֶל (16)
1482	שַׂלְמָה	garment, clothing (16); compare with שִׂמְלָה (#957)
1483	שְׁאֵר	flesh, meat, food, blood relative (16)
1484	שִׁבֹּלֶת	ear of grain; (fp) שִׁבֳּלִים (16)
1485	שָׁוָה	(Q) to be(come) like (the same, the equal of), be equivalent to, resemble; (Pi) make like, make level (16)
1486	שֶׁפֶט	act of judgment, punishment; (mp) שְׁפָטִים (16)
1487	אֲהָהּ	ah! alas! (15)
1488	אָמַל	(Pulal) to dry up, waste away, languish (15)
1489	אַמְתַּחַת	sack, bag; (fp cstr) אַמְתְּחֹת (15); all in Gen 42–44
1490	אֵפוֹא	then, so; also spelled אֵפוֹ (15)
1491	אָרֵךְ	(adj) long, slow (15); 13x אֶרֶךְ־אַפַּיִם (lit) "long of nose;" (idiom) "slow to anger" or "patient"
1492	גְּבִירָה	mistress, lady, queen mother (15)
1493	גָּדֵר	wall (of stone) (15)
1494	גָּזַז	(Q) to shear, cut (15)
1495	גֻּלָּה	bowl, basin; (fp) גֻּלֹּת (15)
1496	גָּלוּת	exile, exiles (15)
1497	גְּעָרָה	rebuke, threat (15)
1498	גָּרָה	(Hith) to strive (against), oppose, battle (15)
1499	דָּגָה	fish (15); compare with (ms) דָּג (#1278)
1500	דֶּשֶׁן	fat, fat-soaked ashes (15)

1501	הָלַל	(Q) to be infatuated, be deluded; (Hithpolel) be mad, act like a madman (15); compare with הָלַל (#282)
1502	הָרָה	(fs adj) pregnant (15); compare with הָרָה (#728)
1503	זוּ	(dmstr pron and adj) this; (rel pron) who, that, which (15)
1504	חָבֵר	associate, companion, friend (15)
1505	חָצָה	(Q) to divide (into) (15)
1506	כָּבַשׁ	(Q) to subdue, subjugate, make subservient, bring into bondage, violate (rape) a woman; (Ni) be subdued, be subjugated (15)
1507	כָּלִיל	(adj) entire, whole, complete (15)
1508	כַּרְמֶל	fertile field, orchard, plantation (15)
1509	מֹאזְנַיִם	balances, scales (15)
1510	מִבְטָח	confidence, trust, security (15)
1511	מְחִיר	price, payment, money (15)
1512	מִלֻּאִים	consecration, ordination (of priest), setting (of stones); also spelled מִלּוּאִים (15)
1513	מִקְנָה	purchase, acquisition (15)
1514	מַשְׂאֵת	something lifted up, gift, tribute (15)
1515	נָגַן	(Pi) to play a stringed instrument (15)
1516	נָוֶה	pasture, dwelling; (fp cstr) נְאוֹת (15); compare with נָוֶה (#930)
1517	סוּפָה	wind (of a storm), tempest, gale (15)
1518	סַל	basket (15)
1519	עָצַב	(Q) to hurt, pain, rebuke, grieve; (Ni) be pained for, be in grieving for, be worried, be distressed (15)
1520	עֵקֶב	(conj) because, on account of; (n) result, wages (15)
1521	עָרָה	(Pi) to uncover, reveal, expose, lay bare, empty; (Hi) uncover, make naked, expose, pour out (15)
1522	עֲרָפֶל	thick darkness, gloom (15)

1523	עָרַץ	(Q) to tremble, be terrified, be in dread, be startled, be alarmed; (Hi) terrify, strike (inspire) with awe, be in terror (15)
1524	עֹשֶׁק	oppression, extortion (15)
1525	פָּצָה	(Q) to open (the mouth), speak (15)
1526	צֶלֶם	image, idol; (mp cstr) צַלְמֵי (15)
1527	צֶמֶד	pair, team (15)
1528	צָמַת	(Hi) to silence, exterminate, annihilate (15)
1529	קָדַד	(Q) to bow down, kneel down (15)
1530	רֹמַח	spear, lance (15)
1531	רְמִיָּה	laziness, slackness, deceit, treachery (15)
1532	רִשְׁעָה	wickedness, guilt (15)
1533	שׁוּר	(Q) to behold, regard, gaze on (15)
1534	שָׁנָה	(Q) to change; (Pi) change, alter, pervert (15); compare with שָׁנָה (#51)
1535	שֶׁרֶץ	swarming things (15); 12x in Lev
1536	תֹּאַר	form, shape, appearance (15)
1537	תָּם	(adj) blameless, complete, perfect; (mp) תַּמִּים (15)
1538	תַּן	(cs) jackal; (cp) תַּנִּים (15)
1539	תַּנּוּר	(cs) oven, firepot, furnace (15)
1540	תַּנִּין	serpent, dragon, monster (15)
1541	תְּרָפִים	images, statues, idols (15)
1542	אֵזוֹר	loincloth, girdle (14)
1543	אֵיתָן	(adj) everflowing, constant, enduring; (mp) אֵתָנִים (14)
1544	אָנַף	(Q) to be angry (14)
1545	אָסִיר	prisoner (14)
1546	בּוּז	(Q) to show contempt, despise (14); compare with בּוּז (#1755)

1547	בַּר	grain, corn, wheat (14)
1548	בָּרִיא	(adj) fat, well fed; (fp) בְּרִיאוֹת (14)
1549	גְּאֻלָּה	right of redemption, next-of-kin (14)
1550	גָּבִיעַ	cup, bowl; (mp) גְּבִעִים (14)
1551	גָּעַר	(Q) to rebuke, reproach (14)
1552	דֶּגֶל	division of a tribe, banner, standard (14); 13x in Num
1553	דַּק	(adj) thin, lean, skinny; (fp) דַּקּוֹת (14)
1554	דֶּשֶׁא	grass, vegetation (14)
1555	חוֹתָם	seal, signet ring (14)
1556	חָכָה	(Pi) to wait (for), tarry, long for, be patient (14)
1557	חַלָּה	cake, ring-shaped bread (14)
1558	טוּל	(Hi) to throw (far), cast, hurl; (Hoph) be thrown, be hurled (14)
1559	יַבָּשָׁה	dry land, dry ground (14)
1560	יָגוֹן	grief, sorrow, agony (14)
1561	יְרֻשָּׁה	possession, inheritance (14)
1562	יֹשֶׁר	uprightness, honesty, straightness (14)
1563	כָּבֵד	(fs) liver (14); compare with כָּבֵד (#353, #773)
1564	כְּהֻנָּה	priesthood (14)
1565	כָּרָה	(Q) to dig, excavate, hollow out (14)
1566	לָוָה	(Q) to borrow; (Hi) lend to (14); compare with לָוָה (#1706)
1567	לוּלֵי	if not, unless, except; also spelled לוּלֵא (14)
1568	לַפִּיד	torch, lightning (14)
1569	מוּר	(Hi) to change, alter, exchange (14)
1570	מָחַץ	(Q) to smash, shatter, beat to pieces, smite (14)
1571	מִכְשׁוֹל	stumbling block, obstacle, offense (14)

1572	מַעֲרָב	west, sunset (14)
1573	מָרַט	(Q) to make smooth (bare or bald), polish, scour, pull out (hair), sharpen (sword); (Pu) be polished, be smooth or bare (14)
1574	מַשְׂכִּיל	undetermined technical term, perhaps indicating a song of "wisdom" or "insight" (14); all in psalm titles
1575	נְגִינָה	music of stringed instrument, song of mockery (14)
1576	נָשָׁא	(Hi) to deceive, cheat, trick (14)
1577	נֶתֶק	skin disease, scab (14); all in Lev
1578	עֲדִי	ornament, jewelry; (with 3ms suff) עֶדְיוֹ (14)
1579	עָכַר	(Q) to disturb, trouble, put into disorder, confuse, bring disaster (ruin); be stirred up, be ruined, be cut off (14)
1580	עָצֵל	(adj) low, lazy; (n) sluggard (14); all in Prov
1581	עָקֵב	heel, footprint, rear guard (of an army) (14)
1582	פָּגַשׁ	(Q) to meet, encounter, confront (14)
1583	פְּנִימָה	inside, within (14)
1584	פִּסֵּחַ	(adj) lame, crippled (14)
1585	פְּעֻלָּה	work, deed, reward, payment; (with 3ms suff) פְּעֻלָּתוֹ (14)
1586	פֶּרֶד	mule (14)
1587	פָּרַס	(Q) to break; (Hi) have a divided hoof (14)
1588	פַּת	piece, scrap, morsel; (fp) פִּתִּים (14)
1589	צָבָא	(Q) to wage war, go to war, fight against, serve (in the cult) (14); compare with צָבָא (#107)
1590	צַיִד	game, hunting, hunter (14)
1591	צִיץ	flower, blossom; (mp) צִצִּים (14)
1592	צַעַד	step, pace (14)
1593	קָבַב	(Q) to curse (14)

1594   קְבוּרָה   grave, burial; (with 3ms suff) קְבֻרָתוֹ (14)

1595   קָבַל   (Pi) to take, receive, accept (14)

1596   קֶמַח   flour (14)

1597   קָצַץ   (Q) to cut (chop) off, trim; (Pi) cut (chop) off, cut in pieces (14)

1598   קָצַר   (Q) to be short(ened), be(come) impatient (14); compare with קָצַר (#855)

1599   רָוָה   (Q) to drink one's fill; (Pi, Hi) drink abundantly, water thoroughly, drench, saturate (14)

1600   רָוַח   (Q) to get relief; (Pu) be wide or spacious; (Hi) smell (14)

1601   רֵיק   (adj) empty, vain; (mp) רֵקִים (14); compare with רִיק (#1308)

1602   שְׂחוֹק   laughter, laughingstock, mockery (14)

1603   שִׂיחַ   complaint, lament (14); compare with שִׂיחַ (#1265)

1604   שָׁאַף   (Q) to gasp, pant (for or after), long for (14)

1605   שְׁבִית   captivity (14)

1606   שָׁלַל   (Q) to plunder, spoil, capture, rob (14)

1607   שָׁרַץ   (Q) to swarm, teem (with), be innumerable (14)

1608   תּוֹר   (fs) turtledove; (fp) תֹּרִים (14)

1609   תּוֹשָׁב   resident alien, stranger, sojourner (14)

1610   תַּחַשׁ   porpoise, dolphin, leather (14)

1611   אֵלָה   oak, terebinth, large tree (13)

1612   אָנָּא   please! I ask you! (preceding a request); also spelled אָנָּה (13)

1613   אָנַח   (Ni) to sigh, groan (13)

1614   אָרַג   (Q) to weave; (Q Ptc) weaver (13)

1615   בָּחִיר   (adj) chosen, elect (13)

1616	בַּת	(ms) liquid measurement, bath; (mp) בַּתִּים (13); compare with בַּת (#82)
1617	גְּדוּלָה	greatness, great deed (13)
1618	גֹּדֶל	greatness, arrogance (13)
1619	גְּוִיָּה	body, corpse (13)
1620	הַוָּה	destruction, ruin; (fp) הַוּוֹת (13)
1621	הָמַם	(Q) to make (a) noise, confuse, bring into motion and confusion (army), discomfit, disturb (13)
1622	וָו	hook, nail, peg; (mp cstr) וָוֵי (13); all in Exod
1623	זֵד	(adj) proud, insolent, presumptuous; (mp) זֵדִים (13)
1624	זוֹב	discharge (of body fluid), hemorrhage (13); all in Lev
1625	זָמַם	(Q) to consider, think, ponder, devise, plan (evil), purpose (13)
1626	חָבַל	(Q) to take, hold or seize (something) in pledge, exact a pledge from someone, bind by taking a pledge (13); compare with חָבַל (#1766)
1627	חָבַק	(Q) to embrace, fold the hands (in idleness); (Pi) embrace (13)
1628	חָזֶה	(ms) breast (of sacrificial animal) (13)
1629	חֹמֶר	dry measurement, heap, pile, homer (13); compare with חֹמֶר (#1370)
1630	חַנּוּן	(adj) gracious, merciful (13)
1631	חָנֵף	(adj) godless, profane (13)
1632	חָפֵץ	(adj) delighting (in), desiring (13); compare with חָפֵץ (#471)
1633	חֹר	noble, free person; (mp) חֹרִים (13)
1634	טָהֳרָה	purification, purity, ceremonial cleanness (13)
1635	טִיט	mud, mire, clay (13)
1636	טַעַם	taste, sense, discernment (13)
1637	יְבוּל	produce, harvest, crop (13)

1638	יָלִיד	(adj) born (of); (n) son, slave (13)
1639	יְשִׁימוֹן	desert, wilderness, waste (13)
1640	כֹּפֶר	ransom, bribe (13)
1641	כֶּשֶׂב	young ram, lamb (13)
1642	לֻלָאֹת	(fp) loops, knots (13); all in Exod
1643	מַבּוּל	flood, deluge (13); 12x in Gen 7–11
1644	מַחְמָד	something desirable, precious thing (13)
1645	מַחְסוֹר	need, lack, poverty (13)
1646	מָן	manna (13)
1647	מַעְגָּל	path, wagon track; (mp cstr) מַעְגְּלוֹת (13)
1648	מֵצַח	forehead, brow (13)
1649	מְצִלְתַּיִם	(cd) cymbals (13)
1650	מְרַאֲשֹׁות	(fp) at the head of, headrest (13)
1651	מִרְעֶה	(ms) pasture, place of grazing (13)
1652	מַרְפֵּא	healing, cure, remedy (13)
1653	מְשׁוּבָה	backsliding, falling away, apostasy; also spelled מְשֻׁבָה (13)
1654	נְבָלָה	outrage, disgrace, willful sin, stupidity (13)
1655	נָעִים	(adj) pleasant, lovely, delightful; (mp) נְעִימִים (13)
1656	נֵתַח	piece of meat (13)
1657	סָכַן	(Q) to be of use or service; (Hi) be accustomed to, be familiar (acquainted) with, be in the habit of (13)
1658	סָתַם	(Q) to plug (stop) up, shut up, close, hide, keep secret, disguise (13)
1659	עָטָה	(Q) to wrap, cover or envelop (oneself) with (13)
1660	פָּאַר	(Pi) to glorify, exalt, beautify; (Hith) show (manifest) one's glory, glorify oneself, be glorified, boast (13)
1661	פֶּלֶא	wonder, miracle, something extraordinary (13)

1662	פָּקִיד	leader, overseer, officer (13)
1663	צָחַק	(Q) to laugh; (Pi) joke (with), play (with), amuse oneself, fondle (13)
1664	צְפַרְדֵּעַ	(fs) frog; (fp) צְפַרְדְּעִים (13); 11x in Exod
1665	קַו	measuring line (13)
1666	קַל	(adj) light, swift, agile; (mp) קַלִּים (13)
1667	קֵן	nest, nestlings; (mp) קִנִּים (13)
1668	רָגַע	(Q) to crust over or become hard (of skin), stir up (sea); (Hi) give rest to, come to rest, make peace, linger (13)
1669	רַחוּם	(adj) compassionate (13)
1670	רָעֵב	(Q) to be hungry, suffer famine (13); compare with רָעָב (#1263)
1671	שְׂרֵפָה	burning, fire (13)
1672	שְׁאֵלָה	request, petition (13)
1673	שׁוּט	(Q) to roam (around), go (rove) about, row (across water); (Polel) roam about (around) (13)
1674	שְׁחִין	boil, blister, skin ulcer (13)
1675	שִׁירָה	song (13); compare with שִׁיר (#418 and #455)
1676	שִׁכּוֹר	(adj) drunk; (n) drunkard (13)
1677	שָׁעָה	(Q) to gaze at, look at, look (regard) with favor, be concerned about (13)
1678	תַּחְתּוֹן	(adj) lower, lowest; (fs) תַּחְתּוֹנָה (13)
1679	תַּעַר	razor, knife, sheath (13)
1680	אַדֶּרֶת	cloak, robe, fur coat (12)
1681	בַּהֶרֶת	white spot on the skin (12); all in Lev
1682	בּוּס	(Q) to tread down, trample under foot (12)
1683	בִּי	please, with your permission (12); בִּי אֲדֹנִי "please, my lord"

1684	בְּכֹרָה	birthright, right of the firstborn (12)
1685	גַּב	something curved, back, eyebrow, rim (of a wheel); (mp cstr) גַּבֵּי (12)
1686	גָּזַר	(Q) to cut (in two, in pieces), divide, cut down, decide; (Ni) be cut off (from), be decided (12)
1687	גֻּלְגֹּלֶת	head, skull; (fp cstr) גֻּלְגְּלֹת (12)
1688	גַּנָּה	garden, orchard; (fp) גַּנּוֹת (12)
1689	דֹּב	bear; (mp) דֻּבִּים (12)
1690	דָּמָה	(Ni) to be destroyed, be ruined (12); compare with דָּמָה (#965)
1691	דָּקַק	(Q) to crush, become fine through grinding; (Hi) crush fine, pulverize; (Hoph) be crushed fine (12)
1692	הֶאָח	aha! (12)
1693	הֲלֹם	here, to here (12)
1694	זְנוּנִים	prostitution, fornication (12)
1695	זָעַם	(Q) to curse, scold, denounce (12)
1696	חֲלִיפָה	change, shift, relief; (fp) חֲלִיפוֹת (12)
1697	חָפָה	(Q) to cover; (Pi) overlay (with) (12)
1698	חֵקֶר	searching, something searched out (12)
1699	טֶבַח	slaughtering, slaughter (12)
1700	יָחִיד	(adj) only (child), lonely, solitary (12)
1701	יֶרַח	month (12)
1702	כַּר	ram, battering ram; (mp) כָּרִים (12)
1703	לָבִיא	(cs) lion, lioness (12)
1704	לְבֵנָה	brick, tile; (fp) לְבֵנִים (12)
1705	לַהַב	flame, blade (of sword) (12)
1706	לָוָה	(Ni) to join oneself to (12); compare with לָוָה (#1566)
1707	לַחַץ	oppression, affliction (12)

1708	מִבְחָר	choicest, finest, best (people or things) (12)
1709	מְהוּמָה	confusion, dismay, panic (12)
1710	מוֹטָה	yoke, bar, carrying pole; (fp) מֹטוֹת (12); 10x in Isa, Ezek
1711	מָנָה	part, portion, share; (fp) מָנוֹת (12); compare with מָנָה (#1010)
1712	מַסַּע	breaking camp, setting out, journey (12)
1713	מְצָד	(fs) stronghold, fortress; (fp) מְצָדוֹת (12); compare with מְצוּדָה (#1338)
1714	מִצְנֶפֶת	turban, headband, diadem (12); 11x in Exod, Lev
1715	מִקְצוֹעַ	corner, angle (12)
1716	מֹר	myrrh, myrrh oil; also spelled מוֹר (12)
1717	מַרְאָה	appearance, vision (12)
1718	מָתוֹק	(adj) sweet, pleasant (12)
1719	נָפַח	(Q) to breathe, blow, blow fire upon (set aflame), gasp, pant (12)
1720	נְצִיב	pillar, post, military garrison (12)
1721	נֶשֶׁךְ	interest, usury (12)
1722	נֶשֶׁף	twilight, dusk (12)
1723	סָלַל	(Q) to pile up, heap up, lift up, exalt, praise (12)
1724	סָעַד	(Q) to support, sustain, strengthen (with food), uphold (12)
1725	עֶגְלָה	heifer, young cow (12)
1726	עָוַת	(Q) to bend, make crooked, pervert (justice), falsify (balances), suppress (12)
1727	עָמִית	(ms) neighbor, friend, community; (ms cstr) עֲמִית (12)
1728	עָמַל	(Q) to labor, toil, exert oneself (12)
1729	עָקָר	(adj) barren, childless; (fs) עֲקָרָה (12)
1730	צְבִי	gazelle (12); compare with צְבִי (#1347)

1731	צוּק	(Hi) to oppress, press hard, harass, constrain (12)
1732	צֶמַח	growth, sprout, branch (12)
1733	קָצִין	commander, leader, ruler (12)
1734	קָרֵב	(adj) approaching, drawing near (12)
1735	רֹאשׁ	poisonous herb, venom (12); compare with רֹאשׁ (#80)
1736	רָבַע	(Q) to provide with four corners, make square (12)
1737	רַגְלִי	(adj) on foot, pedestrian, foot soldier (12)
1738	רִיק	emptiness, vanity (12); compare with רִיק (#1308)
1739	רִקְמָה	(something) embroidered, woven garment (12)
1740	שׁוֹאָה	trouble, ruin, storm (12)
1741	שָׁחַר	(Pi) to seek eagerly for, look diligently for, be intent on (12)
1742	שָׁקַד	(Q) to (keep) watch, be wakeful, be vigilant, watch over, be concerned about (12)
1743	שָׁרַק	(Q) to hiss, whistle (12)s
1744	תּוּשִׁיָּה	wisdom, success (12)
1745	אֲבָל	but, however, indeed, truly (11)
1746	אֹדוֹת	because, on account of; (always with prep עַל אֹדוֹת) עַל (11)
1747	אַיָּל	(male) deer, stag (11)
1748	אַיָּלָה	(female) deer, doe (11)
1749	אֶלֶף	clan, tribe, region (11); compare with אֶלֶף (#101)
1750	אֲנָחָה	sighing, groaning (11)
1751	אִסָּר	obligation, pledge, vow; also spelled אֱסָר (11); all in Num 30
1752	אָרַשׂ	(Pi) to become engaged to or betroth (a wife); (Pu) be(come) engaged or betrothed (11)
1753	אֶתְנַן	wages, payment, gift (11)

1754	בָּדָד	alone, by oneself (11)
1755	בּוּז	contempt (11); compare with בּוּז (#1546)
1756	גָּאַל	(Ni, Pu) to be defiled, become impure; (Hith) defile oneself (11); compare with גָּאַל (#372)
1757	גָּזִית	cut stone (11)
1758	גֵּרָה	cud (11); all in Lev 11 and Deut 14
1759	דָּקַר	(Q) to pierce (through), run through; (Pu) be pierced through (11)
1760	דָּשֵׁן	(Pi) to refresh, revive, clean away fat ashes; (Pu) be made fat (11)
1761	הָדַף	(Q) to thrust (away, out), push (away), drive away (out), shove (11)
1762	זָדוֹן	arrogance, presumption (11)
1763	זֹה	(dmstr adj) this (11); alternate form of זֹאת(#79)
1764	זַךְ	(adj) pure, clean; (fs) זַכָּה (11)
1765	זָנָב	tail (11)
1766	חָבַל	(Q) to act corruptly or ruinously; (Pi) ruin, destroy (11); compare with חָבַל (#1626)
1767	חוֹחַ	thorn, thornbush (11)
1768	חַיָּה	life; (with 3ms suff) חַיָּתוֹ (11); compare with חַיָּה (#390)
1769	חֲלָצַיִם	(md) loins, stomach, waist (11)
1770	חָמוֹת	mother-in-law (11)
1771	חָמֵץ	leaven, something leavened (11)
1772	חָנֵף	(Q) to be godless (of a priest or prophet), be defiled (of land); (Hi) defile, pollute (11)
1773	חַרְטֹם	magician, soothsayer priest; (mp) חַרְטֻמִּים (11)
1774	חָשַׁק	(Q) to be attached to, cling to, love (11)
1775	חָתַן	(Hith) to intermarry with, become related by marriage, become a son-in-law (11)

1776	טָבַח	(Q) to slaughter, butcher, slay (11)
1777	טוּחַ	(Q) to plaster (wall of a house), coat, overlay (11)
1778	טָעַם	(Q) to taste, eat, savor food, perceive (11)
1779	יִדְּעֹנִי	soothsayer; (mp) יִדְּעֹנִים (11)
1780	יָקַץ	(Q) to awake, wake up, become active (11)
1781	יָקַר	(Q) to be difficult, precious, prized, highly valued, esteemed, honored, costly or rare (11)
1782	יֹתֶרֶת	covering, lobe (of animal livers) (11)
1783	כֵּן	base, stand; (with 3ms suff) כַּנּוֹ (11); compare with כֵּן (#69, #1122)
1784	כָּנַס	(Q) to gather, collect, amass; (Pi) gather, assemble (11)
1785	מָגוֹר	place of residence, temporary dwelling; (mp cstr) מְגוּרֵי (11)
1786	מַד	garment, clothes; (with 3ms suff) מִדּוֹ (11)
1787	מוֹרָא	fear, terror (11)
1788	מְחִתָּה	terror, ruin, destruction (11)
1789	מִשְׁעֶנֶת	staff, stick, support (11)
1790	נָבַע	(Hi) to make (something) gush or bubble (forth), pour out or ferment (11)
1791	נָגַח	(Q) to gore (ox); (Pi) push, butt, thrust, knock down (11)
1792	נָחַשׁ	(Pi) to practice divination, seek and give omens, observe signs, foretell (11)
1793	נָעַר	(Q, Pi) to shake (out or off); (Ni) be shaken (out or off) (11)
1794	נָשַׁךְ	(Q, Pi) to bite (11)
1795	סֹלְלָה	mound, siege ramp (11)
1796	סַפִּיר	sapphire, lapis lazuli (11)
1797	עוֹלֵל	child (11)

1798	עָזַז	(Q) to be strong, prevail (against), defy (11)
1799	עָטַף	(Q) to be(come) weak, feeble or faint; (Hith) feel weak or faint (11)
1800	עָנַן	(Poel) to practice soothsaying, conjure up (spirits), interpret signs (11)
1801	עֲצָרָה	assembly, celebration; also spelled עֲצֶרֶת (11)
1802	עָרוּם	(adj) crafty, cunning, clever, prudent (11)
1803	עֲרֵמָה	heap, mound (of grain); (fp) עֲרֵמוֹת (11)
1804	פֶּטֶר	firstborn (11)
1805	פִּתּוּחַ	engraving, inscription (11)
1806	פָּתִיל	cord, thread (11)
1807	צֶאֱצָאִים	offspring, descendants (11)
1808	קָדְקֹד	crown of the head, skull (11)
1809	קָדֵשׁ	cult or temple prostitute; (fs) קְדֵשָׁה (11)
1810	קוֹץ	thorn, thornbush (11)
1811	קֶסֶם	divination, prediction (11)
1812	קָרְחָה	baldness, bald spot (11)
1813	רֹאֶה	seer (11)
1814	רִבּוֹא	(fs) ten thousand, countless number; also spelled רִבּוֹ (11)
1815	רָעַם	(Q) to rage, roar (sea), thunder, storm; (Hi) thunder, storm (11)
1816	רָקַע	(Q) to stamp (down or out), trample, spread out; (Pi) beat out, hammer out (11)
1817	שַׁבָּתוֹן	day of rest, Sabbath, feast (11); 3x in Exod, 8x in Lev
1818	שֹׁהַם	precious stone, carnelian (11)
1819	שׁוּל	hem, skirt (of robe) (11)
1820	שַׁוְעָה	cry for help; (with 1cs suff) שַׁוְעָתִי (11)

1821	שָׁסָה	(Q) to plunder, spoil (11)
1822	שֶׁקֶץ	detestable thing, abomination (11)
1823	תִּיכוֹן	(adj) middle, center; (fs) תִּיכֹנָה (11)
1824	אִגֶּרֶת	letter, document; (fp) אִגְּרוֹת (10)
1825	אָדַם	(Q) to be red; (Pu) be reddened, be dyed red (10)
1826	אוּץ	(Q) to urge, press, be in a hurry, be pressed (10)
1827	אֵזוֹב	hyssop; also spelled אֵזֹב (10)
1828	אֵיפֹה	where? (10)
1829	אַלּוֹן	large tree (10)
1830	אֲפֵלָה	darkness, gloominess (10)
1831	אָשַׁר	(Pi) to call (consider) blessed, fortunate or happy; (Pu) be called blessed, fortunate or happy (10)
1832	בִּגְלַל	because of, on account of (10)
1833	בֶּדֶק	damage, breach, crack (10)
1834	בִּזָּה	spoil, plunder (10)
1835	בַּלָּהָה	sudden terror, horror; (fp) בַּלָּהוֹת (10)
1836	בְּמוֹ	(prep) in, at, with, by, against; alternate (poetic) form of prep בְּ (10)
1837	בְּתוּלִים	virginity, evidence of virginity (10)
1838	גָּדַר	(Q) to build a wall, block a road, wall up (10)
1839	גּוּר	(Q) to be afraid, dread, stand in awe (10); compare with גּוּר (#430)
1840	גָּעַל	(Q) to loathe, abhor, feel disgust (10)
1841	גָּעַשׁ	(Q) to shake (10)
1842	זִיד	(Q) to act insolently; (Hi) boil or cook, become hot (with anger), behave arrogantly (10)
1843	זֵר	frame, border, molding (10); all in Exod
1844	חָדַשׁ	(Pi) to make new, renew, restore (10)

1845	חוּל	(Q) to go around, whirl (about), dance, writhe; also spelled חִיל (10); compare with חִיל (#661)
1846	חָלָק	(adj) smooth, slippery, flattering (10)
1847	חֹם	heat, warmth (10)
1848	חֶמְאָה	butter, cream, curdled milk (10)
1849	חָפַז	(Q) to be in a hurry, hurry away (in alarm or fear), hasten in alarm; (Ni) run away in alarm (10)
1850	חָרֵב	(adj) dry, desolate, wasted; (fs) חֲרֵבָה (10); compare with חָרַב (#840)
1851	חָרַץ	(Q) to decide, cut (10)
1852	חָשַׂף	(Q) to strip, strip off, bare, skim (scoop) off (10)
1853	טָבַע	(Q) to sink, penetrate; (Hoph) be sunk, be settled, be planted (10)
1854	יִתְרוֹן	advantage, profit (10); all in Eccl
1855	כַּבִּיר	(adj) mighty, strong, powerful (10)
1856	כֶּלֶא	prison, confinement (10)
1857	לָהַט	(Q) to blaze, burn; (Pi) set ablaze, devour (with fire or flame), scorch (10)
1858	מָדִין	contention, quarrel; (mp) מִדְיָנִים (10)
1859	מִמְכָּר	something sold, merchandise, sale (10)
1860	מִסְתָּר	secret place, hiding place; (mp) מִסְתָּרִים (10)
1861	מַעֲרֶכֶת	row (of bread), consecrated bread (10)
1862	מַצָּב	military garrison, station (10)
1863	מָקַק	(Ni) to rot (away), fester (wounds), dwindle or waste away, decay, melt, dissolve (10)
1864	מִקְרֶה	(ms) accident, chance, fate (10)
1865	מַרְעִית	pasture, place of grazing (10)
1866	מַשְׁחִית	destroyer, destruction (10)

1867	מָשַׁשׁ	(Q) to feel, touch; (Pi) feel (over, through), grope, search, rummage through (10)
1868	נָאֶה	(adj) lovely, beautiful, desirable, suitable; (fs) נָאוָה (10)
1869	נֵבֶל	jar, bottle (10); compare with נֵבֶל (#1012)
1870	נָגַר	(Ni) to flow, gush forth, be poured (out), be spilled, be stretched out (hands); (Hi) pour (out, down) (10)
1871	נָהַל	(Pi) to lead, guide, escort, help along, give rest to, provide (with food), transport (10)
1872	נָזַר	(Ni) to devote, dedicate or consecrate oneself to (a deity), treat with awe, deal respectfully with, fast; (Hi) restrain from, abstain from, live as a Nazirite (10)
1873	נְחוּשָׁה	copper, bronze (10)
1874	סוּךְ	(Q) to grease (oneself) with oil, anoint (10)
1875	עֵירֹם	(adj) naked; (n) nakedness (10)
1876	עָנַג	(Hith) to pamper oneself, take delight (pleasure) in, refresh oneself (10)
1877	עַפְעַפִּים	(md) eyelids, (flashing of the) eyes (10)
1878	עִקֵּשׁ	(adj) perverted, crooked, false (10)
1879	עֹרֵב	raven (10)
1880	עֶרֶשׂ	(fs) couch, bed (10)
1881	עָשַׂר	(Q) to exact a tithe, take a tenth part of; (Pi) give, pay or receive a tenth, tithe (10)
1882	פּוּחַ	(Hi) to testify (10)
1883	פָּזַר	(Pi) to scatter, disperse (10)
1884	פַּחַת	pit, ravine (10)
1885	פֶּלֶג	water channel, canal (10)
1886	פֶּרֶא	wild donkey (10)

1887	פָּרַק	(Q) to tear away, pull away, rescue; (Pi) pull or tear off; (Hith) pull or tear off from oneself, be pulled or torn off (10)
1888	צֵידָה	food, provisions; also spelled צֵדָה (10)
1889	צָמֵא	(Q) to thirst, be thirsty (10); compare with צָמֵא (#1411)
1890	קַדְמֹנִי	(adj) eastern, former, past (10)
1891	קָמָה	standing grain (10)
1892	קִנְיָן	property, possessions (10)
1893	קֶרֶס	(curtain) hook, clasp; (mp cstr) קַרְסֵי (10); all in Exod
1894	רַעְיָה	darling, beloved; (with 1cs suff) רַעְיָתִי (10); 9x in Song
1895	שָׂבֵעַ	(adj) satisfied, full (10)
1896	שַׁאֲנָן	(adj) at ease, secure, untroubled; (fp) שַׁאֲנַוֹּת (10)
1897	שָׁמַט	(Q) to let loose, let fall, let drop, release, abandon, leave fallow (10)
1898	שָׁמֵן	(adj) fat, rich; (fs) שְׁמֵנָה (10)
1899	שְׁפִי	barren height; (mp) שְׁפָיִים and שְׁפָיִם (10)
1900	שְׁרִרוּת	stubbornness, hardness (10)
1901	שָׁתַל	(Q) to plant, transplant (10)
1902	תַּהְפּוּכָה	perversity, perverse thing; (fp) תַּהְפֻּכוֹת (10)
1903	תְּמוּנָה	form, likeness, image (10)

HEBREW WORDS
ARRANGED BY COMMON ROOT
LISTED ALPHABETICALLY

The following word list contains Hebrew words that occur at least 10 times and share a common root. Note that most of the cognate groupings begin with a verb. Following the verb (if any), entries are arranged by frequency. The words in this list also appear in Word List 1, but not all words that appear in Word List 1 will appear in this list.

אָבַל

אָבַל (Q) to mourn, lament; (Hith) observe mourning rites (36)

אֵבֶל mourning, funeral ceremony (24)

אדר

אַדִּיר (adj) noble, majestic, mighty (27)

אַדֶּרֶת cloak, robe, fur coat (12)

אהב

אָהַב (Q) to love (of human and divine love); (Pi Ptc) lover (217)

אַהֲבָה love (32)

אוה

אָוָה (Pi) to wish, desire, want; (Hith) crave, wish for, long for (30)

תַּאֲוָה desire, longing (26)

אור

אוֹר (Hi) to give light, shine, illuminate, light up (44)

אוֹר (cs) light, daylight, sunshine (120)

מָאוֹר light, luminary, light-bearer (18); 15x in Gen–Num

אזן

אָזַן (Hi) to give ear (to), listen (to), hear, heed (41)

אֹזֶן (fs) ear; (fd cstr) אָזְנֵי (188)

אזר

אָזַר (Q) to gird (on), equip (16)

אֵזוֹר loincloth, girdle (14)

אחז

אָחַז (Q) to seize, grasp, take hold (of), hold fast (63)

אֲחֻזָּה property, possession; (with 3ms suff) אֲחֻזָּתוֹ (66)

אחר

אָחַר   (Pi) to delay, cause one to delay, detain, hesitate, linger (18)

אַחֲרֵי   (prep) after, behind; also spelled (97x) אַחַר (718)

אַחֵר   (adj) other, another, foreign; (fs) אַחֶרֶת; (mp) אֲחֵרִים (166)

אַחֲרִית   end, extremity, last (61)

אַחֲרוֹן   (adj) last, behind, west (51)

אכל

אָכַל   (Q) to eat, consume; (Ni) be eaten, be consumed; (Hi) feed, cause to eat (820)

אֹכֶל   food (38)

מַאֲכָל   food (30)

אָכְלָה   food, nourishment (18)

אמן

אָמַן   (Ni) to (prove to) be reliable, faithful or trustworthy; (Hi) believe (in), trust, have trust in, put trust in (97)

אֱמֶת   truth, fidelity; (with 2ms suff) אֲמִתֶּךָ (127)

אֱמוּנָה   faithfulness, reliability (49)

אָמֵן   amen, surely (30)

אמר

אָמַר   (Q) to say, mention, think; (Ni) be said, be called; (Hi) declare, proclaim (5,316)

אֵמֶר   word, saying, speech; (mp cstr) אִמְרֵי (48)

אִמְרָה   word, saying; (with 1cs suff) אִמְרָתִי (36)

אנח

אָנַח   (Ni) to sigh, groan (13)

אֲנָחָה   sighing, groaning (11)

אנף

אָנַף   (Q) to be angry (14)

אַף   nostril, nose; (metaphorically) anger; (md) אַפַּיִם (277)

אסר

אָסַר	(Q) to tie, bind, fetter, imprison (73)
אָסִיר	prisoner (14)
אִסָּר	obligation, pledge, vow; also spelled אֱסָר (11); all in Num 30

ארך

אָרַךְ	(Hi) to make long, lengthen, extend (34)
אֹרֶךְ	length; (with 3ms suff) אָרְכּוֹ (95)
אָרֵךְ	(adj) long, slow (15); 13x אֶרֶךְ־אַפַּיִם (lit) "long of nose;" (idiom) "slow to anger" or "patient"

אשׁם

אָשַׁם	(Q) to be(come) guilty, commit an offense, do a wrong (35)
אָשָׁם	guilt, guilt offering (46); 27x in Lev
אַשְׁמָה	guilt, blame (19)

אשׁר

אָשַׁר	(Pi) to call (consider) blessed, fortunate or happy; (Pu) be called blessed, fortunate or happy (10)
אַשְׁרֵי	blessed, happy (44); 26x in Pss

בוא

בּוֹא	(Q) to go in, enter, come to, come upon, arrive; (Hi) bring (in), come (in); (Hoph) be brought (2,592)
תְּבוּאָה	produce, harvest (43)
מָבוֹא	entrance, setting (of the sun), west (26)

בוז

בּוּז	(Q) to show contempt, despise (14)
בּוּז	contempt (11)

בושׁ

בּוֹשׁ	(Q) to be ashamed; (Hi) put to shame, be ashamed (125)
בֹּשֶׁת	shame, disgrace (41)

בזז

בָּזַז (Q) to plunder, spoil (43)

בַּז plunder, spoil (25)

בִּזָּה spoil, plunder (10)

בחר

בָּחַר (Q) to choose, test, examine (172)

בָּחִיר (adj) chosen, elect (13)

מִבְחָר choicest, finest, best (people or things) (12)

בטח

בָּטַח (Q) to trust, be confident, rely (upon) (118)

בֶּטַח security, safety (42)

מִבְטָח confidence, trust, security (15)

בין

בִּין (Q) to understand, perceive, consider, give heed to; (Ni) be discerning, have understanding; (Hi) understand, make understand, teach; (Hith) show oneself perceptive, behave intelligently (171)

תְּבוּנָה understanding, skill (42); 19x in Prov

בִּינָה understanding, insight (38)

בכה

בָּכָה (Q) to weep (in grief or joy), weep for (114)

בְּכִי weeping (30)

בכר

בְּכוֹר firstborn, oldest offspring; also spelled בְּכֹר (120)

בִּכּוּרִים firstfruits, early harvest (17)

בְּכֹרָה birthright, right of the firstborn (12)

בלה

בָּלָה (Q) to be(come) worn out, used up or exhausted (16)

בְּלִי without, nothing (59); 22x in Job

בנה

בָּנָה (Q) to build (up), rebuild, build (establish) a family; (Ni) be built, get a child from (with מִן) (377)

תַּבְנִית pattern, form (20)

בעל

בָּעַל   (Q) to rule over, be lord (husband), marry, own (take someone into possession as betrothed) (16)

בַּעַל   owner, master, husband, (divine title) Baal (161)

בצע

בָּצַע   (Q) to cut off, sever, break off (away), make profit (16)

בֶּצַע   unjust gain (23)

בקע

בָּקַע   (Q) to cleave, split, breach, break open; (Ni) be cleft, be split (open); (Pi) split, rip open (51)

בִּקְעָה   valley, plain (19)

ברך

בָּרַךְ   (Q Pass Ptc) blessed, praised, adored; (Pi) bless, praise (327)

בְּרָכָה   blessing, gift (71)

בתל

בְּתוּלָה   virgin (50)

בְּתוּלִים   virginity, evidence of virginity (10)

גאל

גָּאַל   (Q) to redeem, deliver, act as kinsman (perform the responsibilities of the next-of-kin), avenge (104)

גְּאֻלָּה   right of redemption, next-of-kin (14)

גבה

גָּבַה   (Q) to be high, be tall, be lofty, be exalted, be haughty; (Hi) make high, exalt (34)

גָּבֹהַּ   (adj) high, exalted; (fs) גְּבֹהָה (41)

גֹּבַהּ   (ms) height, pride (17)

גבר

גָּבַר　(Q) to be strong, be mighty, be superior, excel, achieve, accomplish, prevail (25)

גִּבּוֹר　(adj) mighty, valiant, heroic (160)

גֶּבֶר　strong man, young man, hero (66)

גְּבוּרָה　power, strength; (fp) גְּבוּרֹת mighty deeds (62)

גְּבִירָה　mistress, lady, queen mother (15)

גדל

גָּדַל　(Q) to grow up, be(come) great, become strong, wealthy or important; (Pi) bring up (children), make great, extol; (Hi) make great, magnify, do great things (117)

גָּדוֹל　(adj) great, big, large (527)

מִגְדָּל　tower; (mp) מִגְדָּלִים and מִגְדָּלוֹת (45)

גֹּדֶל　greatness, arrogance (13)

גְּדוּלָה　greatness, great deed (13)

גדר

גָּדַר　(Q) to build a wall, block a road, wall up (10)

גָּדֵר　wall (of stone) (15)

גור

גּוּר　(Q) to sojourn, dwell (stay) as a foreigner or alien, dwell as a newcomer for a definite or indefinite time (82)

גֵּר　stranger, sojourner, alien (92)

מָגוֹר　sojourning place, dwelling place; (mp cstr) מְגוּרֵי (11)

גלה

גָּלָה　(Q) to uncover, reveal, disclose; (Ni) uncover (reveal) oneself, be revealed, be exposed; (Pi) uncover, reveal, disclose; (Hi) take (carry away) into exile (187)

גּוֹלָה　captivity, exiles (42)

גָּלוּת　exile, exiles (15)

גלל

גָּלַל　(Q) to roll (away) (18)

מְגִלָּה　scroll (21)

גמל

גָּמַל   (Q) to complete, finish, wean, ripen, render, do (to);
recompense, requite (37)

גְּמוּל   recompense, requital (19)

גנב

גָּנַב   (Q) to steal, deceive (40)

גַּנָּב   thief, kidnapper (17); 13x in Ezek

גער

גָּעַר   (Q) to rebuke, reproach (14)

גְּעָרָה   rebuke, threat (15)

דבר

דָּבַר   (Q) to speak (rare in Q); (Pi) speak to, with or about
(someone or something) (1,136)

דָּבָר   word, matter, thing (1,454)

דין

דִּין   (Q) to judge, minister or execute judgment, plead
one's cause, contend with (24)

דִּין   judgment, legal claim (19)

מָדוֹן   strife, dispute, quarrel (17)

דקק

דָּקַק   (Q) to crush, become fine through grinding; (Hi)
crush fine, pulverize; (Hoph) be crushed fine (12)

דַּק   (adj) thin, lean, skinny; (fp) דַּקּוֹת (14)

דרך

דָּרַךְ   (Q) to tread (also in the sense of pressing for wine or
oil), march, bend (draw) the bow; (Hi) cause to tread,
march or walk (63)

דֶּרֶךְ   way, road, journey (712)

דשן

דָּשֵׁן   (Pi) to refresh, revive, clean away fat ashes; (Pu) be
made fat (11)

דֶּשֶׁן   fat, fat-soaked ashes (15)

הלל

הָלַל   (Pi) to praise, sing hallelujah; (Pu) be praised, be praiseworthy; (Hith) boast (146)

תְּהִלָּה   praise, song of praise (58)

המה

הָמָה   (Q) to make (a) noise, make a sound, roar, growl, moan, groan, be boisterous (34)

הָמוֹן   multitude, crowd, sound, roar (85)

הפך

הָפַךְ   (Q) to turn, overturn, overthrow, destroy; (Ni) be destroyed, be turned into, be changed (95)

תַּהְפּוּכָה   perversity, perverse thing; (fp) תַּהְפֻּכוֹת (10)

הרה

הָרָה   (Q) to conceive, be(come) pregnant (43)

הָרָה   (fs adj) pregnant (15)

זבח

זָבַח   (Q) to slaughter (for sacrifice), sacrifice; (Pi) offer sacrifice, sacrifice (134)

מִזְבֵּחַ   altar; (mp) מִזְבְּחוֹת (403)

זֶבַח   sacrifice (162)

זוב

זוּב   (Q) to flow (away), suffer a discharge (42)

זוֹב   discharge (of body fluid), hemorrhage (13); all in Lev

זיד

זִיד   (Q) to act insolently; (Hi) boil or cook, become hot (with anger), behave arrogantly (10)

זֵד   (adj) proud, insolent, presumptuous; (mp) זֵדִים (13)

זָדוֹן   arrogance, presumption (11)

זכר

זָכַר   (Q) to remember, recall, call to mind, mention; (Ni) be remembered, be thought of; (Hi) cause to be remembered, remind, mention (235)

זִכָּרוֹן   memorial, remembrance (24)

זֵכֶר   memory, remembrance; (with 3ms suff) זִכְרוֹ (23)

זמם

זָמַם   (Q) to consider, think, ponder, devise, plan (evil), purpose (13)

מְזִמָּה   purpose, plan, discretion; (fp) מְזִמּוֹת (19)

זמר

זָמַר   (Pi) to sing, praise, make music, play an instrument (45)

מִזְמוֹר   psalm, song (57); all in Pss

זנה

זָנָה   (Q) to commit fornication, be a harlot (prostitute), be unfaithful (60)

זוֹנָה   prostitute, harlot; also spelled זֹנָה (34)

תַּזְנוּת   prostitution, fornication (22); all in Ezek 16 and 23

זְנוּנִים   prostitution, fornication (12)

זעם

זָעַם   (Q) to curse, scold, denounce (12)

זַעַם   anger, indignation, curse (22)

זעק

זָעַק   (Q) to cry (out), call for help, summon (73)

זְעָקָה   outcry, call for help (19)

זקן

זָקֵן   (Q) to be(come) old, grow old (26)

זָקֵן   (adj) old; (n) elder (180)

זָקָן   (cs) beard (19)

זרח

זָרַח   (Q) to rise (sun), shine, come out (leprosy), appear, break out (18)

מִזְרָח   east, sunrise (74)

זרע

זָרַע   (Q) to sow, scatter seed (56)

זֶרַע   seed, offspring, descendants (229)

זרק

זָרַק   (Q) to toss, throw, scatter, sprinkle (34)

מִזְרָק   bowl (perhaps used for sprinkling); (mp) מִזְרָקוֹת (32)

חבר

חָבַר   (Q) to unite, ally oneself (with), be joined, join forces (28)

חָבֵר   associate, companion, friend (15)

חגג

חָגַג   (Q) to stagger, reel, celebrate a pilgrimage festival (16)

חַג   feast, festival, procession; (mp) חַגִּים (62)

חדשׁ

חִדֵּשׁ   (Pi) to make new, renew, restore (10)

חֹדֶשׁ   month, new moon; (mp) חֳדָשִׁים (283)

חָדָשׁ   (adj) new, fresh; (fs) חֲדָשָׁה (53)

חזה

חָזָה   (Q) to see, behold, perceive (55)

חָזוֹן   vision, revelation (35)

חֹזֶה   (ms) seer (16)

חזק

חָזַק   (Q) to be(come) strong, grow firm, have courage; (Pi) make firm, make strong, strengthen; (Hi) strengthen, seize, grasp, take hold of; (Hith) strengthen oneself, show oneself as strong or courageous (290)

חָזָק   (adj) strong, mighty, hard (57)

חטא

חָטָא   (Q) to miss (a goal or mark), sin, commit a sin; (Pi) make a sin offering; (Hi) induce or cause to sin (240)

חַטָּאת   sin, sin offering; (fs cstr) חַטַּאת; (fp cstr) חַטֹּאות and חַטֹּאת (298)

חֵטְא   sin (34)

חַטָּא   (adj) sinful; (n) sinner; (mp) חַטָּאִים (19)

חיה

חָיָה   (Q) to live, be alive, stay alive, revive, restore to life; (Pi) preserve alive, let live, give life; (Hi) preserve, keep alive, revive, restore to life (283)

חַי   (adj) living, alive; (mp) חַיִּים (254)

חַיִּים   (mp) life, lifetime (140)

חַיָּה   animal, beast; (fs cstr) חַיַּת (96)

חַיָּה   life; (with 3ms suff) חַיָּתוֹ (11)

חכם

חָכַם   (Q) to be(come) wise, act wisely (28)

חָכְמָה   wisdom, skill (153)

חָכָם   (adj) wise, skillful, experienced (138)

חלה

חָלָה   (Q) to be(come) weak or tired, be(come) sick; (Ni) be exhausted, be made sick; (Pi) appease, flatter (75)

חֳלִי   illness, sickness (24)

חלל

חָלַל   (Ni) to be defiled, be profaned, defile oneself; (Pi) profane, pollute, defile, dishonor, violate; (Hi) let something be profaned, begin (135)

חָלָל   (adj) pierced, slain, defiled; (mp) חֲלָלִים; (mp cstr) חַלְלֵי (94)

חלם

חָלַם   (Q) to dream (29)

חֲלוֹם   dream (65)

חלף

חָלַף   (Q) to pass on or away (quickly), pass by, vanish; (Hi) change, replace, substitute (26)

חֲלִיפָה   change, shift, relief; (fp) חֲלִיפוֹת (12)

חֵלֶק

חָלַק   (Q) to divide, share (with), share (in), apportion, distribute; (Pi) divide (in pieces), apportion, scatter (55)

חֵלֶק   portion, share (66)

מַחֲלֹקֶת   division, portion; (fp cstr) מַחְלְקוֹת (42)

חֶלְקָה   piece (of land), portion (23)

חמד

חָמַד   (Q) to desire, take pleasure (delight) in, crave, covet (21)

חֶמְדָּה   something desirable, precious or valuable (16)

מַחְמָד   something desirable, precious thing (13)

חמם

חָמַם   (Q) to be(come) warm, grow warm (23)

חֵמָה   wrath, heat, poison; (with 1cs suff) חֲמָתִי (125)

חֹם   heat, warmth (10)

חנה

חָנָה   (Q) to decline, camp, encamp, pitch camp, lay seige to (143)

מַחֲנֶה   (cs) camp, army; (cp) מַחֲנוֹת and מַחֲנִים (215)

חנן

חָנַן   (Q) to be gracious to, show favor to, favor; (Hith) plead for grace, implore favor or compassion (77)

חֵן   favor, grace, charm (69)

תְּחִנָּה   plea, petition (for favor) (25)

תַּחֲנוּן   plea for mercy, supplication (for favor) (18)

חַנּוּן   (adj) gracious, merciful (13)

חנף

חָנֵף   (Q) to be godless (of a priest or prophet), be defiled (of land); (Hi) defile, pollute (11)

חָנֵף   (adj) godless, profane (13)

חסה

חָסָה   (Q) to seek or take refuge (37)

מַחְסֶה   (ms) refuge, shelter (20)

חסר

חָסֵר (Q) to diminish, decrease, lack, be lacking (22)

חָסֵר (adj) lacking, wanting; (ms cstr) חֲסַר (17)

מַחְסוֹר need, lack, poverty (13)

חפץ

חָפֵץ (Q) to delight in, take pleasure in, desire, be willing (74)

חֵפֶץ delight, desire, pleasure, joy (38)

חָפֵץ (adj) delighting (in), desiring (13)

חצה

חָצָה (Q) to divide (into) (15)

חֲצִי half, middle (125)

מַחֲצִית half, middle (16)

חקק

חָקַק (Q) to hew out or carve out (a grave), inscribe, engrave, enact, decree (19)

חֹק statute, appointed time, portion; (mp) חֻקִּים (131)

חֻקָּה statute, ordinance (104)

חקר

חָקַר (Q) to explore, search, spy out (27)

חֵקֶר searching, something searched out (12)

חרב

חָרֵב (Q) to dry up (intransitive), lie in ruins; (Hi) cause to dry up, lay waste, reduce to ruins, make desolate (36)

חֹרֶב dryness, drought, heat, waste (16)

חָרֵב (adj) dry, desolate, wasted; (fs) חֲרֵבָה (10)

חרה

חָרָה (Q) to be(come) hot, burn with anger, become angry (93)

חָרוֹן anger, fury, burning (41)

חרם

חָרַם   (Hi) to devote to the ban, dedicate for destruction, exterminate (50)

חֵרֶם   something set apart for destruction, something banned, devoted thing (29)

חרף

חָרַף   (Q) to taunt, reproach; (Pi) taunt, reproach, revile (38)

חֶרְפָּה   reproach, disgrace, shame (73)

חרשׁ

חָרַשׁ   (Q) to plow, engrave, devise, plan (27)

חָרָשׁ   craftsman; (mp) חָרָשִׁים (36)

חשׁב

חָשַׁב   (Q) to think, consider, devise, plan, value, esteem, reckon; (Ni) be reckoned, be accounted, be esteemed, be considered (as); (Pi) think, consider, devise, plan (124)

מַחֲשָׁבָה   thought, plan, scheme (56)

חשׁך

חָשַׁך   (Q) to be(come) dark, grow dim (eyes) (17)

חֹשֶׁך   darkness (80)

חתם

חָתַם   (Q) to seal (up), affix a seal (27)

חוֹתָם   seal, signet ring (14)

חתן

חָתַן   (Hith) to intermarry with, become related by marriage, become a son-in-law (11)

חֹתֵן   father-in-law (21)

חָתָן   bridegroom, son-in-law (20)

חתת

חָתַת   (Q) to be shattered, be dismayed, be filled with terror (55)

מְחִתָּה   terror, ruin, destruction (11)

טבח

טָבַח (Q) to slaughter, butcher, slay (11)

טַבָּח guard, cook; (mp) טַבָּחִים (32)

טֶבַח slaughtering, slaughter (12)

טהר

טָהֵר (Q) to be clean (ceremonially), be pure (morally); (Pi) cleanse, purify, pronounce clean; (Hith) purify or cleanse oneself (94)

טָהוֹר (adj) clean, pure; also spelled טָהֹר (96)

טָהֳרָה purification, purity, ceremonial cleanness (13)

טוב

טוֹב (Q) to be good, be pleasing, be pleasant, be joyful, be well with (44)

טוֹב (adj) good, pleasant (530)

טוּב goodness, well-being, happiness (32)

טמא

טָמֵא (Q) to be(come) unclean; (Ni) defile oneself; (Pi) defile, pronounce or declare unclean; (Hith) defile oneself, become unclean (162)

טָמֵא (adj) unclean; (fs) טְמֵאָה (88)

טֻמְאָה uncleanness, impurity; (with 3ms suff) טֻמְאָתוֹ (36)

טעם

טָעַם (Q) to taste, eat, savor food, perceive (11)

טַעַם taste, sense, discernment (13)

טרף

טָרַף (Q) to tear (in pieces), rend (25)

טֶרֶף prey, food (22)

יבל

יָבַל (Hi) to bring (as gift or tribute), lead; (Hoph) be brought, be led (18)

יְבוּל produce, harvest, crop (13)

יבשׁ

יָבֵשׁ   (Q) to dry up, be(come) dry, wither; (Hi) make dry
        (up), make wither (59)

יַבָּשָׁה   dry land, dry ground (14)

יגע

יָגַע   (Q) to toil, labor, struggle, grow or be weary (26)

יְגִיעַ   labor, work, product of labor, gain (16)

ידה

יָדָה   (Hi) to thank, praise, confess; (Hith) confess (111)

תּוֹדָה   thanksgiving, thank offering, thanksgiving song (32)

ידע

יָדַע   (Q) to know, have understanding, notice, observe,
        be(come) acquainted with, know sexually; (Ni)
        be(come) known, reveal oneself; (Hi) make known
        (something to someone), inform (956)

דַּעַת   knowledge, understanding, ability (88)

יִדְּעֹנִי   soothsayer; (mp) יִדְּעֹנִים (11)

יחד

יַחְדָּו   together, at the same time (96)

יַחַד   together, along with (46)

יכח

יָכַח   (Hi) to reprove, rebuke, reproach, chasten, punish,
        decide, mediate, arbitrate (59)

תּוֹכַחַת   rebuke, correction (24)

ילד

יָלַד   (Q) to bear (children), give birth, bring forth, beget;
        (Ni) be born; (Pi) help at birth, serve as midwife; (Pu)
        be born; (Hi) beget, become the father of (499)

יֶלֶד   child, boy, youth (89)

יָלִיד   (adj) born; (n) son, slave (13)

מוֹלֶדֶת   relatives, offspring, native (land) (22)

תּוֹלְדוֹת   (fp) generations, descendants; (fp cstr) תּוֹלְדֹת and
        תֹּלְדוֹת (39)

יסד

יָסַד   (Q) to found, establish, appoint, destine, allocate; (Pi) found, appoint, establish (41)

יְסוֹד   foundation wall, base (20)

יסר

יָסַר   (Pi) teach, discipline, correct, chastise, rebuke (41)

מוּסָר   discipline, correction, instruction (50); 41x in Exod

יעד

יָעַד   (Q) to designate, appoint; (Ni) make or have an appointment, meet by appointment, gather or assemble by appointment (29)

מוֹעֵד   appointed time (of feast), meeting place, assembly (223)

עֵדָה   congregation, assembly (171)

יעץ

יָעַץ   (Q) to advise, counsel, plan, decide; (Ni) consult (take counsel) together (80)

עֵצָה   counsel, plan, advice; (fs cstr) עֲצַת (87)

יפה

יָפֶה   (adj) beautiful; (fs) יָפָה (42)

יְפִי   beauty; (with 2fs suff) יָפְיֵךְ (19); 10x in Ezek

יצא

יָצָא   (Q) to go out, go forth, come out, come forth; (Hi) cause to go out or come out, lead out, bring forth (1,076)

מוֹצָא   act of going forth, exit, source, spring (27)

תּוֹצָאוֹת   end, limit, outermost area (25)

צֶאֱצָאִים   offspring, descendants (11)

יקר

יָקַר   (Q) to be difficult, precious, prized, highly valued, esteemed, honored, costly or rare (11)

יָקָר   (adj) precious, valuable; (fs) יְקָרָה (36)

יְקָר   precious thing, something valuable, honor, respect (17)

ירא

יָרֵא	(Q) to fear, be afraid, be in awe of, reverence, hold in deference; (Ni) be feared, be held in honor (317)
יָרֵא	(adj) fearful, afraid of (63)
יִרְאָה	fear; (fs cstr) יִרְאַת (44); יִרְאַת יְהוָה "the fear of the Lord"
מוֹרָא	fear, terror (11)

ירה

יָרָה	(Hi) to instruct, teach (47)
תּוֹרָה	law, instruction, teaching, custom (223)

ירח

יָרֵחַ	moon (27)
יֶרַח	month (12)

ירש

יָרַשׁ	(Q) to inherit, take possession of, dispossess, take away someone's property; (Hi) cause to possess or inherit, dispossess, impoverish (232)
יְרֻשָּׁה	possession, inheritance (14)

ישב

יָשַׁב	(Q) to sit (down), remain, dwell, inhabit; (Hi) cause to sit or dwell, settle (a city) (1,088)
מוֹשָׁב	dwelling, settlement, seat; (mp) מוֹשָׁבוֹת (44)
תּוֹשָׁב	resident alien, stranger, sojourner (14)

ישן

יָשֵׁן	(Q) to sleep, go to sleep, be asleep (16)
שֵׁנָה	sleep (23)

ישע

יָשַׁע	(Ni) to be delivered, be victorious, receive help; (Hi) help, save, deliver, rescue, come to the aid of (205)
יְשׁוּעָה	salvation, help, deliverance; (with 1cs suff) יְשׁוּעָתִי (78)
יֵשַׁע	salvation, deliverance, help; (with 1cs suff) יִשְׁעִי (36)
תְּשׁוּעָה	salvation, deliverance, victory (34)

יָשַׁר

יָשַׁר	(Q) to be straight, be upright, be right, please, go straight (27)
יָשָׁר	(adj) upright, just, level, straight (119)
מִישׁוֹר	plain, level ground, fairness; also spelled מִישֹׁר (23)
מֵישָׁרִים	level path, uprightness, fairness (19)
יֹשֶׁר	uprightness, honesty, straightness (14)

יתר

יָתַר	(Ni) to be left over, remain; (Hi) leave (over), have (something) left over or remaining (106)
יֶתֶר	rest, remainder, excess (97)
יִתְרוֹן	advantage, profit (10); all in Eccl

כבד

כָּבֵד	(Q) to be heavy, be weighty, be honored; (Ni) be honored; (Pi) make insensitive, honor; (Hi) make heavy, dull or insensitive, harden (heart), cause to be honored (114)
כָּבוֹד	glory, splendor, honor, abundance (200); כְּבוֹד יְהוָה "the glory of the Lord"
כָּבֵד	(adj) heavy, severe (41)

כהן

כָּהַן	(Pi) to perform the duties of a priest, minister as a priest (23)
כֹּהֵן	priest; (mp) כֹּהֲנִים (750)
כְּהֻנָּה	priesthood (14)

כון

כּוּן	(Ni) to be established, stand firm, be steadfast, be ready, be arranged; (Hi) establish, set up, prepare, make ready, make firm; (Polel) set up, establish (219)
מְכוֹנָה	stand, base, support; (fp) מְכֹנוֹת (25); 15x in 1 Kgs
כֵּן	(adj) honest, correct, right (24)
מָכוֹן	place, site, foundation, support (17)
כֵּן	base, stand; (with 3ms suff) כַּנּוֹ (11)

כזב

כָּזַב   (Pi) to lie, deceive (16)

כָּזָב   lie, deception, falsehood (31)

כלא

כָּלָא   (Q) to shut up, restrain, withhold, keep back (17)

כֶּלֶא   prison, confinement (10)

כלה

כָּלָה   (Q) to (be) complete, be finished, be at an end, come
to an end, be accomplished, be spent, be exhausted;
(Pi) complete, finish, bring to an end (207)

כֹּל   all, each, every; (cstr) כָּל־ (5,415)

כָּלָה   complete destruction (22)

כָּלִיל   (adj) entire, whole, complete (15)

כלם

כָּלַם   (Ni) to be hurt, be humiliated, be ashamed, be
disgraced, be dishonored, be confounded; (Hi) put to
shame, humiliate, disgrace, harm (38)

כְּלִמָּה   insult, disgrace, humiliation (30)

כסה

כָּסָה   (Q) to cover, conceal, hide; (Pi) cover (up), conceal,
clothe (153)

מִכְסֶה   (ms) cover, covering (16)

כעס

כָּעַס   (Q) to be angry, be vexed; (Hi) vex, provoke, provoke
to anger (God) (55)

כַּעַס   anger, vexation (21)

כפר

כָּפַר   (Pi) to cover (over), atone (for), make atonement (102)

כַּפֹּרֶת   mercy seat, place of atonement, lid (27); 25x in
Exod–Lev

כֹּפֶר   ransom, bribe (13)

כשל

כָּשַׁל   (Q) to stumble, totter, stagger; (Ni) be caused to
          stumble, stumble (65)
מִכְשׁוֹל   stumbling block, obstacle, offense (14)

כתב

כָּתַב   (Q) to write (upon), register, record; (Ni) be written
         (225)
כְּתָב   writing, something written, document, register (17)

לבש

לָבַשׁ   (Q) to put on a garment, clothe, be clothed; (Hi)
         clothe (112)
לְבוּשׁ   clothing, garment (32)

להב

לֶהָבָה   flame (19)
לַהַב   flame, blade (of sword) (12)

לחם

לָחַם   (Q, Ni) to fight, do battle with (rare in Q) (171)
מִלְחָמָה war, battle, struggle (319)

לחץ

לָחַץ   (Q) to squeeze, crowd, press, oppress, torment (19)
לַחַץ   oppression, affliction (12)

מדד

מָדַד   (Q) to measure, measure off (distance or expanse),
         measure out (grain) (52)
מִדָּה   measure, measurement (55)

מהר

מָהַר   (Pi) to hasten, hurry, go or come quickly; Inf often
         used as an adverb with the sense of "hastily" (81)
מְהֵרָה   quickly, at once (20)

מוט

מוֹט   (Q) to totter, shake, waver, sway, stagger; (Ni) be
made to stagger, stumble or totter (39)

מוֹטָה   yoke, bar, carrying pole; (fp) מֹטוֹת (12); 10x in Isa,
Ezek

מות

מוּת   (Q) to die; (Hi) kill, put to death; (Hoph) be killed,
suffer death (845)

מָוֶת   death, dying; (ms cstr) מוֹת (153)

מחר

מָחָר   tomorrow (52)

מָחֳרָת   the next day (32)

מטר

מָטַר   (Hi) to make (let) rain fall, send rain (17)

מָטָר   rain (38)

מכר

מָכַר   (Q) to sell, hand over; (Ni) be sold, sell oneself (80)

מִמְכָּר   something sold, merchandise, sale (10)

מלא

מָלֵא   (Q) to be full, fill (up); (Ni) be filled (with); (Pi) fill,
perform, carry out, consecrate as priest (252)

מָלֵא   (adj) full, filled (61)

מְלֹא   that which fills, fullness, abundance; also spelled
מְלוֹא (38)

מִלֻּאִים   consecration, ordination (of priest), setting (of
stones); also spelled מִלּוּאִים (15)

מֶלֶךְ

מָלַךְ   (Q) to be(come) king or queen, reign, rule; (Hi) make someone king or queen, install someone as king or queen (350)

מֶלֶךְ   king, ruler (2,530)

מַלְכָּה   queen (35)

מַמְלָכָה   kingdom, dominion, reign (117)

מַלְכוּת   kingdom, dominion, royal power (91)

מְלוּכָה   kingship, royalty (24)

מנה

מָנָה   (Q) to count, number, reckon, assign, appoint (28) ·

מָנָה   part, portion, share; (fp) מָנוֹת (12)

מעט

מָעַט   (Q) to be(come) few, be too small; (Hi) make small or few, diminish, reduce, collect or gather little (22)

מְעַט   (adj) little, few (101)

מעל

מָעַל   (Q) to be unfaithful, act unfaithfully or treacherously, act counter to one's duty or legal obligations (36)

מַעַל   unfaithfulness, infidelity (29)

מרה

מָרָה   (Q) to be rebellious, obstinate or contentious; (Hi) behave rebelliously or obstinately (44)

מְרִי   rebellion (23); 16x in Ezek

מרר

מָרַר   (Q) to be bitter (of taste, experience or attitude), be desperate; (Hi) embitter, cause bitterness or grief (16)

מַר   (adj) bitter; (substantive) bitterness (38)

משח

מָשַׁח   (Q) to smear (with a liquid, oil or dye), anoint (70)

מָשִׁיחַ   (adj) anointed; (n) anointed one, Messiah (38)

מִשְׁחָה   anointing (21)

מֹשֵׁל

מָשַׁל to rule (81)

מֶמְשָׁלָה rule, dominion, authority (17)

מָשַׁל

מָשַׁל (Q) to use a proverb, speak in parables or sentences of poetry; (Ni) be(come) like, similar or the same (17)

מָשָׁל proverb, wisdom saying (40)

נבא

נָבָא (Ni) to prophesy, be in a state of prophetic ecstasy; (Hith) speak or behave as a prophet, be in a state of prophetic ecstasy (115)

נָבִיא prophet (317)

נבל

נָבֵל (Q) to fade, wither, decay, crumble away, wear out (20)

נְבֵלָה carcass, corpse (48)

נגן

נָגַן (Pi) to play a stringed instrument (15)

נְגִינָה music of stringed instrument, song of mockery (14)

נגע

נָגַע (Q) to touch, strike, reach; (Hi) touch, reach, throw, arrive (150)

נֶגַע mark, plague, affliction (78)

נגף

נָגַף (Q) to smite, strike, injure; (Ni) be smitten, be struck (with) (49)

מַגֵּפָה plague, slaughter (26)

נדב

נָדַב (Q) to incite, instigate; (Hith) volunteer, make a voluntary decision, enlist as a volunteer, offer voluntarily, give a freewill offering (17)

נְדָבָה freewill offering, voluntary gift (26)

נָדִיב (adj) noble, willing, generous (26)

נדר

נָדַר   (Q) to make (perform) a vow, keep (make) a promise (31)

נֵ֫דֶר   vow; also spelled נֶ֫דֶר (60)

נוח

נוּחַ   (Q) to rest, settle down, repose; (Hi) cause to rest, secure rest, set, lay, leave (behind, untouched) (140)

מְנוּחָה   rest, resting place (21)

נוף

נוּף   (Hi) to move back and forth, wave, brandish, wield (34)

תְּנוּפָה   wave offering (30)

נזר

נָזַר   (Ni) to devote, dedicate or consecrate oneself to (a deity), treat with awe, deal respectfully with, fast; (Hi) restrain from, abstain from, live as a Nazirite (10)

נֵ֫זֶר   consecration, dedication, crown; (with 3ms suff) נִזְרוֹ (25)

נָזִיר   one who is devoted, consecrated one, a Nazirite (16)

נחל

נָחַל   (Q) to take (as a) possession, obtain (receive) property, give as an inheritance; (Hi) give (leave) as an inheritance (59)

נַחֲלָה   inheritance, property, possession (222)

נכה

נָכָה   (Hi) strike, smite, beat, strike dead, destroy, injure; (Hoph) be struck down dead, be beaten (501)

מַכָּה   wound, injury, defeat (48)

נכר

נָכַר   (Hi) to recognize, know, investigate, be acquainted with, acknowledge (50)

נָכְרִי   (adj) foreign, strange; (fs) נָכְרִיָּה (46)

נֵכָר   foreigner, stranger (36)

נסך

נָסַךְ   (Q) to pour out, pour (cast) a metal image or statue;
          (Hi) pour out libations, offer a drink offering (25)

נֶסֶךְ   drink offering; also spelled נֵסֶךְ (60)

מַסֵּכָה   molten (metal) image, idol (26)

נסע

נָסַע   (Q) to pull (out or up), set out, start out, depart,
          journey, march (on) (146)

מַסַּע   breaking camp, setting out, journey (12)

נצב

נָצַב   (Ni) to stand (firm), take one's stand, station oneself,
          be positioned; (Hi) station, set (up), place, establish
          (74)

מַצֵּבָה sacred stone, pillar (33)

נְצִיב   pillar, post, military garrison (12)

מַצָּב   military garrison, station (10)

נקה

נָקָה   (Ni) to be free (of), be without guilt (innocent), be
          exempt from (punishment), be emptied; (Pi) leave
          unpunished, hold innocent (44)

נָקִי   (adj) blameless, innocent; (mp) נְקִיִּם (43)

נקם

נָקַם   (Q) to avenge, take vengeance, take revenge; (Ni)
          avenge oneself, take revenge (35)

נְקָמָה   vengeance, revenge (27)

נָקָם   vengeance, revenge (17)

נשא

נָשָׂא   (Q) to lift, carry, raise, bear (load or burden), take
          (away); (Ni) be carried, be lifted up, be exalted; (Pi)
          lift up, exalt; (Hith) lift oneself up, exalt oneself (659)

נָשִׂיא   chief, leader, prince (130)

מַשָּׂא   load, burden (44)

מַשָּׂא   oracle, pronouncement (20)

מַשְׂאֵת something lifted up, gift, tribute (15)

נתן

נָתַן   (Q) to give, put, set; (Ni) be given (2,014)

מַתָּנָה   gift, present (17)

נתק

נָתַק   (Q) to pull off, tear away; (Ni) be drawn out or away, be torn apart, be separated; (Pi) tear up (out), tear apart, tear to pieces (27)

נֶתֶק   skin disease, scab (14); all in Lev

סבב

סָבַב   (Q) to turn (about), go around, march around, surround; (Ni) turn; (Hi) cause to go around, lead around; (Polel) encompass with protection (163)

סָבִיב   around, about; (n) surroundings, circuit; (fp) סְבִיבוֹת (338)

סגר

סָגַר   (Q) to shut (in), close; (Hi) deliver (up), hand over, surrender, give up (91)

מִסְגֶּרֶת   rim (of table), border, prison; (fp) מִסְגְּרוֹת (18)

סלל

סָלַל   (Q) to pile up, heap up, lift up, exalt, praise (12)

סֹלְלָה   mound, siege ramp (11)

ספד

סָפַד   (Q) to lament, wail, bewail, mourn for someone (30)

מִסְפֵּד   wailing, mourning, funeral ceremony (16)

ספר

סָפַר   (Q) to count; (Pi) count, recount, relate, make known, proclaim, report, tell (107)

סֵפֶר   book, scroll, document (191); סֵפֶר הַתּוֹרָה "the book of the law"

מִסְפָּר   number (134)

סֹפֵר   scribe, secretary; also spelled סוֹפֵר (54)

סתר

סָתַר	(Ni) to be hidden, hide oneself; (Hi) hide (82)
סֵתֶר	hiding place, secret place, shelter (35)
מִסְתָּר	secret place, hiding place; (mp) מִסְתָּרִים (10)

עבד

עָבַד	(Q) to work, serve, toil, till, cultivate (289)
עֶבֶד	slave, servant (803)
עֲבֹדָה	work, labor, service, worship; also spelled עֲבוֹדָה (145)

עבר

עָבַר	(Q) to pass over, pass through, pass by, cross; (Hi) cause to pass over, bring over, cause or allow to pass (through), cause to pass through fire, sacrifice (553)
עֵבֶר	beyond, other side, edge, bank (92)

עגל

עֵגֶל	calf, young bull (35)
עֶגְלָה	heifer, young cow (12)

עגל

עֲגָלָה	cart, wagon (25)
מַעְגָּל	path, wagon track; (mp cstr) מַעְגְּלוֹת (13)

עוד

עוּד	(Hi) to warn, admonish, witness, be a witness, call as witness, testify (40)
עֵד	witness; (mp) עֵדִים (69)
עֵדוּת	witness, testimony; also spelled עֵדָת; (fp) עֵדוֹת (61)

עוה

עָוָה	(Q) to do wrong; (Ni) be disturbed, be irritated; (Hi) twist, pervert, do wrong (17)
עָוֹן	transgression, iniquity, guilt, punishment (of sin); (mp) עֲוֹנוֹת (233)

עוּף

עוּף   (Q) to fly (27)

עוֹף   (coll) flying creatures, birds, insects (71)

עזז

עָזַז   (Q) to be strong, prevail (against), defy (11)

עֹז   strength, power, might; (with 3ms suff) עֻזּוֹ (76)

עַז   (adj) strong, mighty; (mp) עַזִּים (23)

עֹז   refuge, protection; (with 1cs suff) עֻזִּי (17)

עזר

עָזַר   (Q) to help, assist, come to the aid of (82)

עֶזְרָה   help, assistance, support; (with 1cs suff) עֶזְרָתִי (26)

עֵזֶר   help, assistance (17)

עלה

עָלָה   (Q) to go up, ascend; (Ni) be taken up; (Hi) bring or lead up or out, offer up (sacrifice) (894)

עֹלָה   whole burnt offering (sacrifice that is completely burned); also spelled עוֹלָה (286)

מַעַל   above, upward, on top of (140)

עֶלְיוֹן   (adj) upper; (divine title) Most High (53)

מַעֲלָה   ascent, step, stairs; (fp) מַעֲלוֹת (49)

מַעֲלֶה   ascent, stairs, rise; (ms cstr) מַעֲלֵה (22)

עֲלִיָּה   upper room (20)

עלל

עָלַל   (Poel) to deal (act) severely with, treat violently, glean (19)

מַעֲלָל   deed, act (42); 18x in Jer

עֲלִילָה   deed, action; (fp) עֲלִילוֹת (24)

עמד

עָמַד   (Q) to stand (up), take one's stand, stand still; (Hi) station, set up, set in position, appoint, designate (524)

עַמּוּד   pillar, column, tent pole (112)

עמל

עָמַל   (Q) to labor, toil, exert oneself (12)

עָמָל   trouble, labor, toil (54)

עמק

עֵמֶק   valley, plain (70)

עָמֹק   (adj) deep, unfathomable, mysterious; (fs) עֲמֻקָּה (17)

ענה

עָנָה   (Q) to be afflicted, be humbled, become low; (Pi) afflict, oppress, humiliate, violate (79)

עָנִי   (adj) poor, humble, afflicted; (mp) עֲנִיִּים (80)

עֳנִי   poverty, affliction, misery (36)

עָנָו   (adj) afflicted, oppressed, humble, meek; (mp) עֲנָוִים (25)

עצם

עָצַם   (Q) to be vast, mighty, powerful or numerous (17)

עָצוּם   (adj) mighty, numerous (31)

ערב

עֶרֶב   evening, sunset (134)

מַעֲרָב   west, sunset (14)

ערה

עָרָה   (Pi) to uncover, reveal, expose, lay bare, empty; (Hi) uncover, make naked, expose, pour out (15)

עֶרְוָה   nakedness (54)

עָרוֹם   (adj) naked; (mp) עֲרוּמִּים (16)

עֵירֹם   (adj) naked; (n) nakedness (10)

ערך

עָרַךְ   (Q) to lay out, set in rows, arrange, set in order, stack (wood), draw up a battle formation (75)

עֵרֶךְ   value, assessment; (with 2ms suff) עֶרְכְּךָ (33)

מַעֲרָכָה   row, battle line (19)

מַעֲרֶכֶת   row (of bread), consecrated bread (10)

עָרַץ

עָרַץ   (Q) to tremble, be terrified, be in dread, be startled, be alarmed; (Hi) terrify, strike (inspire) with awe, be in terror (15)

עָרִיץ   (adj) ruthless, fierce; (mp) עָרִיצִים (20)

עשׂה

עָשָׂה   (Q) to do, make, create, acquire, prepare, carry out; (Ni) be done, be made (2,632)

מַעֲשֶׂה   (ms) work, deed, act (235)

עשׂר

עָשַׂר   (Q) to exact a tithe, take a tenth part of; (Pi) give, pay or receive a tenth, tithe (10)

עֶשֶׂר   ten; (fs) עֲשָׂרָה; (mp) עֶשְׂרִים twenty, twentieth (492)

עָשָׂר   ten; (fs) עֶשְׂרֵה; used in constructions to express numerals eleven to nineteen; אַחַד עָשָׂר eleven, etc. (337)

עָשׂוֹר   ten, tenth (day) (16)

עשׁק

עָשַׁק   (Q) to oppress, exploit, wrong (someone) (37)

עֹשֶׁק   oppression, extortion (15)

עשׁר

עָשַׁר   (Q) to be(come) rich; (Hi) make rich, gain riches (17)

עֹשֶׁר   wealth, riches (37)

עָשִׁיר   (adj) rich, wealthy (23)

פאר

פָּאַר   (Pi) to glorify, exalt, beautify; (Hith) show (manifest) one's glory, glorify oneself, be glorified, boast (13)

תִּפְאֶרֶת   beauty, glory, splendor (49)

פחד

פָּחַד   (Q) to tremble, shiver, be startled, be in dread, be in awe (25)

פַּחַד   trembling, terror, dread (49)

פלא

פָּלָא   (Ni) to be extraordinary, be wonderful, be too difficult; (Hi) do something wonderful (71)

פֶּלֶא   wonder, miracle, something extraordinary (13)

פלט

פָּלַט   (Pi) to bring out, bring forth, bring to safety, save (27)

פְּלֵיטָה   survivor, escape, deliverance (28)

פָּלִיט   fugitive, survivor (19)

פלל

פָּלַל   (Hith) to pray, make intercession (84)

תְּפִלָּה   prayer; (with 1cs suff) תְּפִלָּתִי (77)

פנה

פָּנָה   (Q) to turn (toward, from, to the side, away) (134)

פָּנִים   (cp) face, front; (cp cstr with prep לְ) לִפְנֵי (1102x) before, in front of (2,126)

פְּנִימִי   (adj) inner; (fs) פְּנִימִית (32)

פִּנָּה   corner, cornerstone (30)

פְּנִימָה   inside, within (14)

פסל

פֶּסֶל   idol, carved image (31)

פָּסִיל   idol, cultic statue (23)

פעל

פָּעַל   (Q) to do, make, perform, practice (58)

פֹּעַל   work, deed; (with 3ms suff) פָּעֳלוֹ (36)

פְּעֻלָּה   work, deed, reward, payment; (with 3ms suff) פְּעֻלָּתוֹ (14)

פקד

פָּקַד   (Q) to attend (to), pay attention to, take care of, miss, muster, number, appoint, visit; (Ni) be missed, be visited, be appointed; (Hi) appoint, entrust (304)

פְּקֻדָּה   appointment, service, watch, punishment (32)

פִּקּוּדִים   precepts, directions, instructions; (with 2ms suff) פִּקּוּדֶיךָ (24); all in Pss, 21x in Ps 119

פָּקִיד   leader, overseer, officer (13)

פרה

פָּרָה   (Q) to bear fruit, be fruitful (29)

פְּרִי   fruit, offspring (119)

פרח

פָּרַח   (Q) to bud, sprout, bloom, shoot, break out, break open (34)

פֶּרַח   blossom, bud, flower (17)

פרס

פָּרַס   (Q) to break; (Hi) have a divided hoof (14)

פַּרְסָה   hoof (21)

פרץ

פָּרַץ   (Q) to break through, break (out or into), make a breach, burst open, spread out (46)

פֶּרֶץ   breach, gap (19)

פשׁע

פָּשַׁע   (Q) to revolt, rebel (against), transgress, break with, break away from, behave as a criminal (41)

פֶּשַׁע   transgression, rebellion, crime; (mp cstr) פִּשְׁעֵי (93)

פתה

פָּתָה   (Q) to be simple, be inexperienced, be gullible; (Pi) fool, deceive, persuade, seduce (27)

פֶּתִי   naïve person, simpleton; (mp) פְּתָאִים (17)

פתח

פָּתַח   (Q) to open (up); (Ni) be opened, be loosened, be set free; (Pi) let loose, loosen, free, unsaddle (136)

פֶּתַח   opening, entrance, doorway (164)

צבא

צָבָא   (Q) to wage war, go to war, fight against, serve (in the cult) (14)

צָבָא   host, army, war, service; (mp) צְבָאוֹת (487); יְהוָה

צְבָאוֹת   "Lord of Hosts"

צדק

צָדַק	(Q) to be in the right, have a just cause, be just (justified), be righteous; (Hi) declare righteous, just or innocent, justify (41)
צַדִּיק	(adj) righteous, just, innocent (206)
צְדָקָה	righteousness, righteous act, justice (159)
צֶדֶק	righteousness, equity (123)

צוד

צוּד	(Q) to hunt (for) (17)
צַיִד	game, hunting, hunter (14)
צֵידָה	food, provisions; also spelled צָדָה (10)

צוה

צָוָה	(Pi) to command, give an order, charge; (Pu) be ordered, be told, receive a command (496)
מִצְוָה	commandment; (fp) מִצְוֹת (184); מִצְוֹת יְהוָה "the commandments of the Lord"

צום

צוּם	(Q) to fast, abstain from food and drink (21)
צוֹם	fast, (period of) fasting (26)

צמא

צָמֵא	(Q) to thirst, be thirsty (10)
צָמָא	thirst (17)

צמח

צָמַח	(Q) to sprout, spring up, grow; (Hi) make grow or sprout (33)
צֶמַח	growth, sprout, branch (12)

צרע

צָרַע	(Q) to be afflicted with a skin disease (traditionally leprosy); (Pu) be struck with a skin disease (20)
צָרַעַת	leprosy, skin disease (35)

צרר

צָרַר (Q: transitive) to wrap (up), tie up, bind, shut away; (Q: intransitive) be cramped, be restricted, be hampered, be depressed; (Hi) oppress, harass, afflict (47)

צָרָה distress, anxiety, trouble (70)

צַר (adj) narrow; (n) anxiety, distress (27)

מָצוֹר distress, siege (20)

צרר

צָרַר (Q) to be hostile (toward), treat with hostility, attack (26)

צַר adversary, enemy; (mp cstr) צָרֵי (72)

קבר

קָבַר (Q) to bury; (Ni) be buried (133)

קֶבֶר grave, burial site; (mp) קְבָרִים and קְבָרוֹת (67)

קְבוּרָה grave, burial; (with 3ms suff) קְבֻרָתוֹ (14)

קדם

קָדַם (Pi) to be in front, confront, meet, go before, walk at the head, do something early or for the first time (26)

קָדִים east, eastern, east wind (69)

קֶדֶם east, ancient times (61)

קֵדְמָה eastward, toward the east (26); קֶדֶם plus directional ה

קַדְמֹנִי (adj) eastern, former, past (10)

קדשׁ

קָדַשׁ (Q) to be holy, set apart or consecrated; (Ni) show oneself holy (of God), be honored or treated as holy; (Pi) set apart, consecrate or dedicate as holy, observe as holy; (Hi) consecrate, dedicate or declare as holy; (Hith) show or keep oneself holy (171)

קֹדֶשׁ holiness, something that is holy; (mp) קָדָשִׁים (470)

קָדוֹשׁ (adj) holy, set apart (117)

מִקְדָּשׁ sanctuary (75); 31x in Ezek

קָדֵשׁ cult or temple prostitute; (fs) קְדֵשָׁה (11)

קהל

קָהַל   (Ni) to assemble (intransitive); (Hi) assemble (transitive), summon (39)

קָהָל   assembly, community, crowd (123)

קוה

קָוָה   (Pi) to wait (for), wait with eagerness, hope (47)

תִּקְוָה   hope, expectation (32)

קום

קוּם   (Q) to rise, arise, get up, stand (up); (Hi) set up, erect, put up, cause to arise, establish (627)

מָקוֹם   place, location; (mp) מְקֹמוֹת (401)

קוֹמָה   height; (with 3ms suff) קוֹמָתוֹ (46)

קָמָה   standing grain (10)

קטר

קָטַר   (Pi) to make a sacrifice go up in smoke, offer (a sacrifice) by burning; (Hi) cause a sacrifice to go up in smoke (115)

קְטֹרֶת   incense, smoke (60)

קלל

קָלַל   (Q) to be small, be insignificant, be of little account, be swift; (Ni, Pi) declare cursed; (Hi) lighten, make lighter, treat with contempt (82)

קְלָלָה   curse (33)

קַל   (adj) light, swift, agile; (mp) קַלִּים (13)

קנא

קָנָא   (Pi) to envy, be envious of, be jealous, be zealous for (34)

קִנְאָה   jealousy, zeal (43)

קנה

קָנָה   (Q) to get, acquire, buy (85)

מִקְנֶה   (ms) cattle, livestock, property (76)

מִקְנָה   purchase, acquisition (15)

קִנְיָן   property, possessions (10)

קסם

קָסַם   (Q) to practice divination, consult a spirit of the dead, predict (22)

קֶסֶם   divination, prediction (11)

קצף

קָצַף   (Q) to be(come) angry or furious (34)

קֶצֶף   wrath, anger (28)

קצץ

קָצַץ   (Q) to cut (chop) off, trim; (Pi) cut (chop) off, cut in pieces (14)

קָצֶה   (ms) end, border, outskirts; (ms cstr) קְצֵה (92)

קֵץ   end, border, limit (67)

קצר

קָצַר   (Q) to gather in, reap, harvest (36)

קָצִיר   harvest (49)

קרא

קָרָא   (Q) to call, summon, proclaim, announce, shout, read aloud, give a name to; (Ni) be called, be summoned, be proclaimed (739)

מִקְרָא   summons, assembly (23); 20x in Exod–Num

קרב

קָרַב   (Q) to approach, draw near, come near, make a sexual advance; (Hi) bring (near), present, offer a sacrifice or offering (280)

קֶרֶב   inner part(s), organ(s), body; (prep) בְּקֶרֶב (155x) in the middle of, among (227)

קָרְבָּן   gift, offering (80)

קָרוֹב   (adj) near, close; also spelled קָרֹב (75)

קָרֵב   (adj) approaching, drawing near (12)

קרה

קָרָה   (Q) to encounter, meet, befall, happen to (22)

מִקְרֶה   (ms) accident, chance, fate (10)

קשׁה

קָשָׁה   (Q) to be heavy, hard or difficult; (Hi) make hard, harden, make stubborn or obstinate (28)

קָשֶׁה   (adj) difficult, hard, severe; (fs) קָשָׁה (36)

קשׁר

קָשַׁר   (Q) to bind, be in league together, conspire (against) (44)

קֶשֶׁר   alliance, conspiracy, treason (16)

ראה

רָאָה   (Q) to see, perceive, understand; (Ni) appear, become visible; (Pu) be seen; (Hi) let or cause someone to see (something), show someone (something) (1,311)

מַרְאֶה   (ms) vision, sight, appearance (103)

מַרְאָה   appearance, vision (12)

רֹאֶה   seer (11)

ראשׁ

רֹאשׁ   head, top, chief; (mp) רָאשִׁים (600)

רִאשׁוֹן   (adj) first, former; (fs) רִאשֹׁנָה; (mp) רִאשֹׁנִים (182)

רֵאשִׁית   beginning, first (51)

מְרַאֲשׁוֹת   (fp) at the head of, headrest (13)

רבב

רָבַב   (Q) to be(come) many, numerous or great (23)

רַב   (adj) great, many; (mp) רַבִּים (419)

רֹב   multitude, abundance, greatness (150)

רַב   chief, captain, ruler (30)

רְבָבָה   ten thousand, great multitude, immense number (18)

רִבּוֹא   (fs) ten thousand, countless number; also spelled רִבּוֹ (11)

רבה

רָבָה   (Q) to be(come) numerous, be(come) great, increase; (Hi) make many, make great, multiply, increase (229)

אַרְבֶּה   (ms) locust (24)

רבע

רָבַע	(Q) to provide with four corners, make square (12)
אַרְבַּע	four; (fs) אַרְבָּעָה; (mp) אַרְבָּעִים forty (455)
רְבִיעִי	(adj) fourth; (fs) רְבִיעִית (55)

רגל

רָגַל	(Pi) to spy (out), scout (26)
רֶגֶל	(fs) foot (251)
רַגְלִי	pedestrian, foot soldier (12)

רגע

רָגַע	(Q) to crust over or become hard (of skin), stir up (sea); (Hi) give rest to, come to rest, make peace, linger (13)
רֶגַע	moment, instant (22)

רוח

רָוַח	(Q) to get relief; (Pu) be wide or spacious; (Hi) smell (14)
רוּחַ	(cs) spirit, wind, breath; (cp) רוּחוֹת (378)
רֵיחַ	smell, odor, scent (58)

רום

רוּם	(Q) to be high, be exalted, rise, arise; (Hi) raise, lift up, exalt, take away; (Hoph) be exalted; (Polel) exalt, bring up, extol, raise (children) (197)
תְּרוּמָה	offering, contribution, tribute (76)
מָרוֹם	height, elevation, pride (54)

רוע

רוּעַ	(Hi) to shout, cry (out), shout a war cry (alarm of battle), sound a signal for war, cheer, shout in triumph (44)
תְּרוּעָה	shout, alarm, signal (36)

רחב

רָחַב   (Q) to open wide; (Hi) make wide (large), enlarge, extend (26)

רֹחַב   width, breadth, expanse (101)

רְחוֹב   (fs) public square, street; (fp) רְחֹבוֹת (43)

רָחָב   (adj) wide, spacious; (fp) רְחָבָה (20)

רחם

רָחַם   (Pi) to show love for, have compassion, take pity on someone, greet (meet) someone with love (47)

רַחֲמִים   compassion, mercy (40)

רֶחֶם   womb (26)

רַחוּם   (adj) compassionate (13)

רחק

רָחַק   (Q) to be(come) far or distant, keep far from; (Hi) remove, put (keep) far away, keep at a distance (59)

רָחוֹק   (adj) distant, remote, far away; also spelled רָחֹק (84)

מֶרְחָק   distance, distant place (18)

ריב

רִיב   (Q) to strive, contend, quarrel, dispute, conduct a legal case (72)

רִיב   dispute, quarrel, lawsuit (62)

ריק

רִיק   (Hi) to empty out, pour out (19)

רֵיקָם   empty-handed, without success (16)

רִיק   (adj) empty, vain; (mp) רֵקִים (14)

רִיק   emptiness, vanity (12)

רכב

רָכַב   (Q) to mount and ride, ride; (Hi) cause or make to ride (78)

רֶכֶב   chariot, (coll) chariots or chariot riders, upper millstone (120)

מֶרְכָּבָה   chariot (44)

רמשׂ

רָמַשׂ   (Q) to crawl, creep, swarm, teem (17)

רֶמֶשׂ   creeping thing, animal that creeps upon the earth (17); 10x in Gen

רנן

רָנַן   (Q) to call or cry aloud, shout with joy; (Pi) cry out (with joy), exult (53)

רִנָּה   shout of joy, shout of lament (33)

רעב

רָעֵב   (Q) to be hungry, suffer famine (13)

רָעָב   famine, hunger (101)

רָעֵב   (adj) hungry; (mp) רְעֵבִים (20)

רעה

רָעָה   (Q) to pasture, tend (flocks), graze, shepherd, feed (167)

מִרְעֶה   (ms) pasture, place of grazing (13)

מַרְעִית   pasture, place of grazing (10)

רעע

רָעַע   (Q) to be bad, evil or displeasing; (Hi) do evil, do wickedly, do injury, harm, treat badly (98)

רָעָה   evil, wickedness, calamity, disaster (354)

רַע   (adj) bad, evil, wicked, of little worth; also spelled רָע (312)

רֹעַ   corruption, evil (19)

רעשׁ

רָעַשׁ   (Q) to quake, shake (29)

רַעַשׁ   earthquake, clatter, commotion (17)

רפא

רָפָא   (Q) to heal; (Ni) be healed, become whole; (Pi) heal, make healthy (69)

מַרְפֵּא   healing, cure, remedy (13)

רצה

רָצָה   (Q) to be pleased with, be favorable to, be well disposed toward, accept (with pleasure), become friends with (48)

רָצוֹן   pleasure, acceptance, favor (56)

רשע

רָשַׁע   (Hi) to condemn, declare or pronounce guilty (35)

רָשָׁע   (adj) wicked, guilty; (mp) רְשָׁעִים (264)

רֶשַׁע   evil, wickedness, offense, injustice (30)

רִשְׁעָה   wickedness, guilt (15)

שׂבע

שָׂבַע   (Q) to be satisfied or satiated, have one's fill (of), eat or drink one's fill; (Hi) satisfy (97)

שָׂבֵעַ   (adj) satisfied, full (10)

שׂגב

שָׂגַב   (Ni) to be high, be exalted, be inaccessible; (Pi) make high, make inaccessible, protect (20)

מִשְׂגָּב   high point, fortress, refuge (17)

שׂושׂ

שׂוּשׂ   (Q) to rejoice; also spelled שִׂישׂ (27)

שָׂשׂוֹן   joy, exultation (22)

מָשׂוֹשׂ   joy, delight (16)

שׂחק

שָׂחַק   (Q) to laugh, play; (Pi) play, entertain, amuse (37)

שְׂחוֹק   laughter, laughingstock, mockery (14)

שׂיח

שִׂיחַ   (Q) to consider, meditate, complain, lament, praise (20)

שִׂיחַ   complaint, lament (14)

שׂכל

שָׂכַל   (Hi) to understand, comprehend, have insight, make wise, have success (60)

שֶׂכֶל   insight, understanding, success; also spelled שֵׂכֶל (16)

מַשְׂכִּיל   undetermined technical term, perhaps indicating a song of "wisdom" or "insight" (14); all in psalm titles

שָׂכַר

שָׂכַר	(Q) to hire (for wages) (20)
שָׂכָר	wages, payment, reward (28)
שָׂכִיר	(adj) hired (worker); (n) day-laborer (18)

שָׂמַח

שָׂמַח	(Q) to rejoice, be joyful, be glad; (Pi) cause to rejoice, gladden, make someone happy (156)
שִׂמְחָה	joy, gladness (94)
שָׂמֵחַ	(adj) joyful, glad, happy; (mp) שְׂמֵחִים (21)

שָׂנֵא

| שָׂנֵא | (Q) to hate; (Pi Ptc) enemy, (lit) the one who hates (148) |
| שִׂנְאָה | hatred, enmity, malice (17) |

שָׂרַף

| שָׂרַף | (Q) to burn (completely), destroy; (Ni) be burned (117) |
| שְׂרֵפָה | burning, fire (13) |

שָׁאַל

| שָׁאַל | (Q) to ask (of), inquire (of), request, demand (176) |
| שְׁאֵלָה | request, petition (13) |

שָׁאַר

שָׁאַר	(Ni) to remain, be left over, survive; (Hi) leave (someone or something) remaining, spare (133)
שְׁאֵרִית	remnant, remainder (66); 37x in Isa, Jer, Ezek
שְׁאָר	remnant, remainder (26)

שָׁבָה

שָׁבָה	(Q) to take captive, deport (47)
שְׁבִי	captivity, captives (48)
שְׁבוּת	captivity, exile, imprisonment (29)
שְׁבִית	captivity (14)

שָׁבַע

| שָׁבַע | (Ni) to swear, swear (take) an oath, adjure; (Hi) cause to take an oath, adjure, plead with someone (186) |
| שְׁבוּעָה | oath; also spelled שְׁבֻעָה (30) |

שׁבר

שָׁבַר   (Q) to break (up), break in pieces, smash, shatter; (Ni) be smashed, broken, shattered or destroyed; (Pi) shatter, smash, break (148)

שֶׁבֶר   break, fracture, collapse (44)

שׁבת

שָׁבַת   (Q) to stop, cease, rest; (Hi) put an end to, bring to a stop, remove, put away (71)

שַׁבָּת   (cs) Sabbath, period of rest; (cp) שַׁבָּתוֹת (111)

שַׁבָּתוֹן   day of rest, Sabbath feast (11); 3x in Exod, 8x in Lev

שׁדד

שָׁדַד   (Q) to devastate, ruin, deal violently with, violently destroy; (Pu) be devastated (59)

שֹׁד   violence, destruction (25)

שׁוב

שׁוּב   (Q) to turn back, return, go back, come back, turn away from; (Hi) cause to return, bring back, lead back, give back, restore; (Polel) bring back, restore (1,075)

מְשׁוּבָה   backsliding, falling away, apostasy; also spelled מְשֻׁבָה (13)

שׁוע

שִׁוַּע   (Pi) to cry (call) for help (21)

שַׁוְעָה   cry for help; (with 1cs suff) שַׁוְעָתִי (11)

שׁחת

שָׁחַת   (Pi, Hi) to ruin, destroy, spoil, annihilate (152)

מַשְׁחִית   destroyer, destruction (10)

שׁיר

שִׁיר   (Q) to sing (of); (Q and Polel Ptc) singer (88)

שִׁיר   song (78)

שִׁירָה   song (13)

שׁכב

שָׁכַב   (Q) to lie down, have sexual intercourse (with) (213)

מִשְׁכָּב   bed, couch (46)

שׁכן

שָׁכַן   (Q) to settle (down), abide, reside, dwell, inhabit; (Pi) abide, dwell (130)

מִשְׁכָּן   dwelling place, tabernacle; (mp) מִשְׁכָּנוֹת (139)

שָׁכֵן   neighbor, resident (19)

שׁכר

שָׁכַר   (Q) to be(come) drunk; (Pi, Hi) make drunk (18)

שֵׁכָר   intoxicating drink, beer (23)

שִׁכּוֹר   (adj) drunk; (n) drunkard (13)

שׁלל

שָׁלַל   (Q) to plunder, spoil, capture, rob (14)

שָׁלָל   plunder, spoil, loot (74)

שׁלם

שָׁלֵם   (Q) to be complete, be finished; (Pi) complete, finish, make whole, restore, repay, requite, recompense, reward, perform (a vow); (Hi) bring to completion, consummate, make peace (116)

שָׁלוֹם   peace, welfare, wholeness, deliverance (237)

שֶׁלֶם   peace offering; (mp) שְׁלָמִים (87)

שָׁלֵם   (adj) whole, complete, safe (28)

שׁמם

שָׁמֵם   (Q) to be deserted, be uninhabited, be desolated, be appalled; (Ni) be made uninhabited, desolate or deserted; (Hi) cause to be deserted or desolated (92)

שְׁמָמָה   desolation, waste, ruin (56)

שַׁמָּה   desolation, horror (39)

שׁמע

שָׁמַע   (Q) to hear, listen to, understand, obey; (Ni) be heard; (Hi) cause to hear, proclaim (1,165)

שְׁמוּעָה   message, report, news (27)

שֵׁמַע   report, news, rumor (17)

שׁמר

שָׁמַר   (Q) to watch (over), guard, keep, observe, preserve, protect, take care of; (Ni) be kept, be protected, be on one's guard (469)

מִשְׁמֶרֶת   watch, guard, responsibility (78)

מִשְׁמָר   prison, guard(ing), custody, watch (22)

שׁנה

שָׁנָה   (Q) to change; (Pi) change, alter, pervert (15)

שָׁנָה   year; (fp) שָׁנִים (878)

שׁען

שָׁעַן   (Ni) to lean (on or against), support oneself on, depend on (22)

מִשְׁעֶנֶת   staff, stick, support (11)

שׁפט

שָׁפַט   (Q) to judge, make a judgment, decide (between), settle (a dispute or controversy); (Ni) go to court, plead, dispute (204)

מִשְׁפָּט   judgment, decision, ordinance, law, custom, manner (425)

שֶׁפֶט   act of judgment, punishment; (mp) שְׁפָטִים (16)

שׁפל

שָׁפֵל   (Q) to be(come) low, be(come) humble, humiliated or abased; (Hi) bring down, overthrow, abase, humiliate (30)

שְׁפֵלָה   foothills, Shephelah (20)

שָׁפָל   (adj) low, lowly, humble, deep; (fs) שְׁפָלָה (17)

שׁקה

שָׁקָה   (Hi) to give drink to, provide drink for, irrigate (62)

מַשְׁקֶה   (ms) cupbearer, drink; (mp) מַשְׁקִים (19)

שׁקל

שָׁקַל   (Q) to weigh (out) (23)

שֶׁקֶל   measurement of weight, shekel (88)

מִשְׁקָל   weight (49)

שרץ

שָׁרַץ	(Q) to swarm, teem (with), be innumerable (14)
שֶׁרֶץ	swarming things (15); 12x in Lev

שתה

שָׁתָה	(Q) to drink (217)
מִשְׁתֶּה	(ms) feast, banquet (46); 20x in Esther

תחת

תַּחַת	(prep) under, below, instead of (510)
תַּחְתִּית	(fs adj) lower; (fp) תַּחְתִּיּוֹת (19)
תַּחְתּוֹן	(adj) lower, lowest; (fs) תַּחְתּוֹנָה (13)

תמם

תָּמַם	(Q) to be(come) complete or finished, come to an end, cease, be consumed, be spent, be burned out (64)
תָּמִים	(adj) blameless, perfect, honest, devout; (mp) תְּמִימִם and תְּמִימִים (91)
תֹּם	integrity, innocence, perfection; (with 3ms suff) תֻּמּוֹ (23)
תָּם	(adj) blameless, complete, perfect; (mp) תַּמִּים (15)

תעב

תָּעַב	(Pi) to abhor, loathe, make an abomination (22)
תּוֹעֵבָה	abomination, abhorrence, offensive thing (118)

PROPER NOUNS
LISTED ALPHABETICALLY

In the Hebrew Old Testament, there are almost 3,000 proper nouns with a total occurrence of over 35,000 times. Just over 400 proper nouns occur more than 10 times.

אֲבִיגַיִל	Abigail (19)	אִיזֶבֶל	Jezebel (22)
אֲבִיָּה	Abijah (23)	אַיָּלוֹן	Aijalon (10)
אֲבִיהוּא	Abihu (12)	אִישׁ־בֹּשֶׁת	Ish-Bosheth (11)
אֲבִימֶלֶךְ	Abimelech (67)	אִיתָמָר	Ithamar (21)
אֲבִינָדָב	Abinadab (13)	אָכִישׁ	Achish (21)
אֲבִירָם	Abiram (11)	אֵלָה	Elah (13)
אֲבִישַׁי	Abishai (25)	אֱלִיאָב	Eliab (21)
אֶבְיָתָר	Abiathar (30)	אֱלִיאֵל	Eliel (10)
אַבְנֵר	Abner (63)	אֵלִיָּהוּ	Elijah (71)
אַבְרָהָם	Abraham (175)	אֱלִיהוּא	Elihu (11)
אַבְרָם	Abram (61)	אֱלִיעֶזֶר	Eliezer (14)
אַבְשָׁלוֹם	Absalom (109)	אֱלִיפַז	Eliphaz (15)
אֱדוֹם	Edom (100)	אֶלְיָקִים	Eliakim (12)
אֲדוֹמִי	Edomite (12)	אֶלְיָשִׁיב	Eliashib (17)
אֲדֹנִיָּהוּ	Adonijah (26)	אֱלִישָׁמָע	Elishama (17)
אַהֲרֹן	Aaron (347)	אֱלִישָׁע	Elisha (58)
אוּרִיָּה	Uriah (36)	אֶלְעָזָר	Eleazar (72)
אַחְאָב	Ahab (93)	אֶלְקָנָה	Elkanah (21)
אָחָז	Ahaz (41)	אָמוֹן	Amon (17)
אֲחַזְיָהוּ	Ahaziah (30)	אָמוֹץ	Amoz (13)
אֲחִיָּה	Ahijah (19)	אַמְנוֹן	Amnon (28)
אֲחִיטוּב	Ahitub (15)	אֲמַצְיָהוּ	Amaziah (40)
אֲחִימֶלֶךְ	Ahimelech (17)	אֱמֹרִי	Amorite (87)
אֲחִימַעַץ	Ahimaaz (15)	אֲמַרְיָה	Amariah (13)
אֲחִיקָם	Ahikam (20)	אָסָא	Asa (58)
אֲחִיתֹפֶל	Ahithophel (20)	אָסָף	Asaph (46)
אֲחַשְׁוֵרוֹשׁ	Ahasuerus (32)	אֶסְתֵּר	Esther (55)
אִיּוֹב	Job (58)	אֶפְרַיִם	Ephraim (180)

אֲרַוְנָה	Araunah (11)	בָּרוּךְ	Baruch (26)
אֲרָם	Aram (149)	בַּרְזִלַּי	Barzillai (12)
אֲרַמִּי	Aramean (13)	בְּרִיעָה	Beriah (11)
אַרְנוֹן	Arnon (25)	בָּרָק	Barak (13)
אַרְנָן	Arnan (12)	בָּשָׁן	Bashan (60)
אַרְתַּחְשַׁסְתְּא	Artaxerxes (10)	בַּת־שֶׁבַע	Bathsheba (11)
אַשּׁוּר	Assyria (151)	גֶּבַע	Geba (19)
אַשְׁקְלוֹן	Ashkelon (12)	גִּבְעָה	Gibeah (42)
אָשֵׁר	Asher (43)	גִּבְעוֹן	Gibeon (37)
בְּאֵר	Beer (39)	גָּד	Gad (76)
בָּבֶל	Babylon (262)	גָּדִי	Gadite (16)
בֵּית חוֹרוֹן	Beth Horon (14)	גְּדַלְיָהוּ	Gedaliah (26)
בֵּית לֶחֶם	Bethlehem (41)	גִּדְעוֹן	Gideon (39)
בֵּית־שֶׁמֶשׁ	Beth Shemesh (21)	גּוֹג	Gog (12)
בִּלְהָה	Bilhah (10)	גֶּזֶר	Gezer (15)
בֶּלַע	Bela (12)	גֵּיחֲזִי	Gehazi (12)
בִּלְעָם	Balaam (60)	גִּלְגָּל	Gilgal (40)
בָּלָק	Balak (43)	גִּלְעָד	Gilead (134)
בֶּן־הֲדַד	Ben Hadad (25)	גִּלְעָדִי	Gileadite (11)
בֶּן־הִנֹּם	Ben Hinnom (11)	גְּרָר	Gerar (10)
בָּנִי	Bani (15)	גֵּרְשׁוֹם	Gershom (14)
בְּנָיָהוּ	Benaiah (42)	גֵּרְשׁוֹן	Gershon (17)
בִּנְיָמִן	Benjamin (169)	גֵּרְשֻׁנִּי	Gershonite (13)
בְּעוֹר	Beor (10)	גֹּשֶׁן	Goshen (15)
בֹּעַז	Boaz (22)	גַּת	Gath (33)
בַּעַל	Baal (122)	גִּתִּי	Gittite (10)
בַּעֲנָה	Baanah (12)	דְּבוֹרָה	Deborah (10)
בַּעְשָׁא	Baasha (28)	דְּבִר	Debir (11)

דָּגוֹן	Dagon (15)	חִוִּי	Hivite (25)
דָּוִד	David (1075)	חוּר	Hur (16)
דִּיבוֹן	Dibon (11)	חוּרָם	Huram (13)
דַּמֶּשֶׂק	Damascus (43)	חוּשַׁי	Hushai (14)
דָּן	Dan (70)	חֲזָאֵל	Hazael (23)
דָּנִיֵּאל	Daniel (32)	חִזְקִיָּהוּ	Hezekiah (125)
דָּרְיָוֶשׁ	Darius (10)	חִירוֹם	Hiram (25)
דָּתָן	Dathan (10)	חִלְקִיָּהוּ	Hilkiah (34)
הָגָר	Hagar (12)	חָם	Ham (16)
הֲדַד	Hadad (37)	חֲמוֹר	Hamor (13)
הֲדַדְעֶזֶר	Hadadezer (21)	חֲמָת	Hamath (37)
הוֹשֵׁעַ	Hoshea, Hosea (16)	חַנָּה	Hannah (13)
הֵימָן	Heman (17)	חֲנוֹךְ	Enoch (15)
הָמָן	Haman (54)	חָנוּן	Hanun (11)
הֹר	Hor (12)	חָנָן	Hanan (19)
וַשְׁתִּי	Vashti (10)	חֲנָנִי	Hanani (11)
זְבוּלוּן	Zebulun (45)	חֲנַנְיָה	Hananiah (25)
זֶבַח	Zebah (12)	חָצוֹר	Hazor (21)
זַכּוּר	Zaccur (10)	חֶצְרוֹן	Hezron (16)
זִכְרִי	Zichri (12)	חֹרֵב	Horeb (17)
זְכַרְיָה	Zechariah (25)	חָרִם	Harim (11)
זְכַרְיָהוּ	Zechariah (16)	חֶרְמוֹן	Hermon (16)
זִמְרִי	Zimri (14)	חָרָן	Haran (10)
זְרֻבָּבֶל	Zerubbabel (21)	חֶשְׁבּוֹן	Heshbon (38)
זֶרַח	Zerah (21)	חֲשַׁבְיָה	Hashabiah (12)
חֶבֶר	Zeber (11)	חֵת	Heth (14)
חֶבְרוֹן	Hebron (62)	חִתִּי	Hittite (46)
		טוֹבִיָּה	Tobiah (17)

יָאִיר	Jair (12)	יוֹנָה	Jonah (19)
יֹאשִׁיָּהוּ	Josiah (52)	יוֹסֵף	Joseph (214)
יְבוּסִי	Jebusite (41)	יוֹתָם	Jotham (24)
יְדוּתוּן	Jeduthun (20)	יִזְרְעֶאל	Jezreel (34)
יְדַעְיָה	Jedaiah (11)	יִזְרְעֵאלִי	Jezreelite (13)
יָהּ	Yah, Yahweh (49)	יְחִיאֵל	Jehiel (15)
יָהּ	Yah, Yahweh (15)	יְמִינִי	Benjaminite (13)
יֵהוּא	Jehu (58)	יְעוּשׁ	Jeush (12)
יְהוֹאָחָז	Jehoahaz (24)	יַעְזֵר	Jazer (13)
יְהוֹאָשׁ	Jehoash (64)	יְעִיאֵל	Jeiel (17)
יְהוּדָה	Judah (820)	יַעֲקֹב	Jacob (349)
יְהוּדִי	Judean, Jew (88)	יְפֻנֶּה	Jephunneh (16)
יהוה	Yahweh, LORD (6828)	יֶפֶת	Japheth (11)
		יִפְתָּח	Jephthah (29)
יְהוֹזָבָד	Jehozabad (15)	יִצְחָק	Isaac (112)
יְהוֹחָנָן	Jehohanan (33)	יְרֻבַּעַל	Jerubbaal (14)
יְהוֹיָדָע	Jehoiada (56)	יָרָבְעָם	Jeroboam (104)
יְהוֹיָכִין	Jehoiachin (14)	יַרְדֵּן	Jordan (183)
יְהוֹיָקִים	Jehoiakim (41)	יְרוּשָׁלַ͏ִם	Jerusalem (643)
יְהוֹנָדָב	Jehonadab (15)	יְרֹחָם	Jeroham (10)
יְהוֹנָתָן	Jonathan (124)	יְרִיחוֹ	Jericho (56)
יְהוֹצָדָק	Jehozadak (12)	יִרְמְיָה	Jeremiah (17)
יְהוֹרָם	Jehoram (48)	יִרְמְיָהוּ	Jeremiah (130)
יְהוֹשֻׁעַ	Joshua (227)	יִשְׂרָאֵל	Israel (2507)
יְהוֹשָׁפָט	Jehoshaphat (84)	יִשָּׂשכָר	Issachar (43)
יוֹאָב	Joab (146)	יֵשׁוּעַ	Jeshua (19)
יוֹאָח	Joah (11)	יִשַׁי	Jesse (42)
יוֹאֵל	Joel (19)	יִשְׁמָעֵאל	Ishmael (48)

יְשַׁעְיָהוּ	Isaiah (35)	מִיכָיְהוּ	Michaiah, Micah (21)
כּוֹרֶשׁ	Cyrus (15)	מִיכַל	Michal (18)
כּוּשׁ	Cush (29)	מָכִיר	Machir (22)
כּוּשִׁי	Cushite (25)	מִכְמָס	Michmas (11)
כְּנַעַן	Canaan (93)	מִלְכָּה	Milcah (11)
כְּנַעֲנִי	Canaanite (73)	מַלְכִּיָּה	Malchiah (16)
כַּרְמֶל	Carmel (14)	מָנוֹחַ	Manoah (18)
כְּרֵתִי	Cherethite (10)	מְנַשֶּׁה	Manasseh (146)
כַּשְׂדִּים	Chaldea (82)	מַעֲשֵׂיָה	Maaseiah (16)
כִּתִּיִּם	Kittim (10)	מְפִיבֹשֶׁת	Mephibosheth (18)
לֵאָה	Leah (34)	מִצְפָּה	Mizpah (40)
לָבָן	Laban (54)	מִצְרִי	Egyptian (30)
לִבְנָה	Libnah (18)	מִצְרַיִם	Egypt (682)
לְבָנוֹן	Lebanon (71)	מָרְדְּכַי	Mordecai (60)
לוֹט	Lot (33)	מְרִיבָה	Meribah (11)
לֵוִי	Levi, Levite (350)	מִרְיָם	Miriam (15)
לָכִישׁ	Lachish (24)	מְרָרִי	Merari (35)
לֶמֶךְ	Lamech (11)	מֹשֶׁה	Moses (766)
מְגִדּוֹ	Megiddo (12)	מְשֻׁלָּם	Meshullam (25)
מָדַי	Medes, Media (16)	מַתַּנְיָה	Mattaniah (13)
מִדְיָן	Midian (59)	נְבוֹ	Nebo (12)
מוֹאָב	Moab (187)	נְבוּזַרְאֲדָן	Nebuzaradan (16)
מוֹאָבִי	Moabite (16)	נְבוּכַדְנֶאצַּר	Nebuchadnezzar (10)
מַחְלִי	Mahli (11)	נְבוּכַדְרֶאצַּר	Nebuchadrezzar (52)
מַחֲנַיִם	Mahanaim (13)		
מִיכָאֵל	Michael (13)	נָבוֹת	Naboth (22)
מִיכָה	Micah (34)		

נְבָט	Nebat (25)	עִבְרִי	Hebrew (34)
נָבָל	Nabal (22)	עֵדֶן	Eden (13)
נֶּגֶב	Negev (83)	עוֹבֵד	Obed (10)
נָדָב	Nadab (20)	עוֹג	Og (22)
נוּן	Nun (30)	עֻזָּא	Uzza (15)
נֹחַ	Noah (46)	עַזָּה	Gaza (20)
נָחוֹר	Nahor (18)	עֻזִּיאֵל	Uzziel (16)
נַחְשׁוֹן	Nahshon (10)	עֻזִּיָּהוּ	Uzziah (19)
נְטֹפָתִי	Netophathite (11)	עֶזְרָא	Ezra (22)
נִינְוֵה	Nineveh (17)	עֲזַרְיָה	Azariah (32)
נָעֳמִי	Naomi (21)	עֲזַרְיָהוּ	Azariah (16)
נַעֲמָן	Naaman (16)	עַי	Ai (38)
נַפְתָּלִי	Naphtali (51)	עֵילָם	Elam (30)
נֵר	Ner (16)	עֵלִי	Eli (33)
נֵרִיָּה	Neriah (10)	עַמּוֹן	Ammon (106)
נָתָן	Nathan (42)	עַמּוֹנִי	Ammonite (22)
נְתַנְאֵל	Nethanel (14)	עַמִּיהוּד	Ammihud (10)
נְתַנְיָה	Nethaniah (15)	עַמִּינָדָב	Amminadab (13)
סְדֹם	Sodom (39)	עֲמָלֵק	Amalek (39)
סִיחוֹן	Sihon (37)	עֲמָלֵקִי	Amalekite (12)
סִינַי	Sinai (35)	עֲמֹרָה	Gomorrah (19)
סִיסְרָא	Sisera (21)	עָמְרִי	Omri (18)
סֻכּוֹת	Succoth (19)	עַמְרָם	Amram (14)
סַנְבַלַּט	Sanballat (10)	עֲמָשָׂא	Amasa (16)
סַנְחֵרִיב	Sennacherib (13)	עֲנָה	Anah (12)
עֹבֵד אֱדֹם	Obed Edom (20)	עֲנָק	Anak (17)
עֹבַדְיָה	Obadiah (11)	עֲנָתוֹת	Anathoth (13)
עֵבֶר	Eber (15)	עֶפְרוֹן	Ephron (12)

עֶקְרוֹן	Ekron (22)
עֵר	Er (10)
עֲרוֹעֵר	Aroer (15)
עֲשָׂהאֵל	Asahel (24)
עֵשָׂו	Esau (97)
עֲתַלְיָהוּ	Athaliah (17)
פָּארָן	Paran (12)
פִּינְחָס	Phinehas (25)
פְּלִשְׁתִּי	Philistine (290)
פְּעוֹר	Peor (15)
פֶּקַח	Pekah (11)
פְּרִזִּי	Perizzite (23)
פָּרַס	Persia (28)
פַּרְעֹה	Pharaoh (274)
פֶּרֶץ	Perez (12)
פְּרָת	Euphrates (19)
פַּשְׁחוּר	Pashur (14)
צָדוֹק	Zadok (53)
צִדְקִיָּהוּ	Zedekiah (56)
צוֹבָה	Zobah (11)
צִיבָא	Ziba (16)
צִידוֹן	Sidon (22)
צִידֹנִי	Sidonian (16)
צִיּוֹן	Zion (154)
צַלְמֻנָּע	Zalmunna (12)
צְלָפְחָד	Zelophehad (11)
צִן	Zin (10)
צֹעַר	Zoar (10)

צִקְלַג	Ziklag (15)
צֹר	Tyre (42)
צְרוּיָה	Zeruiah (26)
צָרְעָה	Zorah (10)
קֵדָר	Kedar (12)
קִדְרוֹן	Kidron (11)
קֶדֶשׁ	Kedesh (12)
קָדֵשׁ	Kadesh (18)
קָדֵשׁ בַּרְנֵעַ	Kadesh Barnea (10)
קְהָת	Kohath (32)
קְהָתִי	Kohathite (15)
קַיִן	Cain (16)
קֵינִי	Kenite (12)
קִישׁ	Kish (21)
קְנַז	Kenaz (11)
קְעִילָה	Keilah (18)
קֹרַח	Korah (37)
קָרֵחַ	Kareah (14)
קִרְיַת יְעָרִים	Kiriath Jearim (19)
רְאוּבֵן	Reuben (72)
רְאוּבֵנִי	Reubenite (18)
רָאמֹות	Ramoth (20)
רַבָּה	Rabbah (16)
רִבְלָה	Riblah (11)
רִבְקָה	Rebekah (30)
רוּת	Ruth (12)
רְחַבְעָם	Rehoboam (50)

רָחֵל	Rachel (47)	שַׁלּוּם	Shallum (27)
רֵכָב	Rechab (13)	שְׁלֹמֹה	Solomon (293)
רָמָה	Ramah (36)	שֵׁם	Shem (17)
רְמַלְיָהוּ	Remaliah (13)	שְׁמוּאֵל	Samuel (140)
רְעוּאֵל	Reuel (11)	שִׁמְעוֹן	Simeon (44)
רְפָאִים	Rephaim (19)	שִׁמְעִי	Shimei (44)
רְצִין	Rezin (11)	שְׁמַעְיָה	Shemaiah (34)
שֵׂעִיר	Seir (38)	שֹׁמְרוֹן	Samaria (109)
שָׂרָה	Sarah (38)	שִׁמְשׁוֹן	Samson (38)
שָׂרַי	Sarai (17)	שְׁפַטְיָה	Shephatiah (10)
שְׂרָיָה	Seraiah (19)	שָׁפָן	Shaphan (30)
שָׁאוּל	Saul (405)	תָּבוֹר	Tabor (11)
שְׁבָא	Sheba (23)	תִּמְנָה	Timnah (12)
שֶׁבַע	Sheba (45)	תָּמָר	Tamar (21)
שׁוּשַׁן	Susa (21)	תֶּרַח	Terah (11)
שְׁכֶם	Shechem (58)	תִּרְצָה	Tirzah (14)
שִׁלֹה	Shiloh (33)	תַּרְשִׁישׁ	Tarshish (26)

NOUNS WITH COMMON GENDER
LISTED ALPHABETICALLY

In the Hebrew Old Testament, there are 43 common
nouns with common gender with a total occurrence of
approximately 5,700 times. 34 of these nouns occur 10
times or more.

אוֹר   light, daylight, sunshine (120)

אוֹת   sign, mark, pledge; (cp) אֹתוֹת (79)

אָרוֹן   ark, chest, coffin (202); אֲרוֹן הַבְּרִית "the ark of the covenant"

אֹרַח   road, path, way; (cp cstr) אָרְחוֹת (59)

אֵשׁ   fire (376)

גַּיְא   valley; (cp) גֵּאָיוֹת; also spelled גֵּיְא (64)

גַּן   garden; (cp) גַּנִּים (41)

גֶּפֶן   vine, grapevine (55)

דֶּרֶךְ   way, road, journey (712)

זָקָן   beard (19)

חַלּוֹן window; (cp) חַלּוֹנוֹת and חַלּוֹנִים (32)

חָצֵר   courtyard, village, settlement; (cp) חֲצֵרִים and חֲצֵרוֹת (192)

לָבִיא   lion, lioness (12)

לָשׁוֹן tongue, language (117)

מָגֵן   shield; (cp) מָגִנִּים (60)

מַחֲנֶה camp, army; (cp) מַחֲנוֹת and מַחֲנִים (215)

מְצִלְתַּיִם (cd) cymbals (13)

מַקֵּל   rod, staff, branch; (cp) מַקְלוֹת (18)

סִיר   basin, pot, tub (29)

עֲבֹת   cord, rope; (cp) עֲבֹתֹת and עֲבֹתִים (19)

עַיִן   eye, spring; (cs cstr) עֵין; (cd cstr) עֵינֵי (900)

עֵת   time, point of time; (cp) עִתִּים and עִתּוֹת (296)

פָּנִים (cp) face, front; (cp cstr) פְּנֵי (2,126)

צֹאן   (cs) flock(s), flock of sheep and goats (274)

צָבָא   host, army, war, service; (cp) צְבָאוֹת (487); יְהוָה צְבָאוֹת "Lord of Hosts"

צִפּוֹר   bird; also spelled צִפֹּר; (cp) צִפֳּרִים (40)

רוּחַ   spirit, wind, breath; (cp) רוּחוֹת (378)

שְׁאוֹל   underworld, Sheol (65)

שַׁבָּת   Sabbath, period of rest; (cp) שַׁבָּתוֹת (111)

שֶׁמֶשׁ   sun (134)

שֵׁן   tooth, ivory; (cd cstr) שִׁנֵּי (55)

תְּהוֹם   primeval ocean, deep, depth; (cp) תְּהֹמוֹת (36)

תַּן   jackal; (cp) תַּנִּים (15)

תַּנּוּר   oven, firepot, furnace (15)

ENDINGLESS
FEMININE SINGULAR NOUNS
LISTED ALPHABETICALLY

In the Hebrew Old Testament, there are some 1,500 feminine nouns with a total occurrence of approximately 28,000 times. 974 feminine nouns (occurring 13,664) end with הָ . 353 feminine nouns (occurring 4,194 times) end with ת. 165 feminine nouns (occurring 10,336 times) are "endingless," meaning that they do not end with either הָ or the ת that is characteristic of the feminine gender. There are 44 "endingless" feminine nouns that occur more than 10 times in the Hebrew Bible.

אֶבֶן   stone; (p) אֲבָנִים (276)

אֹזֶן   ear; (d cstr) אָזְנֵי (188)

אֵם   mother; (with 3ms suff) אִמּוֹ (220)

אֶצְבַּע   finger, toe; (p cstr) אֶצְבְּעֹת (31)

אֶרֶץ   land, earth, ground (2,505)

אָתוֹן   female donkey; (p) אֲתֹנוֹת (34)

בְּאֵר   well, pit (37)

בֶּטֶן   belly, stomach, womb (72)

בֶּרֶךְ   knee; (d) בִּרְכַּיִם (26)

גֹּרֶן   threshing floor (37)

זְרוֹעַ   arm, forearm; (metaphorically) strength or power; (p) זְרֹעוֹת (91)

חֶרֶב   sword (413)

יָד   hand; (metaphorically) side, power (1,627)

יָמִין   right hand, south (141)

יָרֵךְ   thigh, loin, side (34)

יָתֵד   tent peg, stake, pin; (p) יְתֵדֹת (24)

כָּבֵד   liver (14)

כַּד   jar, pitcher; (p) כַּדִּים (18)

כּוֹס   cup (31)

כִּכָּר   something round, talent (weight), valley; (p) כִּכָּרִים (68)

כָּנָף   wing, edge, extremity; (d) כְּנָפַיִם (111)

כַּף   hand, palm, sole of the foot; (p) כַּפּוֹת (195)

כָּתֵף   side, shoulder; (p) כְּתֵפוֹת (67)

לְחִי   jaw, cheek, chin (21)

מְצָד   stronghold, fortress; (fp) מְצָדוֹת (12)

נַעַל   sandal, shoe (22)

נֶפֶשׁ   soul, life, person, neck, throat (757)

עֵז   goat, goat's hair; (p) עִזִּים (74)

עִיר   city, town; (p) עָרִים (1,088)

עֶצֶם   bone, skeleton (126)

עֶרֶשׂ   couch, bed (10)

פִּילֶגֶשׁ   concubine; also spelled פִּלֶגֶשׁ; (p) פִּילַגְשִׁים (37)

פַּעַם   foot, pace, time; (p) פְּעָמִים (118)

צֵלָע   rib, side (40)

צָפוֹן   north, northern (153)

צְפַרְדֵּעַ   frog; (p) צְפַרְדְּעִים (13); 11x in Exod

קֶרֶן   horn; (p cstr) קַרְנוֹת (76)

רְבוֹא   ten thousand, countless number; also spelled רִבּוֹ (11)

רֶגֶל   foot (251)

רְחוֹב   public square, street; (p) רְחֹבוֹת (43)

שׁוֹק   thigh, leg (19)

תֵּבֵל   world (36)

תּוֹר   turtledove; (p) תֹּרִים (14)

תֵּימָן   south; (with directional ה) תֵּימָנָה "southward" (24)

WORD LIST 3D

SEGHOLATE PATTERN NOUNS
LISTED ALPHABETICALLY

The following list contains 194 two-syllable nouns that are accented on the penultima (next-to-last syllable).

אֵבֶל   mourning, funeral ceremony (24)

אֶבֶן   (fs) stone; (fp) אֲבָנִים (276)

אֶדֶן   base, pedestal; (mp) אֲדָנִים; (mp cstr) אַדְנֵי (57)

אֹהֶל   tent (348)

אָוֶן   iniquity, wickedness, evildoer (81)

אֹזֶן   (fs) ear; (fd cstr) אָזְנֵי (188)

אֹכֶל   food (38)

אֶלֶף   thousand (496)

אֶלֶף   clan, tribe, region (11)

אֹמֶר   word, saying, speech; (mp cstr) אִמְרֵי (48)

אֶפֶס   end, nothing (43)

אֵפֶר   ashes, dust (22)

אֶרֶז   cedar; (mp) אֲרָזִים (73)

אֹרַח   (cs) road, path, way; (cp cstr) אָרְחוֹת (59)

אֹרֶךְ   length; (with 3ms suff) אָרְכּוֹ (95)

אֶרֶץ   (fs) land, earth, ground (2,505)

בֶּגֶד   clothes, garment, covering (216)

בֶּדֶק   damage, breach, crack (10)

בֹּהֶן   thumb, big toe (16)

בֶּטַח   security, safety (42)

בֶּטֶן   (fs) belly, stomach, womb (72)

בַּעַל   owner, master, husband, (divine title) Baal (161)

בֶּצַע   unjust gain (23)

בֹּקֶר   morning (213)

בֶּרֶךְ   (fs) knee; (fd) בִּרְכַּיִם (26)

בֹּשֶׂם   spice, perfume (30)

בֹּשֶׁת   shame, disgrace (41)

גֶּבֶר   strong man, young man (66)

גֹּדֶל   greatness, arrogance (13)

גֶּפֶן (cs) vine, grapevine (55)

גֹּרֶן (fs) threshing floor (37)

גֶּשֶׁם rain, showers (35)

דֶּבֶר plague, pestilence (46)

דֶּגֶל division of a tribe, banner, standard (14); 13x in Num

דֶּלֶת door; (fp cstr) דַּלְתוֹת (88)

דַּעַת knowledge, understanding, ability (88)

דֶּרֶךְ (cs) way, road, journey (712)

דֶּשֶׁא grass, vegetation (14)

דֶּשֶׁן fat, fat-soaked ashes (15)

הֶבֶל vanity, futility, breath (73); 38x in Eccl

זֶבַח sacrifice (162)

זֵכֶר memory, remembrance; (with 3ms suff) זִכְרוֹ (23)

זַעַם anger, indignation, curse (22)

זֶרַע seed, offspring, descendants (229)

חֶבֶל rope, cord, field, region (48)

חֶדֶר room, chamber (38)

חֹדֶשׁ month, new moon; (mp) חֳדָשִׁים (283)

חֵלֶב fat; (metaphorically) best, choice part (92)

חֵלֶק portion, share (66)

חֹמֶר mud, clay, mortar (17)

חֹמֶר dry measurement, heap, pile, homer (13)

חֶסֶד loyalty, faithfulness, steadfast love, lovingkindness (249)

חֵפֶץ delight, desire, pleasure (38)

חֵקֶר searching, something searched out (12)

חֶרֶב (fs) sword (413)

חֹרֶב dryness, drought, heat, waste (16)

חֵרֶם set apart for destruction, something banned, devoted thing (29)

חֶ֫רֶשׂ	earthenware, potsherd (20)
חֹ֫שֶׁךְ	darkness (80)
חֹ֫שֶׁן	breastplate (of the high priest) (25); 23x in Exod
טֶ֫בַח	slaughtering, slaughter (12)
טַ֫עַם	taste, sense, discernment (13)
טֶ֫רֶף	prey, food (22)
יֶ֫לֶד	child, boy, youth (89)
יַ֫עַר	forest, woods, thicket (57)
יֶ֫קֶב	wine vat, winepress (16)
יֶ֫רַח	month (12)
יֶ֫שַׁע	salvation, deliverance, help; (with 1cs suff) יִשְׁעִי (36)
יֹ֫שֶׁר	uprightness, honesty, straightness (14)
יֶ֫תֶר	rest, remainder, excess (97)
כֶּ֫בֶשׂ	lamb, sheep; (mp) כְּבָשִׂים (107)
כֶּ֫לֶא	prison, confinement (10)
כֶּ֫לֶב	dog, male temple prostitute (32)
כֶּ֫סֶף	silver, money (403)
כַּ֫עַס	anger, vexation (21)
כֹּ֫פֶר	ransom, bribe (13)
כֶּ֫רֶם	vineyard; (mp) כְּרָמִים (94)
כֶּ֫שֶׂב	young ram, lamb (13)
לַ֫הַב	flame, blade (of sword) (12)
לֶ֫חֶם	bread, food (340)
לַ֫חַץ	oppression, affliction (12)
מֶ֫לַח	salt (23)
מֶ֫לֶךְ	king, ruler (2,530)
מַ֫עַל	unfaithfulness, infidelity (29)
מֵ֫צַח	forehead, brow (13)
נֵ֫בֶל	stringed instrument, harp; (mp) נְבָלִים (28)

נֵבֶל   jar, bottle (10)

נֶגֶב   south, Negev (29)

נֹגַהּ   brightness, radiance (19)

נֶגַע   mark, plague, affliction (78)

נֶדֶר   vow; also spelled נֵדֶר (60)

נֶזֶם   earring, nose-ring (17)

נֵזֶר   consecration, dedication, crown; (with 3ms suff) נִזְרוֹ (25)

נַחַל   stream, brook, wadi (137)

נֶסֶךְ   drink offering; also spelled נֵסֶךְ (60)

נַעַל   (fs) sandal, shoe (22)

נַעַר   boy, youth, servant (240)

נֶפֶשׁ   (fs) soul, life, person, neck, throat (757)

נֶצַח   forever, everlasting; also spelled לָנֶצַח with prep לְ (43)

נֶשֶׁךְ   interest, usury (12)

נֶשֶׁף   twilight, dusk (12)

נֶשֶׁר   eagle, vulture (26)

נֵתַח   piece of meat (13)

נֶתֶק   skin disease, scab (14); all in Lev

סֶלַע   rock, stone, cliff (59)

סֹלֶת   flour (53)

סֵפֶר   book, scroll, document (191); סֵפֶר הַתּוֹרָה "the book of the law"

סֶרֶן   ruler, lord; (mp cstr) סַרְנֵי (21); 19x in Judg, 1 Sam

סֵתֶר   hiding place, secret place, shelter (35)

עֶבֶד   slave, servant (803)

עֵבֶר   beyond, other side, edge, bank (92)

עֵגֶל   calf, young bull (35)

עֵדֶר   flock, herd (38)

עָוֶל   iniquity, injustice, wrong (21)

עֵזֶר   help, assistance (17)

עֵמֶק   valley, plain (70)

עֶצֶם   (fs) bone, skeleton; (fp) עֲצָמוֹת (126)

עֵקֶב   result, wages (15)

עֶרֶב   evening, sunset (134)

עֵרֶךְ   value, assessment; (with 2ms suff) עֶרְכְּךָ (33)

עֹרֶף   (back of) neck (33)

עֶרֶשׂ   (fs) couch, bed (10)

עֵשֶׂב   green plant, grass (33)

עֹשֶׁק   oppression, extortion (15)

עֹשֶׁר   wealth, riches (37)

פֶּגֶר   corpse, carcass; (mp cstr) פִּגְרֵי (22)

פַּחַד   trembling, terror, dread (49)

פַּחַת   pit, ravine (10)

פֶּטֶר   firstborn (11)

פֶּלֶא   wonder, miracle, something extraordinary (13)

פֶּלֶג   water channel, canal (10)

פֶּסַח   Passover (49)

פֶּסֶל   idol, carved image (31)

פֹּעַל   work, deed; (with 3ms suff) פָּעֳלוֹ (36)

פַּעַם   (fs) foot, pace, time; (fp) פְּעָמִים (118)

פֶּרֶא   wild donkey (10)

פֶּרֶד   mule (14)

פֶּרַח   blossom, bud, flower (17)

פֶּרֶץ   breach, gap (19)

פֶּשַׁע   transgression, rebellion, crime; (mp cstr) פִּשְׁעֵי (93)

פֵּשֶׁת   linen, flax; (fp) פִּשְׁתִּים (16)

פֶּתַח   opening, entrance, doorway (164)

צֶדֶק   righteousness, equity (123)

צֶלֶם   image, idol; (mp cstr) צַלְמֵי (15)

צֶמֶד   pair, team (15)

צֶמַח   growth, sprout, branch (12)

צֶמֶר   wool (16)

צַעַד   step, pace (14)

קֶבֶר   grave, burial site; (mp) קְבָרִים and קְבָרוֹת (67)

קֶדֶם   east, ancient times (61)

קֹדֶשׁ   holiness, something that is holy; (mp) קֳדָשִׁים (470)

קֶלַע   curtain; (mp) קְלָעִים (16)

קֶמַח   flour (14)

קֶסֶם   divination, prediction (11)

קֶצֶף   wrath, anger (28)

קֶרֶב   inner part(s), organ(s), body; (prep) בְּקֶרֶב (155x) in the middle of, among (227)

קֶרֶן   (fs) horn; (fp cstr) קַרְנוֹת (76)

קֶרֶס   (curtain) hook, clasp; (mp cstr) קַרְסֵי (10); all in Exod

קֶרֶשׁ   board, plank (51); 48x in Exod

קֶשֶׁר   alliance, conspiracy, treason (16)

קֶשֶׁת   bow, weapon (76)

רֶגֶל   (fs) foot (251)

רֶגַע   moment, instant (22)

רֶחֶם   womb (26)

רֶכֶב   chariot, (coll) chariots or chariot riders, upper millstone (120)

רֹמַח   spear, lance (15)

רֶמֶשׂ   creeping thing, animal that creeps upon the earth (17); 10x in Gen

רַעַשׁ   earthquake, clatter, commotion (17)

רֶשַׁע   evil, wickedness, offense, injustice (30)

רֶשֶׁת   net, trap (22)

שֵׂכֶל   insight, understanding, success; also spelled שֶׂכֶל (16)

שֵׁבֶט   rod, staff, scepter, tribe (190); שִׁבְטֵי יִשְׂרָאֵל "the tribes of Israel"

שֶׁבֶר   break, fracture, collapse (44)

שֹׁהַם   precious stone, (perhaps) onyx (11)

שֹׁחַד   bribe, gift (23)

שַׁחַק   layer of dust, cloud of dust, cloud; (mp) שְׁחָקִים (21)

שַׁחַר   dawn, daybreak (23)

שַׁחַת   pit, grave (23)

שֶׁלֶג   snow (20)

שֶׁלֶם   peace offering; (mp) שְׁלָמִים (87)

שֶׁמֶן   oil, fat (193)

שֵׁמַע   report, news, rumor (17)

שֶׁמֶשׁ   (cs) sun (134)

שַׁעַר   gate (373)

שֶׁפֶט   act of judgment, punishment; (mp) שְׁפָטִים (16)

שֶׁקֶל   measurement of weight, shekel (88)

שֶׁקֶץ   detestable thing, abomination (11)

שֶׁקֶר   lie, deception, falsehood (113)

שֶׁרֶץ   swarming things (15); 12x in Lev

שֹׁרֶשׁ   root; (mp with 3ms suff) שָׁרָשָׁיו (33)

תֹּאַר   form, shape, appearance (15)

תֶּבֶן   straw, chaff (17)

תַּחַשׁ   porpoise, dolphin, leather (14)

תַּעַר   razor, knife, sheath (13)

ADJECTIVES
LISTED ALPHABETICALLY

In the Hebrew Old Testament, there are approximately 500 adjectives with a total occurrence of some 17,000 times. Excluding demonstrative adjectives and most numerals, there are 116 adjectives that occur more than 10 times.

אֶבְיוֹן   poor, needy (61)

אַבִּיר   mighty, strong, powerful (17)

אַדִּיר   noble, majestic, mighty (27)

אַחֵר   other, another, foreign; (fs) אַחֶרֶת (166)

אַחֲרוֹן   last, behind, west (51)

אֵיתָן   ever flowing, constant, enduring; (mp) אֵתָנִים (14)

אָרֵךְ   long, slow (15); 13x אֶרֶךְ־אַפַּיִם (lit) "long
of nose;" (idiom) "slow to anger" or "patient"

בָּחִיר   chosen, elect (13)

בְּלִיַּעַל   useless, worthless (27)

בָּצוּר   fortified, inaccessible; (fp) בְּצֻרוֹת (26)

בָּרִיא   fat, well fed; (fp) בְּרִיאוֹת (14)

גָּבֹהַּ   high, exalted; (fs) גְּבֹהָה (41)

גִּבּוֹר   mighty, valiant, heroic (160)

גָּדוֹל   great, big, large (527)

דַּל   poor, weak, needy; (mp) דַּלִּים (48)

דַּק   thin, lean, skinny; (fp) דַּקּוֹת (14)

הָרָה   (fs) pregnant (15)

זֵד   proud, insolent, presumptuous; (mp) זֵדִים (13)

זַךְ   pure, clean; (fs) זַכָּה (11)

זָקֵן   old (180)

זָר   foreign, strange; (mp) זָרִים (70)

חָדָשׁ   new, fresh; (fs) חֲדָשָׁה (53)

חָזָק   strong, mighty, hard (57)

חַטָּא   sinful; (mp) חַטָּאִים (19)

חַי   living, alive; (mp) חַיִּים (254)

חִיצוֹן   outer, external; (fs) חִיצוֹנָה (25)

חָכָם   wise, skillful, experienced (138)

חָלָל   pierced, slain, defiled; (mp) חֲלָלִים; (mp cstr) חַלְלֵי (94)

חָלָק   smooth, slippery, flattering (10)

חַנּוּן   gracious, merciful (13)

חָנֵף   godless, profane (13)

חָסִיד   godly, faithful, pious (34)

חָסֵר   lacking, wanting; (ms cstr) חֲסַר (17)

חָפֵץ   delighting (in), desiring (13)

חָפְשִׁי free, exempt; (mp) חָפְשִׁים (17)

חָרֵב   dry, desolate, wasted; (fs) חֲרֵבָה (10)

טָהוֹר   clean, pure; also spelled טָהֹר (96)

טוֹב   good, pleasant (530)

טָמֵא   unclean; (fs) טְמֵאָה (88)

יָחִיד   only (child), lonely, solitary (12)

יָלִיד   born (of) (13)

יְמָנִית (fs) right, southern; (ms) יְמָנִי (33)

יָפֶה   beautiful; (fs) יָפָה (42)

יָקָר   precious, valuable; (fs) יְקָרָה (36)

יָרֵא   fearful, afraid of (63)

יָשָׁר   upright, just, level, straight (119)

כָּבֵד   heavy, severe (41)

כַּבִּיר   mighty, strong, powerful (10)

כָּלִיל   entire, whole, complete (15)

כֵּן   honest, correct, right (24)

לָבָן   white (29)

מָלֵא   full, filled (61)

מְעַט   little, few (101)

מַר   bitter (38)

מָשִׁיחַ   anointed (38)

מָתוֹק   sweet, pleasant (12)

נָאֶה   lovely, beautiful, desirable, suitable; (fs) נָאוָה (10)

נָבָל   foolish, good-for-nothing (18)

נָדִיב   noble, willing, generous (26)

נָכְרִי   foreign, strange; (fs) נָכְרִיָּה (46)

נָעִים   pleasant, lovely, delightful; (mp) נְעִימִים (13)

נָקִי   blameless, innocent; (mp) נְקִיִּם (43)

עִוֵּר   blind; (mp) עִוְרִים (26)

עַז   strong, mighty; (mp) עַזִּים (23)

עָיֵף   tired, exhausted, weary; (fs) עֲיֵפָה (17)

עֵירֹם   naked (10)

עֶלְיוֹן   upper; (divine title) Most High (53)

עָמֹק   deep, unfathomable, mysterious; (fs) עֲמֻקָּה (17)

עָנָו   afflicted, oppressed, humble, meek; (mp) עֲנָוִים (25)

עָנִי   poor, humble, afflicted; (mp) עֲנִיִּים (80)

עָצוּם   mighty, numerous (31)

עָצֵל   low, lazy (14); all in Prov

עָקָר   barren, childless; (fs) עֲקָרָה (12)

עִקֵּשׁ   perverted, crooked, false (10)

עָרוּם   crafty, cunning, clever, prudent (11)

עָרוֹם   naked; (mp) עֲרוּמִּים (16)

עָרִיץ   ruthless, fierce, violent; (mp) עָרִיצִים (20)

עָרֵל   uncircumcised; (mp) עֲרֵלִים (35)

עָשִׁיר rich, wealthy (23)

פְּנִימִי inner; (fs) פְּנִימִית (32)

פִּסֵּחַ lame, crippled (14)

צַדִּיק righteous, just, innocent (206)

צָעִיר little, small, young (23)

צַר narrow (27)

קָדוֹשׁ holy, set apart (117)

קַדְמֹנִי eastern, former, past (10)

קָטֹן small, young, insignificant; (fs) קְטַנָּה (74)

קָטָן small, young; (mp) קְטַנִּים (27)

קַל light, swift, agile; (mp) קַלִּים (13)

קָרֵב approaching, drawing near (12)

קָרוֹב near, close; also spelled קָרֹב (75)

קָשֶׁה difficult, hard, severe; (fs) קָשָׁה (36)

רִאשׁוֹן first, former; (fs) רִאשֹׁנָה (182)

רַב great, many; (mp) רַבִּים (419)

רַגְלִי on foot, pedestrian, foot soldier (12)

רָחָב wide, spacious; (fp) רְחָבָה (20)

רַחוּם compassionate (13)

רָחוֹק distant, remote, far away; also spelled רָחֹק (84)

רֵיק empty, vain; (mp) רֵקִים (14)

רַךְ tender, frail, weak, soft; (fs) רַכָּה (16)

רַע bad, evil, of little worth; (mp) רָעִים; also spelled רָע (312)

רָעֵב hungry; (mp) רְעֵבִים (20)

רַעֲנָן green, fresh, luxuriant (19)

רָשָׁע wicked, guilty; (mp) רְשָׁעִים (264)

שָׂבֵעַ satisfied, full (10)

שָׂכִיר   hired (worker) (18)

שָׂמֵחַ   joyful, glad, happy; (mp) שְׂמֵחִים (21)

שַׁאֲנָן   at ease, secure, untroubled; (fp) שַׁאֲנַנּוֹת (10)

שִׁכּוֹר   drunk (13)

שָׁלֵם   whole, complete, safe (28)

שָׁמֵן   fat, rich; (fs) שְׁמֵנָה (10)

שָׁפָל   low, lowly, humble, deep; (fs) שְׁפָלָה (17)

תַּחְתּוֹן   lower, lowest; (fs) תַּחְתּוֹנָה (13)

תַּחְתִּית   (fs) lower; (fp) תַּחְתִּיּוֹת (19)

תִּיכוֹן   middle, center; (fs) תִּיכֹנָה (11)

תָּם   blameless, complete, perfect; (mp) תַּמִּים (15)

תָּמִים   blameless, perfect, honest, devout; (mp) תְּמִימִם (91)

PREPOSITIONS
LISTED ALPHABETICALLY

In the Hebrew Old Testament, there are approximately 50 prepositions with a total occurrence of approximately 57,000 times. There are 31 prepositions that occur more than 10 times.

אַחֲרֵי   after, behind; also spelled אַחַר (718)

אֶל־   to, toward, in, into; (with 3ms suff) אֵלָיו (5,518)

אֵצֶל   beside, near (62)

אֵת   with, beside; also spelled אֶת־; (with 3ms suff) אִתּוֹ (890)

בְּ   in, at, with, by, against (15,559)

בֵּין   between (409)

בִּלְעֲדֵי   apart from, except for, without (17)

בְּמוֹ   in, at, with, by, against; alternate (poetic) form of prep בְּ (10)

בַּעֲבוּר   on account of, in order that (49)

בַּעַד   behind, through (104)

בְּקֶרֶב   in the middle of, among (155)

בְּתוֹךְ   in the midst (middle) of (319)

זוּלָה   except, only; (with 1cs suff) זוּלָתִי (16)

יַעַן   on account of (100)

כְּ   as, like, according to; (with 2ms suff) כָּמוֹךָ (3,053)

לְ   to, toward, for (20,321)

לְמַעַן   on account of, for the sake of (272)

לְעֻמַּת   beside, alongside, corresponding to; combination of prep לְ and עֻמָּה (32)

לִפְנֵי   before, in front of (1,102)

מוּל   in front of, opposite (36); compare with מוּל (#925)

מִן   from, out of; (with 3ms suff) מִמֶּנּוּ; (prefixed to a nominal) · מִ (7,592)

מֵעַל   above, upward, on top of (140)

נֶגֶד   opposite, in front of (151)

נֹכַח   in front of, opposite (25)

סָבִיב   around, about; (fp) סְבִיבוֹת (338)

עַד   until, as far as, during (1,263); compare with עַד (#678)

עַל   on, upon, on account of, according to (5,777)

עִם   with, together with; (with 3ms suff) עִמּוֹ (1,048)

עִמָּד   with; (with 1cs suff) עִמָּדִי (45)

תַּחַת   under, below, instead of (510)

WORD LIST 4A

VERBS
LISTED ALPHABETICALLY

In the Hebrew Old Testament, there are approximately 1,600 verbs with a total occurrence of some 73,000 times. 629 of these verbs occur more than 10 times.

אָבַד (Q) to perish, vanish, be(come) lost, go astray; (Pi) cause to perish, destroy; (Hi) exterminate (185)

אָבָה (Q) to be willing, consent, yield to, accede to, want something (54)

אָבַל (Q) to mourn, lament; (Hith) observe mourning rites (36)

אָדַם (Q) to be red; (Pu) be reddened, be dyed red (10)

אָהַב (Q) to love (of human and divine love); (Pi Ptc) lover (217)

אָוָה (Pi) to wish, desire, want; (Hith) crave, wish for, long for (30)

אוּץ (Q) to urge, press, be in a hurry, be pressed (10)

אוֹר (Hi) to give light, shine, illuminate, light up (44)

אָזַן (Hi) to give ear (to), listen (to), hear, heed (41)

אָזַר (Q) to gird (on), equip (16)

אָחַז (Q) to seize, grasp, take hold (of), hold fast (63)

אָחַר (Pi) to delay, cause one to delay, detain, hesitate, linger (18)

אָכַל (Q) to eat, consume; (Ni) be eaten, be consumed; (Hi) feed, cause to eat (820)

אָמַל (Pulal) to dry up, waste away, languish (15)

אָמַן (Ni) to (prove to) be reliable, faithful or trustworthy; (Hi) believe (in), trust, have trust in, put trust in (97)

אָמֵץ (Q) to be strong, be bold; (Pi) make firm, strengthen, harden someone's heart (41)

אָמַר (Q) to say, mention, think; (Ni) be said, be called; (Hi) declare, proclaim (5,316)

אָנַח (Ni) to sigh, groan (13)

אָנַף (Q) to be angry (14)

אָסַף   (Q) to gather (in), take in, take away, destroy; (Ni) be gathered, assemble, be taken away (200)

אָסַר   (Q) to tie, bind, fetter, imprison (73)

אָפָה   (Q) to bake (25)

אָרַב   (Q) to lie in ambush, lie in wait, ambush (41)

אָרַג   (Q) to weave; (Q Ptc) weaver (13)

אָרַךְ   (Hi) to make long, lengthen, extend (34)

אָרַר   (Q) to curse (63)

אָרַשׂ   (Pi) to become engaged to or betroth (a wife); (Pu) be(come) engaged or betrothed (11)

אָשַׁם   (Q) to be(come) guilty, commit an offense, do a wrong (35)

אָשַׁר   (Pi) to call (consider) blessed, fortunate or happy; (Pu) be called blessed, fortunate or happy (10)

אָתָה   (Q) to come; (Hi) bring (21)

בָּאַשׁ   (Q) to stink, have a bad smell; (Hi) make odious, become hated (18)

בָּגַד   (Q) to act or deal treacherously, faithlessly or deceitfully with (49)

בָּדַל   (Ni) to separate oneself, withdraw; (Hi) divide, separate, set apart, make a distinction (between), single out (42)

בָּהַל   (Ni) to be terrified, be horrified, be dismayed, be disturbed, make haste, be hasty; (Pi) terrify, make haste, act hastily (39)

בּוֹא   (Q) to go in, enter, come to, come upon, arrive; (Hi) bring (in), come (in); (Hoph) be brought (2,592)

בּוּז   (Q) to show contempt, despise (14)

בּוּס   (Q) to tread down, trample under foot (12)

בּוֹשׁ   (Q) to be ashamed (125)

בָּזָה   (Q) to despise, regard with contempt (42)

בָּזַז (Q) to plunder, spoil (43)

בָּחַן (Q) to test, put to the test, try, examine (29)

בָּחַר (Q) to choose, test, examine (172)

בָּטַח (Q) to trust, be confident, rely (upon) (118)

בִּין (Q) to understand, perceive, consider, give heed to; (Ni) be discerning, have understanding; (Hi) understand, make understand, teach; (Hith) show oneself perceptive, behave intelligently (171)

בָּכָה (Q) to weep (in grief or joy), weep for (114)

בָּלָה (Q) to be(come) worn out, used up or exhausted (16)

בָּלַל (Q) to mix (up), confuse or confound (languages), mingle (44)

בָּלַע (Q, Pi) to swallow (up), engulf (42)

בָּנָה (Q) to build (up), rebuild, build (establish) a family; (Ni) be built, get a child from (with מִן) (377)

בָּעַל (Q) to rule over, be lord (husband), marry, own (take someone into possession as betrothed) (16)

בָּעַר (Q) to burn (up), consume; (Pi) kindle, burn (60)

בָּעַר (Pi) to graze, sweep away, remove, get rid of, purge (27)

בָּעַת (Pi) to terrify, frighten, startle (16)

בָּצַע (Q) to cut off, sever, break off (away), make profit (16)

בָּקַע (Q) to cleave, split, breach, break open; (Ni) be cleft, be split (open); (Pi) split, rip open (51)

בָּקַשׁ (Pi) to seek, seek to find, seek to obtain, search for, look for, discover, demand, require; (Pu) be sought (225)

בָּרָא (Q) to create (only with God as subject); (Ni) be created (48)

בָּרַח (Q) to run away, flee, go (pass) through (63)

בֵּרַךְ (Q Pass Ptc) blessed, praised, adored; (Pi) bless, praise (327)

בָּרַר (Q) to purify, purge out, sort, choose, select (16)

בִּשֵּׂר (Pi) to bring good news, tell, announce (24)

בָּשַׁל (Q) to boil; (Pi) boil, cook, roast (28)

גָּאַל (Q) to redeem, deliver, act as kinsman (perform the responsibilities of the next-of-kin), avenge (104)

גָּאַל (Ni, Pu) to be defiled, become impure; (Hith) defile oneself (11)

גָּבַה (Q) to be high, be tall, be lofty, be exalted, be haughty; (Hi) make high, exalt (34)

גָּבַר (Q) to be strong, be mighty, be superior, excel, achieve, accomplish, prevail (25)

גָּדַל (Q) to grow up, be(come) great, become strong, wealthy or important; (Pi) bring up (children), make great, extol; (Hi) make great, magnify, do great things (117)

גָּדַע (Q) to cut off, cut down; (Ni) be cut off, be cut down, be cut into pieces; (Pi) cut down (through, off), cut to pieces (22)

גָּדַר (Q) to build a wall, block a road, wall up (10)

גָּוַע (Q) to die, expire, pass away, perish (24)

גּוּר (Q) to sojourn, dwell (stay) as a foreigner or alien, dwell as a newcomer for a definite or indefinite time (82)

גּוּר (Q) to be afraid, dread, stand in awe (10)

גָּזַז (Q) to shear, cut (15)

גָּזַל (Q) to tear off, tear away, seize, rob, take away by force (30)

גָּזַר (Q) to cut (in two, in pieces), divide, cut down, decide; (Ni) be cut off (from), be decided (12)

גִּיל   (Q) to shout with joy, rejoice (47)

גָּלָה   (Q) to uncover, reveal, disclose; (Ni) uncover (reveal) oneself, be revealed, be exposed; (Pi) uncover, reveal, disclose; (Hi) take (carry away) into exile (187)

גָּלַח   (Pi) to shave (23)

גָּלַל   (Q) to roll (away) (18)

גָּמַל   (Q) to complete, finish, wean, ripen, render, do (to), recompense, requite (37)

גָּנַב   (Q) to steal, deceive (40)

גָּעַל   (Q) to loathe, abhor, feel disgust (10)

גָּעַר   (Q) to rebuke, reproach (14)

גָּעַשׁ   (Q) to shake (10)

גָּרָה   (Hith) to strive (against), oppose, battle (15)

גָּרַע   (Q) to shave, trim (a beard), diminish, restrain, withdraw, take (away) (21)

גָּרַשׁ   (Q) to drive out, banish; (Pi) drive out (away) (45)

דָּבַק   (Q) to cling, cleave to, stick to; (Hi) cause to cling, cleave or stick to, pursue closely (55)

דָּבַר   (Q) to speak (rare in Q); (Pi) speak to, with or about (someone or something) (1,136)

דּוּשׁ   (Q) to tread on, trample down (out), thresh, exterminate, destroy; also spelled דִּישׁ (16)

דִּין   (Q) to judge, minister or execute judgment, plead one's cause, contend with (24)

דָּכָא   (Pi) to crush, beat to pieces (18)

דָּמָה   (Q) to be like, resemble; (Pi) liken, compare, imagine, ponder, devise (30)

דָּמָה   (Ni) to be destroyed, be ruined (12)

דָּמַם   (Q) to be silent, keep quiet, be still, be motionless, stand still, be (struck) dumb (19)

דָּקַק   (Q) to crush, become fine through grinding; (Hi) crush fine, pulverize; (Hoph) be crushed fine (12)

דָּקַר   (Q) to pierce (through), run through; (Pu) be pierced through (11)

דָּרַךְ   (Q) to tread (also in the sense of pressing for wine or oil), march, bend (draw) the bow; (Hi) cause to tread, march or walk (63)

דָּרַשׁ   (Q) to seek, inquire (of or about), investigate, ask for, require, demand (165)

דָּשֵׁן   (Pi) to refresh, revive, clean away fat ashes; (Pu) be made fat (11)

הָגָה   (Q) to utter a sound, growl, moan, groan, coo (of a dove), speak, proclaim (25)

הָדַף   (Q) to thrust (away, out), push (away), drive away (out), shove (11)

הָיָה   (Q) to be, become, take place, happen, occur; (Ni) be done, be brought about, come to pass, occur (3,576)

הָלַךְ   (Q) to go, walk (metaphorically, behave), die, pass away; (Pi) go, walk; (Hith) walk about, move to and fro (1,554)

הָלַל   (Pi) to praise, sing hallelujah; (Pu) be praised, be praiseworthy; (Hith) boast (146)

הָלַל   (Q) to be infatuated, be deluded; (Hithpolel) be mad, act like a madman (15)

הָמָה   (Q) to make (a) noise, make a sound, roar, growl, moan, groan, be boisterous (34)

הָמַם   (Q) to make (a) noise, confuse, bring into motion and confusion (army), discomfit, disturb (13)

הָפַךְ   (Q) to turn, overturn, overthrow, destroy; (Ni) be destroyed, be turned into, be changed (95)

הָרַג   (Q) to kill, slay (167)

הָרָה   (Q) to conceive, be(come) pregnant (43)

הָרַס   (Q) to tear down, demolish, destroy, throw down, overthrow, break through; (Ni) be ruined (43)

זָבַח (Q) to slaughter (for sacrifice), sacrifice; (Pi) offer sacrifice, sacrifice (134)

זָהַר (Hi) to warn (about), admonish, caution (22)

זוּב (Q) to flow (away), suffer a discharge (42)

זִיד (Q) to act insolently; (Hi) boil or cook, become hot (with anger), behave arrogantly (10)

זָכַר (Q) to remember, recall, call to mind, mention; (Ni) be remembered, be thought of; (Hi) cause to be remembered, remind, mention (235)

זָמַם (Q) to consider, think, ponder, devise, plan (evil), purpose (13)

זָמַר (Pi) to sing, praise, make music, play an instrument (45)

זָנָה (Q) to commit fornication, be a harlot (prostitute), be unfaithful (60)

זָנַח (Q) to reject, spurn, exclude from (19)

זָעַם (Q) to curse, scold, denounce (12)

זָעַק (Q) to cry (out), call for help, summon (73)

זָקֵן (Q) to be(come) old, grow old (26)

זָרָה (Q) to scatter; (Pi) scatter, disperse, spread (38)

זָרַח (Q) to rise (sun), shine, come out (leprosy), appear, break out (18)

זָרַע (Q) to sow, scatter seed (56)

זָרַק (Q) to toss, throw, scatter, sprinkle (34)

חָבָא (Ni) to hide (oneself), be hidden; (Hith) keep oneself hidden (34)

חָבַל (Q) to take, hold or seize (something) in pledge, exact a pledge from someone, bind by taking a pledge (13)

חָבַל (Q) to act corruptly or ruinously; (Pi) ruin, destroy (11)

חָבַק (Q) to embrace, fold the hands (in idleness); (Pi) embrace (13)

חָבַר   (Q) to unite, ally oneself (with), be joined, join forces (28)

חָבַשׁ   (Q) to saddle, bind, bind on (buckle on), bind up (wound), wrap, twist (rope), imprison (33)

חָגַג   (Q) to stagger, reel, celebrate a pilgrimage festival (16)

חָגַר   (Q) to gird (on), gird (oneself or someone), get ready (44)

חָדַל   (Q) to cease, end, stop, refrain (from), desist, discontinue (55)

חָדַשׁ   (Pi) to make new, renew, restore (10)

חָוָה   (Hishtaphel) to bow down, worship (173)

חוּל   (Q) to go around, whirl (about), dance, writhe; also spelled חִיל (10)

חוּס   (Q) to pity, look upon with compassion, spare (24)

חוּשׁ   (Q) to hurry, make haste (18)

חָזָה   (Q) to see, behold, perceive (55)

חָזַק   (Q) to be(come) strong, grow firm, have courage; (Pi) make firm, make strong, strengthen; (Hi) strengthen, seize, grasp, take hold of; (Hith) strengthen oneself, show oneself as strong or courageous (290)

חָטָא   (Q) to miss (a goal or mark), sin, commit a sin; (Pi) make a sin offering; (Hi) induce or cause to sin (240)

חָיָה   (Q) to live, be alive, stay alive, revive, restore to life; (Pi) preserve alive, let live, give life; (Hi) preserve, keep alive, revive, restore to life (283)

חִיל   (Q) to writhe, travail, be in labor, tremble; also spelled חוּל (48)

חָכָה   (Pi) to wait (for), tarry, long for, be patient (14)

חָכַם   (Q) to be(come) wise, act wisely (28)

חָלָה   (Q) to be(come) weak or tired, be(come) sick; (Ni) be exhausted, be made sick; (Pi) appease, flatter (75)

חָלַל	(Ni) to be defiled, be profaned, defile oneself; (Pi) profane, pollute, defile, dishonor, violate; (Hi) let something be profaned, begin (135)
חָלַם	(Q) to dream (29)
חָלַף	(Q) to pass on or away (quickly), pass by, vanish; (Hi) change, replace, substitute (26)
חָלַץ	(Q) to draw (off), draw out, take off, withdraw, be girded (ready for battle); (Pi) rescue, deliver (44)
חָלַק	(Q) to divide, share (with), share (in), apportion, distribute; (Pi) divide (in pieces), apportion, scatter (55)
חָמַד	(Q) to desire, take pleasure (delight) in, crave, covet (21)
חָמַל	(Q) to have compassion (for), have pity (for), spare (41)
חָמַם	(Q) to be(come) warm, grow warm (23)
חָנָה	(Q) to decline, camp, encamp, pitch camp, lay seige to (143)
חָנַן	(Q) to be gracious to, show favor to, favor; (Hith) plead for grace, implore favor or compassion (77)
חָנַף	(Q) to be godless (of a priest or prophet), be defiled (of land); (Hi) defile, pollute (11)
חָסָה	(Q) to seek or take refuge (37)
חָסֵר	(Q) to diminish, decrease, lack, be lacking (22)
חָפָה	(Q) to cover; (Pi) overlay (with) (12)
חָפַז	(Q) to be in a hurry, hurry away (in alarm or fear), hasten in alarm; (Ni) run away in alarm (10)
חָפֵץ	(Q) to delight in, take pleasure in, desire, be willing (74)
חָפַר	(Q) to dig, track, search (for), scout out, spy out (23)
חָפַר	(Q) to be ashamed (17)

חָפַשׂ (Q) to search (out), examine; (Pi) search thoroughly, track down; (Hith) disguise oneself (23)

חָצַב (Q) to quarry, hew (out), dig, dress (stones) (16)

חָצָה (Q) to divide (into) (15)

חָקַק (Q) to hew out or carve out (a grave), inscribe, engrave, enact, decree (19)

חָקַר (Q) to explore, search, spy out (27)

חָרֵב (Q) to dry up (intransitive), lie in ruins; (Hi) cause to dry up, lay waste, reduce to ruins, make desolate (36)

חָרַד (Q) to tremble, do something with trembling, shudder, quake; (Hi) startle (39)

חָרָה (Q) to be(come) hot, burn with anger, become angry (93)

חָרַם (Hi) to devote to the ban, dedicate for destruction, exterminate (50)

חָרַף (Q) to taunt, reproach; (Pi) taunt, reproach, revile (38)

חָרַץ (Q) to decide, cut (10)

חָרֵשׁ (Q) to be silent, be deaf; (Hi) be(come) silent, be deaf, keep still (47)

חָרַשׁ (Q) to plow, engrave, devise, plan (27)

חָשַׂךְ (Q) to withhold, keep back, refrain, spare, save, restrain (28)

חָשַׂף (Q) to strip, strip off, bare, skim (scoop) off (10)

חָשַׁב (Q) to think, consider, devise, plan, value, esteem, reckon; (Ni) be reckoned, be accounted, be esteemed, be considered (as); (Pi) think, consider, devise, plan (124)

חָשָׁה (Q) to be silent; (Hi) be silent, order (someone) to be silent, hesitate, delay (16)

חָשַׁךְ (Q) to be(come) dark, grow dim (eyes) (17)

חָשַׁק (Q) to be attached to, cling to, love (11)

חָתַם   (Q) to seal (up), affix a seal (27)

חָתַן   (Hith) to intermarry with, become related by marriage, become a son-in-law (11)

חָתַת   (Q) to be shattered, be dismayed, be filled with terror (55)

טָבַח   (Q) to slaughter, butcher, slay (11)

טָבַל   (Q) to dip (something into), dip into (16)

טָבַע   (Q) to sink, penetrate; (Hoph) be sunk, be settled, be planted (10)

טָהֵר   (Q) to be clean (ceremonially), be pure (morally); (Pi) cleanse, purify, pronounce clean; (Hith) purify or cleanse oneself (94)

טוֹב   (Q) to be good, be pleasing, be pleasant, be joyful, be well with (44)

טוּחַ   (Q) to plaster (wall of a house), coat, overlay (11)

טוּל   (Hi) to throw (far), cast, hurl; (Hoph) be thrown, be hurled (14)

טָמֵא   (Q) to be(come) unclean; (Ni) defile oneself; (Pi) defile, pronounce or declare unclean; (Hith) defile oneself, become unclean (162)

טָמַן   (Q) to hide (31)

טָעַם   (Q) to taste, eat, savor food, perceive (11)

טָרַף   (Q) to tear (in pieces), rend (25)

יָאַל   (Hi) to be intent (keen) on something, be determined, be resolved, show willingness (undertake) to do something, agree to (18)

יָבַל   (Hi) to bring (as gift or tribute), lead; (Hoph) be brought, be led (18)

יָבֵשׁ   (Q) to dry up, be(come) dry, wither; (Hi) make dry (up), make wither (59)

יָגַע   (Q) to toil, labor, struggle, grow or be weary (26)

יָדָה   (Hi) to thank, praise, confess; (Hith) confess (111)

יָדַע   (Q) to know, have understanding, notice, observe,
           be(come) acquainted with, know sexually (have
           intercourse with); (Ni) be(come) known, reveal
           oneself; (Hi) make known (something to someone),
           inform (956)

יָהַב   (Q) to give, come (33)

יָחַל   (Pi, Hi) to wait (for), hope for (42)

יָחַשׂ   (Hith) to have oneself (to be) registered in a
           genealogical table, be enrolled in a genealogical list;
           (Hith Inf as noun) genealogy, registration (20)

יָטַב   (Q) to be well with, go well with, be pleasing (to);
           (Hi) make things go well for, do good to, deal well
           with, treat kindly (117)

יָכַח   (Hi) to reprove, rebuke, reproach, chasten, punish,
           decide, mediate, arbitrate (59)

יָכֹל   (Q) to be able, be capable of, endure, prevail, be
           victorious (193)

יָלַד   (Q) to bear (children), give birth, bring forth, beget;
           (Ni) be born; (Pi) help at birth, serve as midwife; (Pu)
           be born; (Hi) beget, become the father of (499)

יָלַל   (Hi) to howl, lament, wail (31)

יָנָה   (Q, Hi) to oppress, mistreat (19)

יָנַק   (Q) to suck; (Hi) suckle, nurse (33)

יָסַד   (Q) to found, establish, appoint, destine, allocate; (Pi)
           found, appoint, establish (41)

יָסַף   (Q) to add, continue (do something more or again);
           (Hi) add, increase, do again or more (213)

יָסַר   (Pi) to teach, discipline, correct, chastise, rebuke (41)

יָעַד   (Q) to designate, appoint; (Ni) make or have an
           appointment, meet by appointment, gather or
           assemble by appointment (29)

יָעַל   (Hi) to profit, gain profit, benefit (23)

יָעַץ (Q) to advise, counsel, plan, decide; (Ni) consult (take counsel) together (80)

יָצָא (Q) to go out, go forth, come out, come forth; (Hi) cause to go out or come out, lead out, bring forth (1,076)

יָצַב (Hith) to take one's stand, stand firm, station oneself, present oneself before, resist (48)

יָצַג (Hi) to set, place, establish, take one's stand (17)

יָצַק (Q) to pour, pour out (liquid), cast (metal), flow (into); (Hoph) be cast, be poured out, be emptied out (53)

יָצַר (Q) to form, fashion, shape, create (63)

יָצַת (Q) to kindle, burn; (Hi) set on fire, set fire to (27)

יָקַץ (Q) to awake, wake up, become active (11)

יָקַר (Q) to be difficult, precious, prized, highly valued, esteemed, honored, costly or rare (11)

יָרֵא (Q) to fear, be afraid, be in awe of, reverence, hold in deference; (Ni) be feared, be held in honor (317); compare with יָרָא (#539)

יָרַד (Q) to go down, come down, descend; (Hi) bring down, lead down (382)

יָרָה (Hi) to instruct, teach (47)

יָרָה (Q) to throw, shoot, cast (lots); (Hi) throw, shoot, cast (28)

יָרַשׁ (Q) to inherit, take possession of, dispossess, take away someone's property; (Hi) cause to possess or inherit, dispossess, impoverish (232)

יָשַׁב (Q) to sit (down), remain, dwell, inhabit; (Hi) cause to sit or dwell, settle (a city) (1,088)

יָשֵׁן (Q) to sleep, go to sleep, be asleep (16)

יָשַׁע (Ni) to be delivered, be victorious, receive help; (Hi) help, save, deliver, rescue, come to the aid of (205)

יָשַׁר   (Q) to be straight, be upright, be right, please, go straight (27)

יָתַר   (Ni) to be left over, remain; (Hi) leave (over), have (something) left over or remaining (106)

כָּבֵד   (Q) to be heavy, be weighty, be honored; (Ni) be honored; (Pi) make insensitive, honor; (Hi) make heavy, dull or insensitive, harden (heart), cause to be honored (114)

כָּבָה   (Q) to go out, be quenched, be extinguished; (Pi) put out, quench, extinguish (24)

כָּבַס   (Pi) to clean, cleanse, wash away guilt (51)

כָּבַשׁ   (Q) to subdue, subjugate, make subservient, bring into bondage, violate (rape) a woman; (Ni) be subdued, be subjugated (15)

כָּהַן   (Pi) to perform the duties of a priest, minister as a priest (23)

כּוּל   (Q) to comprehend; (Pilpel) contain, sustain, provide, support; (Hi) contain, hold (in), sustain, endure (38)

כּוּן   (Ni) to be established, stand firm, be steadfast, be ready, be arranged; (Hi) establish, set up, prepare, make ready, make firm; (Polel) set up, establish (219)

כָּזַב   (Pi) to lie, deceive (16)

כָּחַד   (Ni) to be hidden, effaced; (Pi) hide, conceal (32)

כָּחַשׁ   (Pi) to deny, delude, deceive, lie, act deceptively, feign submission or obedience (22)

כָּלָא   (Q) to shut up, restrain, withhold, keep back (17)

כָּלָה   (Q) to (be) complete, be finished, be at an end, come to an end, be accomplished, be spent, be exhausted; (Pi) complete, finish, bring to an end (207)

כָּלַם   (Ni) to be hurt, be humiliated, be ashamed, be disgraced, be dishonored, be confounded; (Hi) put to shame, humiliate, disgrace, harm (38)

כָּנַס   (Q) to gather, collect, amass; (Pi) gather, assemble (11)

כָּנַע   (Ni) to be subdued, be humbled, humble oneself; (Hi)
         humble or subdue someone (36)

כָּסָה   (Q) to cover, conceal, hide; (Pi) cover (up), conceal,
         clothe (153)

כָּעַס   (Q) to be angry, be vexed; (Hi) vex, provoke, provoke
         to anger (God) (55)

כָּפַר   (Pi) to cover (over), atone (for), make atonement (102)

כָּרָה   (Q) to dig, excavate, hollow out (14)

כָּרַע   (Q) to bow (down), kneel (down), fall to one's knees
         (36)

כָּרַת   (Q) to cut off, cut down, make a covenant (with
         בְּרִית); (Ni) be cut off (down); (Hi) cut off, eliminate,
         destroy, exterminate (289)

כָּשַׁל   (Q) to stumble, totter, stagger; (Ni) be caused to
         stumble, stumble (65)

כָּתַב   (Q) to write (upon), register, record; (Ni) be written
         (225)

כָּתַת   (Q) to beat, crush fine, hammer (into pieces); (Pi)
         beat, hammer, crush to pieces (17)

לָאָה   (Q) to be(come) tired or weary; (Ni) tire (oneself) out,
         weary oneself, be tired of something; (Hi) make
         weary (19)

לָבַשׁ   (Q) to put on a garment, clothe, be clothed; (Hi)
         clothe (112)

לָהַט   (Q) to blaze, burn; (Pi) set ablaze, devour (with fire or
         flame), scorch (10)

לָוָה   (Q) to borrow; (Hi) lend to (14)

לָוָה   (Ni) to join oneself to (12)

לוּן   (Ni, Hi) to murmur (against), grumble (17)

לָחַם   (Q, Ni) to fight, do battle with (rare in Q) (171)

לָחַץ   (Q) to squeeze, crowd, press, oppress, torment (19)

לִין (Q) to remain overnight, spend the night, stay, dwell (71)

לִיץ (Q) to boast (28)

לָכַד (Q) to take, capture, catch, seize; (Ni) be caught, be captured (121)

לָמַד (Q) to learn; (Pi) teach (87)

לָעַג (Q, Hi) to mock, ridicule, deride (18)

לָקַח (Q) to take, grasp, capture, seize, lay hold of, accept, receive; (Ni) be captured, be taken away; (Pu) be taken (away) (967)

לָקַט (Q) to gather (together), glean; (Pi) gather (up), collect (37)

מָאֵן (Pi) to refuse (41)

מָאַס (Q) to refuse, reject, despise (74)

מָדַד (Q) to measure, measure off (distance or expanse), measure out (grain) (52)

מָהַר (Pi) to hasten, hurry, go or come quickly; Inf often used as an adverb with the sense of "hastily" (81)

מוּג (Q) to waver, melt; (Ni) wave, sway back and forth, undulate (17)

מוֹט (Q) to totter, shake, waver, sway, stagger; (Ni) be made to stagger, stumble or totter (39)

מוּל (Q) to circumcise; (Ni) be circumcised (32)

מוּר (Hi) to change, alter, exchange (14)

מוּשׁ (Q) to withdraw (from a place), cease from, leave off, depart (21)

מוּת (Q) to die; (Hi) kill, put to death; (Hoph) be killed, suffer death (845)

מָחָה (Q) to wipe, wipe out, destroy, annihilate (34)

מָחַץ (Q) to smash, shatter, beat to pieces, smite (14)

מָטַר (Hi) to make (let) rain fall, send rain (17)

מָכַר   (Q) to sell, hand over; (Ni) be sold, sell oneself (80)

מָלֵא   (Q) to be full, fill (up); (Ni) be filled (with); (Pi) fill, perform, carry out, consecrate as priest (252)

מָלַט   (Ni) to escape, flee to safety, slip away; (Pi) let someone escape, save someone, leave undisturbed (94)

מָלַךְ   (Q) to be(come) king or queen, reign, rule; (Hi) make someone king or queen, install someone as king or queen (350)

מָנָה   (Q) to count, number, reckon, assign, appoint (28)

מָנַע   (Q) to withhold, hold back, retain, refuse, restrain (29)

מָסַס   (Ni) to melt (away), dissolve, become weak (21)

מָעַט   (Q) to be(come) few, be too small; (Hi) make small or few, diminish, reduce, collect or gather little (22)

מָעַל   (Q) to be unfaithful, act unfaithfully or treacherously, act counter to one's duty or legal obligations (36)

מָצָא   (Q) to find (out), reach, obtain, achieve; (Ni) be found, be found sufficient (457)

מָקַק   (Ni) to rot (away), fester (wounds), dwindle or waste away, decay, melt, dissolve (10)

מָרַד   (Q) to rebel, revolt (25)

מָרָה   (Q) to be rebellious, obstinate or contentious; (Hi) behave rebelliously or obstinately (44)

מָרַט   (Q) to make smooth (bare or bald), polish, scour, pull out (hair), sharpen (sword); (Pu) be polished, be smooth or bare (14)

מָרַר   (Q) to be bitter (of taste, experience or attitude), be desperate; (Hi) embitter, cause bitterness or grief (16)

מָשַׁח   (Q) to smear (with a liquid, oil or dye), anoint (70)

מָשַׁךְ   (Q) to draw, pull, drag, draw out, prolong, stretch (36)

מָשַׁל (Q) to rule, reign, govern, have dominion (81)

מָשַׁל (Q) to use a proverb, speak in parables or sentences of poetry; (Ni) be(come) like, similar or the same (17)

מָשַׁשׁ (Q) to feel, touch; (Pi) feel (over, through), grope, search, rummage through (10)

נָאַף (Q) to commit adultery; (metaphorically) commit idolatry; (Pi) commit adultery (31)

נָאַץ (Q) to spurn, despise; (Pi) treat disrespectfully or with irreverence (24)

נָבָא (Ni) to prophesy, be in a state of prophetic ecstasy; (Hith) speak or behave as a prophet, be in a state of prophetic ecstasy (115)

נָבַט (Hi) to look (at or out), gaze, behold (70)

נָבֵל (Q) to fade, wither, decay, crumble away, wear out (20)

נָבַע (Hi) to make (something) gush or bubble (forth), pour out or ferment (11)

נָגַד (Hi) to tell, announce, report, declare, inform; (Hoph) be told, be announced, be reported (371)

נָגַח (Q) to gore (ox); (Pi) push, butt, thrust, knock down (11)

נָגַן (Pi) to play a stringed instrument (15)

נָגַע (Q) to touch, strike, reach; (Hi) touch, reach, throw, arrive (150)

נָגַף (Q) to smite, strike, injure; (Ni) be smitten, be struck (with) (49)

נָגַר (Ni) to flow, gush forth, be poured (out), be spilled, be stretched out (hands); (Hi) pour (out, down) (10)

נָגַשׂ (Q) to oppress, press, force to work, be a slave driver or taskmaster, exact (contributions), collect (offerings) (23)

נָגַשׁ (Q) to draw near, come near, approach; (Ni) draw near; (Hi) bring (near), offer (sacrifice) (125)

נָדַב (Q) to incite, instigate; (Hith) volunteer, make a voluntary decision, enlist as a volunteer, offer voluntarily, give a freewill offering (17)

נָדַד (Q) to flee, wander (about), depart, move, flutter (of wings) (28)

נָדַח (Ni) to be scattered, be banished, be driven away, be thrust out; (Hi) scatter, drive away, disperse, thrust out, tempt, seduce (51)

נָדַר (Q) to make (perform) a vow, keep (make) a promise (31)

נָהַג (Q) to drive (flocks), lead, guide; (Pi) lead (people), lead away, drive away (30)

נָהַל (Pi) to lead, guide, escort, help along, give rest to, provide (with food), transport (10)

נוּד (Q) to move to and fro, sway, wander, be(come) aimless or homeless, express grief or sympathy (by shaking the head) (25)

נוּחַ (Q) to rest, settle down, repose; (Hi) cause to rest, secure rest, set, lay, leave (behind, untouched) (140)

נוּס (Q) to flee, escape (160)

נוּעַ (Q) to tremble, shake, totter, wave (of trees); (Hi) make unstable or unsteady, shake (up), disturb (42)

נוּף (Hi) to move back and forth, wave, brandish, wield (34)

נָזָה (Q) to spatter (blood); (Hi) sprinkle (24)

נָזַל (Q) to trickle, drip down, flow (16)

נָזַר (Ni) to devote, dedicate or consecrate oneself to (a deity), treat with awe, deal respectfully with, fast; (Hi) restrain from, abstain from, live as a Nazirite (10)

נָחָה (Q) to lead; (Hi) lead, guide, conduct (39)

נָחַל (Q) to take (as a) possession, obtain (receive) property, give as an inheritance; (Hi) give (leave) as an inheritance (59)

נָחַם   (Ni) to be sorry, regret, console oneself, comfort oneself, have compassion; (Pi) comfort, console (108)

נָחַשׁ   (Pi) to practice divination, seek and give omens, observe signs, foretell (11)

נָטָה   (Q) to spread out, stretch out, extend, pitch (a tent), turn, bend; (Hi) turn, incline, stretch out, spread out (216)

נָטַע   (Q) to plant (59)

נָטַף   (Q) to drop, drip, secrete; (Hi) cause to drip, cause to flow (metaphorically, of prophetic speech), drivel (18)

נָטַשׁ   (Q) to leave, forsake, abandon, give up (something); (Ni) be forsaken (40)

נָכָה   (Hi) to strike, smite, beat, strike dead, destroy, injure; (Hoph) be struck down dead, be beaten (501)

נָכַר   (Hi) to recognize, know, investigate, be acquainted with, acknowledge (50)

נָסָה   (Pi) to test, put someone to the test, try, tempt (36)

נָסַךְ   (Q) to pour out, pour (cast) a metal image or statue; (Hi) pour out libations, offer a drink offering (25)

נָסַע   (Q) to pull (out or up), set out, start out, depart, journey, march (on) (146)

נָעַר   (Q, Pi) to shake (out or off); (Ni) be shaken (out or off) (11)

נָפַח   (Q) to breathe, blow, blow fire upon (set aflame), gasp, pant (12)

נָפַל   (Q) to fall, fall prostrate, fall upon; (Hi) cause to fall, bring to ruin (435)

נָפַץ   (Q) to shatter, smash to pieces; (Pi) smash (19)

נָצַב   (Ni) to stand (firm), take one's stand, station oneself, be positioned; (Hi) station, set (up), place, establish (74)

נָצַח   (Pi) to supervise, oversee or inspect works and activities related to the temple; מְנַצֵּחַ (Ptc) used as title (superscription) in 55 psalms (65)

נָצַל   (Ni) to be rescued, be delivered, be saved, save oneself; (Hi) tear from, snatch away, take away, deliver from (213)

נָצַר   (Q) to keep watch, watch over, guard, protect, preserve (63)

נָקַב   (Q) to pierce, bore (through), stipulate, specify, designate, curse, slander (19)

נָקָה   (Ni) to be free (of), be without guilt (innocent), be exempt from (punishment), be emptied; (Pi) leave unpunished, hold innocent (44)

נָקַם   (Q) to avenge, take vengeance, take revenge; (Ni) avenge oneself, take revenge (35)

נָקַף   (Hi) to surround, go around, encircle, encompass, enclose, complete a circuit (17)

נָשָׂא   (Q) to lift, carry, raise, bear (load or burden), take (away); (Ni) be carried, be lifted up, be exalted; (Pi) lift up, exalt; (Hith) lift oneself up, exalt oneself (659)

נָשַׂג   (Hi) to reach, overtake (50)

נָשָׁא   (Hi) to deceive, cheat, trick (14)

נָשָׁה   (Q) to forget (18)

נָשַׁךְ   (Q, Pi) to bite (11)

נָשַׁק   (Q) to kiss (32)

נָתַךְ   (Q) to gush forth, pour out, be poured out; (Ni) gush forth, be poured (out or forth) (21)

נָתַן   (Q) to give, put, set; (Ni) be given (2,014)

נָתַץ   (Q) to tear down, pull down, break down, demolish (42)

נָתַק   (Q) to pull off, tear away; (Ni) be drawn out or away, be torn apart, be separated; (Pi) tear up (out), tear apart, tear to pieces (27)

נָתַשׁ   (Q) to uproot, pull out, extract, pull up, remove, drive out (nations) (21)

סָבַב   (Q) to turn (about), go around, march around, surround; (Ni) turn; (Hi) cause to go around, lead around; (Polel) encompass with protection (163)

סָגַר   (Q) to shut (in), close; (Hi) deliver (up), hand over, surrender, give up (91)

סוּג   (Q) to backslide, be disloyal; (Ni) turn back, withdraw, become disloyal (24)

סוּךְ   (Q) to grease (oneself) with oil, anoint (10)

סוּר   (Q) to turn aside, turn off, leave (off), desist; (Hi) remove, take away, get rid of (298)

סוּת   (Hi) to incite (against), stir up, provoke, instigate, seduce, mislead, lead astray (18)

סָחַר   (Q) to pass through (of shepherds), travel about (conducting business); (Q Ptc) trader, merchant (21)

סָכַךְ   (Q) to overshadow, cover (protectively), protect (16)

סָכַן   (Q) to be of use or service; (Hi) be accustomed to, be familiar (acquainted) with, be in the habit of (13)

סָלַח   (Q) to pardon, forgive; (Ni) be forgiven (47)

סָלַל   (Q) to pile up, heap up, lift up, exalt, praise (12)

סָמַךְ   (Q) to support, uphold, sustain, help, lean or lay (hand upon); (Ni) lean (on or against), support oneself (48)

סָעַד   (Q) to support, sustain, strengthen (with food), uphold (12)

סָפַד   (Q) to lament, wail, bewail, mourn for someone (30)

סָפָה   (Q) to take, sweep, snatch or carry away; (Ni) be carried, swept or snatched away (19)

סָפַר   (Q) to count; (Pi) count, recount, relate, make known, proclaim, report, tell (107)

סָקַל   (Q) to stone, put to death by stoning; (Ni) be stoned (to death) (22)

סָרַר   (Q) to be stubborn or rebellious (17)

סָתַם   (Q) to plug (stop) up, shut up, close, hide, keep secret, disguise (13)

סָתַר   (Ni) to be hidden, hide oneself; (Hi) hide (82)

עָבַד   (Q) to work, serve, toil, till, cultivate (289)

עָבַר   (Q) to pass over, pass through, pass by, cross; (Hi) cause to pass over, bring over, cause or allow to pass (through), cause to pass through fire, sacrifice (553)

עוּד   (Hi) to warn, admonish, witness, be a witness, call as witness, testify (40)

עָוָה   (Q) to do wrong; (Ni) be disturbed, be irritated; (Hi) twist, pervert, do wrong (17)

עוּף   (Q) to fly (27)

עוּר   (Q) to be awake, stir up; (Hi) arouse, rouse, wake up, stir up; (Polel) arouse, disturb, awaken (80)

עָוַת   (Q) to bend, make crooked, pervert (justice), falsify (balances), suppress (12)

עָזַב   (Q) to leave, leave behind, forsake, abandon, set free, let go (214)

עָזַז   (Q) to be strong, prevail (against), defy (11)

עָזַר   (Q) to help, assist, come to the aid of (82)

עָטָה   (Q) to wrap, cover or envelop (oneself) with (13)

עָטַף   (Q) to be(come) weak, feeble or faint; (Hith) feel weak or faint (11)

עָכַר   (Q) to disturb, trouble, put into disorder, confuse, bring disaster (ruin); be stirred up, be ruined, be cut off (14)

עָלָה   (Q) to go up, ascend; (Ni) be taken up; (Hi) bring or lead up or out, offer up (sacrifice) (894)

עָלַז   (Q) to exult, triumph (17)

עָלַל   (Poel) to deal (act) severely with, treat violently, glean (19)

עָלַם (Ni) to be concealed, be hidden; (Hi) conceal, hide, cover up; (Hith) hide oneself (28)

עָמַד (Q) to stand (up), take one's stand, stand still; (Hi) station, set up, set in position, appoint, designate (524)

עָמַל (Q) to labor, toil, exert oneself (12)

עָנַג (Hith) to pamper oneself, take delight (pleasure) in, refresh oneself (10)

עָנָה (Q) to answer, respond, reply, testify; (Ni) be answered, receive answer (316)

עָנָה (Q) to be afflicted, be humbled, become low; (Pi) afflict, oppress, humiliate, violate (79)

עָנָה (Q) to sing (16)

עָנַן (Poel) to practice soothsaying, conjure up (spirits), interpret signs (11)

עָצַב (Q) to hurt, pain, rebuke, grieve; (Ni) be pained for, be in grieving for, be worried, be distressed (15)

עָצַם (Q) to be vast, mighty, powerful or numerous (17)

עָצַר (Q) to hold back, restrain, hinder, imprison; (Ni) be restrained, be shut up, be brought to a halt, be detained (46)

עָרַב (Q) to stand (as) surety for, pledge oneself (as surety for debts), be responsible for someone, conduct trade, barter (17)

עָרָה (Pi) to uncover, reveal, expose, lay bare, empty; (Hi) uncover, make naked, expose, pour out (15)

עָרַךְ (Q) to lay out, set in rows, arrange, set in order, stack (wood), draw up a battle formation (75)

עָרַץ (Q) to tremble, be terrified, be in dread, be startled, be alarmed; (Hi) terrify, strike (inspire) with awe, be in terror (15)

עָשָׂה (Q) to do, make, create, acquire, prepare, carry out; (Ni) be done, be made (2,632)

עָשַׂר   (Q) to exact a tithe, take a tenth part of; (Pi) give, pay or receive a tenth, tithe (10)

עָשַׁק   (Q) to oppress, exploit, wrong (someone) (37)

עָשַׁר   (Q) to be(come) rich; (Hi) make rich, gain riches (17)

עָתַר   (Q) to pray, plead, entreat; (Ni) be pleaded with, be entreated; (Hi) pray, plead (20)

פָּאַר   (Pi) to glorify, exalt, beautify; (Hith) show (manifest) one's glory, glorify oneself, be glorified, boast (13)

פָּגַע   (Q) to meet, encounter, fall upon, attack, assail, reach (46)

פָּגַשׁ   (Q) to meet, encounter, confront (14)

פָּדָה   (Q) to ransom, redeem, buy out (60)

פּוּחַ   (Hi) to testify (10)

פּוּץ   (Q) to be spread, be dispersed, be scattered, overflow; (Ni) be scattered, be dispersed; (Hi) scatter, disperse (65)

פָּזַר   (Pi) to scatter, disperse (10)

פָּחַד   (Q) to tremble, shiver, be startled, be in dread, be in awe (25)

פָּלָא   (Ni) to be extraordinary, be wonderful, be too difficult; (Hi) do something wonderful (71)

פָּלַט   (Pi) to bring out, bring forth, bring to safety, save (27)

פָּלַל   (Hith) to pray, make intercession (84)

פָּנָה   (Q) to turn (toward, from, to the side, away) (134)

פָּעַל   (Q) to do, make, perform, practice (58)

פָּצָה   (Q) to open (the mouth), speak (15)

פָּקַד   (Q) to attend, attend to, pay attention to, take care of, miss (someone), muster, number, appoint, visit; (Ni) be missed, be visited, be appointed; (Hi) appoint, entrust (304)

פָּקַח   (Q) to open (the) eyes (21)

פָּרַד   (Ni) to divide, separate (intransitive), be scattered, be separated (26)

פָּרָה   (Q) to bear fruit, be fruitful (29)

פָּרַח   (Q) to bud, sprout, bloom, shoot, break out, break open (34)

פָּרַס   (Q) to break; (Hi) have a divided hoof (14)

פָּרַע   (Q) to let go, loose or free (i.e., remove restraint from), let the hair of the head hang loose, allow to run wild, leave unattended, neglect (16)

פָּרַץ   (Q) to break through, break (out or into), make a breach, burst open, spread out (46)

פָּרַק   (Q) to tear away, pull away, rescue; (Pi) pull or tear off; (Hith) pull or tear off from oneself, be pulled or torn off (10)

פָּרַר   (Hi) to break (out), destroy, put an end to, frustrate, make ineffectual (47)

פָּרַשׂ   (Q) to spread out (as with wings or hands in prayer), stretch (out or over) (67)

פָּשָׂה   (Q) to spread (the symptoms of disease) (22)

פָּשַׁט   (Q) to take off (clothes), strip off, rush out, dash out, make a raid; (Hi) take off (clothes or armor), strip off (skin), flay (43)

פָּשַׁע   (Q) to revolt, rebel (against), transgress, break with, break away from, behave as a criminal (41)

פָּתַח   (Q) to open (up); (Ni) be opened, be loosened, be set free; (Pi) let loose, loosen, free, unsaddle (136)

צָבָא   (Q) to wage war, go to war, fight against, serve (in the cult) (14)

צָדֵק   (Q) to be in the right, have a just cause, be just (justified), be righteous; (Hi) declare righteous (just or innocent), justify (41)

צוּד   (Q) to hunt (for) (17)

צָוָה   (Pi) to command, give an order, charge; (Pu) be ordered, be told, receive a command (496)

צוּם   (Q) to fast, abstain from food and drink (21)

צוּק   (Hi) to oppress, press hard, harass, constrain (12)

צוּר   (Q) to tie up, bind, shut in, shut up, enclose, encircle, besiege (31)

צָחַק   (Q) to laugh; (Pi) joke (with), play (with), amuse oneself, fondle (13)

צָלַח   (Q) to succeed, prosper, be successful; (Hi) be successful, succeed, cause to succeed or prosper (65)

צָמֵא   (Q) to thirst, be thirsty (10)

צָמַח   (Q) to sprout, spring up, grow; (Hi) make grow or sprout (33)

צָמַת   (Hi) to silence, exterminate, annihilate (15)

צָעַק   (Q) to shout, cry (out), call for help; (Ni) be called together, be summoned (55)

צָפָּה   (Pi) to overlay, plate (with gold) (47)

צָפָה   (Q) to keep watch, watch attentively, spy (37)

צָפַן   (Q) to hide, store (up), treasure (up), keep, save up (34)

צָרַע   (Q) to be afflicted with a skin disease (traditionally leprosy); (Pu) be struck with a skin disease (20)

צָרַף   (Q) to smelt (metal), refine (by smelting), test (34)

צָרַר   (Q: transitive) to wrap (up), tie up, bind, shut away; (Q: intransitive) be cramped, be restricted, be hampered, be depressed; (Hi) oppress, harass, afflict (47)

צָרַר   (Q) to be hostile (toward), treat with hostility, attack (26)

קָבַב   (Q) to curse (14)

קָבַל   (Pi) to take, receive, accept (14)

קָבַץ   (Q) to collect, gather, assemble; (Ni) be gathered, be assembled; (Pi) gather together, assemble (127)

קָבַר (Q) to bury; (Ni) be buried (133)

קָדַד (Q) to bow down, kneel down (15)

קָדַם (Pi) to be in front, confront, meet, go before, walk at the head, do something early or for the first time (26)

קָדַר (Q) to be(come) dark or dirty, be untidy, be dressed in the clothes of a mourner (17)

קָדַשׁ (Q) to be holy, set apart or consecrated; (Ni) show oneself holy (of God), be honored or treated as holy; (Pi) set apart, consecrate or dedicate as holy, observe as holy; (Hi) consecrate, dedicate or declare as holy; (Hith) show or keep oneself holy (171)

קָהַל (Ni) to assemble (intransitive); (Hi) assemble (transitive), summon (39)

קָוָה (Pi) to wait (for), wait with eagerness, hope (47)

קוּם (Q) to rise, arise, get up, stand (up); (Hi) set up, erect, put up, cause to arise, establish (627)

קָטַר (Pi) to make a sacrifice go up in smoke, offer (a sacrifice) by burning; (Hi) cause a sacrifice to go up in smoke (115)

קִיץ (Hi) to awake, wake up (22)

קָלַל (Q) to be small, be insignificant, be of little account, be swift; (Ni, Pi) declare cursed; (Hi) lighten, make lighter, treat with contempt (82)

קָנָא (Pi) to envy, be envious of, be jealous, be zealous for (34)

קָנָה (Q) to get, acquire, buy (85)

קָסַם (Q) to practice divination, consult a spirit of the dead, predict (22)

קָצַף (Q) to be(come) angry or furious (34)

קָצַץ (Q) to cut (chop) off, trim; (Pi) cut (chop) off, cut in pieces (14)

קָצַר (Q) to gather in, reap, harvest (36)

קָצַר   (Q) to be short(ened), be(come) impatient (14)

קָרָא   (Q) to call, summon, proclaim, announce, shout, read aloud, give a name to; (Ni) be called, be summoned, be proclaimed (739)

קָרָא   (Q) to meet, encounter, befall, happen; Inf Cstr with prep לְ (לִקְרַאת) toward, against, opposite (136)

קָרַב   (Q) to approach, draw near, come near, make a sexual advance; (Hi) bring (near), present, offer a sacrifice or offering (280)

קָרָה   (Q) to encounter, meet, befall, happen to (22)

קָרַע   (Q) to tear, rend, cut up, tear away (63)

קָשַׁב   (Hi) to give (pay) attention, listen carefully or attentively (46)

קָשָׁה   (Q) to be heavy, hard or difficult; (Hi) make hard, harden, make stubborn or obstinate (28)

קָשַׁר   (Q) to bind, be in league together, conspire (against) (44)

רָאָה   (Q) to see, perceive, understand; (Ni) appear, become visible; (Pu) be seen; (Hi) let or cause someone to see (something), show someone (something) (1,311)

רָבַב   (Q) to be(come) many, numerous or great (23)

רָבָה   (Q) to be(come) numerous, be(come) great, increase; (Hi) make many, make great, multiply, increase (229)

רָבַע   (Q) to provide with four corners, make square (12)

רָבַץ   (Q) to lie down, couch (of animals), rest, stretch out (30)

רָגַז   (Q) to shake, quake, tremble, be agitated, be perturbed, be excited, be upset (41)

רָגַל   (Pi) to spy (out), scout (26)

רָגַם   (Q) to stone, kill by stoning (16)

רָגַע   (Q) to crust over or become hard (of skin), stir up (sea); (Hi) give rest to, come to rest, make peace, linger (13)

רָדָה   (Q) to rule (over), have dominion over, govern (with the nuance of oppression), tread (in) the winepress (22)

רָדַף   (Q) to pursue, follow after, chase, persecute (144)

רָוָה   (Q) to drink one's fill; (Pi, Hi) drink abundantly, water thoroughly, drench, saturate (14)

רָוַח   (Q) to get relief; (Pu) be wide or spacious; (Hi) smell (14)

רוּם   (Q) to be high, be exalted, rise, arise; (Hi) raise, lift up, exalt, take away; (Hoph) be exalted; (Polel) exalt, bring up, extol, raise (children) (197)

רוּעַ   (Hi) to shout, cry (out), shout a war cry (alarm of battle), sound a signal for war, cheer, shout in triumph (44)

רוּץ   (Q) to run (104)

רוּשׁ   (Q) to be poor (24)

רָחַב   (Q) to open wide; (Hi) make wide (large), enlarge, extend (26)

רָחַם   (Pi) to show love for, have compassion, take pity on someone, greet (meet) someone with love (47)

רָחַץ   (Q) to wash (with water), wash (off or away), bathe, bathe oneself (72)

רָחַק   (Q) to be(come) far or distant, keep far from; (Hi) remove, put (keep) far away, keep at a distance (59)

רִיב   (Q) to strive, contend, quarrel, dispute, conduct a legal case (72)

רִיק   (Hi) to empty out, pour out (19)

רָכַב   (Q) to mount and ride, ride; (Hi) cause or make to ride (78)

רָכַל   (Q Ptc) to go about as a trader (tradesman), merchant (17)

רָמַס   (Q) to trample (down, out), tread (potter's clay, grapes), crush to pieces (19)

רָמַשׂ   (Q) to crawl, creep, swarm, teem (17)

רָנַן   (Q) to call or cry aloud, shout with joy; (Pi) cry out (with joy), exult (53)

רָעֵב   (Q) to be hungry, suffer famine (13)

רָעָה   (Q) to pasture, tend (flocks), graze, shepherd, feed (167)

רָעַם   (Q) to rage, roar (sea), thunder, storm; (Hi) thunder, storm (11)

רָעַע   (Q) to be bad, evil or displeasing; (Hi) do evil, do wickedly, do injury, harm, treat badly (98)

רָעַשׁ   (Q) to quake, shake (29)

רָפָא   (Q) to heal; (Ni) be healed, become whole; (Pi) heal, make healthy (69)

רָפָה   (Q) to sink, drop, relax, grow slack; (Hi) abandon, forsake, desert, leave (someone) alone (46)

רָצָה   (Q) to be pleased with, be favorable to, be well disposed toward, accept (with pleasure), become friends with (48)

רָצַח   (Q) to kill, murder, slay (47)

רָצַץ   (Q) to crush, oppress, mistreat (19)

רָקַע   (Q) to stamp (down or out), trample, spread out; (Pi) beat out, hammer out (11)

רָשַׁע   (Hi) to condemn, declare or pronounce guilty (35)

שָׂבַע   (Q) to be satisfied or satiated, have one's fill (of), eat or drink one's fill; (Hi) satisfy (97)

שָׂגַב   (Ni) to be high, be exalted, be inaccessible; (Pi) make high, make inaccessible, protect (20)

שׂוּשׂ   (Q) to rejoice; also spelled שִׂישׂ (27)

שָׂחַק   (Q) to laugh, play; (Pi) play, entertain, amuse (37)

שִׂיחַ   (Q) to consider, meditate, complain, lament, praise (20)

שִׂים   (Q) to set (up), put, place, lay (upon), set in place, establish, confirm; also spelled שׂוֹם (588)

שָׂכַל   (Hi) to understand, comprehend, have insight, make wise, have success (60)

שָׂכַר   (Q) to hire (for wages) (20)

שָׂמַח   (Q) to rejoice, be joyful, be glad; (Pi) cause to rejoice, gladden, make someone happy (156)

שָׂנֵא   (Q) to hate; (Pi Ptc) enemy, (lit) the one who hates (148)

שָׂרַף   (Q) to burn (completely), destroy; (Ni) be burned (117)

שָׁאַב   (Q) to draw water (19)

שָׁאַג   (Q) to roar (21)

שָׁאַל   (Q) to ask (of), inquire (of), request, demand (176)

שָׁאַף   (Q) to gasp, pant (for or after), long for (14)

שָׁאַר   (Ni) to remain, be left over, survive; (Hi) leave (someone or something) remaining, spare (133)

שָׁבָה   (Q) to take captive, deport (47)

שָׁבַע   (Ni) to swear, swear (take) an oath, adjure; (Hi) cause to take an oath, adjure, plead with someone (186)

שָׁבַר   (Q) to break (up), break in pieces, smash, shatter; (Ni) be smashed, broken, shattered or destroyed; (Pi) shatter, smash, break (148)

שָׁבַר   (Q) to buy grain (for food) (21)

שָׁבַת   (Q) to stop, cease, rest; (Hi) put an end to, bring to a stop, remove, put away (71)

שָׁגָה   (Q) to stray (of sheep), go astray (morally), err, do or go wrong (unintentionally), stagger, reel (21)

שָׁדַד   (Q) to devastate, ruin, deal violently with, violently destroy; (Pu) be devastated (59)

שׁוּב (Q) to turn back, return, go back, come back, turn away from; (Hi) cause to return, bring back, lead back, give back, restore; (Polel) bring back, restore (1,075)

שָׁוָה (Q) to be(come) like (the same, the equal of), be equivalent to, resemble; (Pi) make like, make level (16)

שׁוּט (Q) to roam (around), go (rove) about, row (across water); (Polel) roam about (around) (13)

שָׁוַע (Pi) to cry (call) for help (21)

שׁוּר (Q) to behold, regard, gaze on (15)

שָׁזַר (Hoph Ptc) twisted; always spelled מָשְׁזָר (21); all in Exod 26–39

שָׁחַח (Q) to cower, crouch, bow down (18)

שָׁחַט (Q) to slaughter (esp. animals for sacrifice) (81)

שָׁחַר (Pi) to seek eagerly for, look diligently for, be intent on (12)

שָׁחַת (Pi, Hi) to ruin, destroy, spoil, annihilate (152)

שָׁטַף (Q) to flood (over), overflow, rinse, wash (away) (31)

שִׁיר (Q) to sing (of); (Q and Polel Ptc) singer (88)

שִׁית (Q) to set, put, place, lay (hand upon), set one's mind to (86)

שָׁכַב (Q) to lie down, have sexual intercourse (with) (213)

שָׁכַח (Q) to forget; (Ni) be forgotten (102)

שָׁכַל (Q) to become childless; (Pi) make someone childless, deprive of children, cause a miscarriage (24)

שָׁכַם (Hi) to get up early, rise early, do (something) early (65)

שָׁכַן (Q) to settle (down), abide, reside, dwell, inhabit; (Pi) abide, dwell (130)

שָׁכַר (Q) to be(come) drunk; (Pi, Hi) make (someone) drunk (18)

שָׁלַח (Q) to send, stretch out; (Pi) send, stretch out, send away, expel, let go free; (Pu) be sent away (off) (847)

שָׁלַךְ (Hi) to send, throw (down, into or away), cast; (Hoph) be thrown, be cast (125)

שָׁלַל (Q) to plunder, spoil, capture, rob (14)

שָׁלֵם (Q) to be complete, be finished; (Pi) complete, finish, make whole, restore, repay, requite, recompense, reward, perform (a vow); (Hi) bring to completion, consummate, make peace (116)

שָׁלַף (Q) to draw out (sword), pull out, take out, pull off (25)

שָׁמַד (Ni) to be exterminated, destroyed or annihilated; (Hi) exterminate, annihilate, destroy (90)

שָׁמַט (Q) to let loose, let fall, let drop, release, abandon, leave fallow (10)

שָׁמֵם (Q) to be deserted, be uninhabited, be desolated, be appalled; (Ni) be made uninhabited, desolate or deserted; (Hi) cause to be deserted or desolated (92)

שָׁמַע (Q) to hear, listen to, understand, obey; (Ni) be heard; (Hi) cause to hear, proclaim (1,165)

שָׁמַר (Q) to watch (over), guard, keep, observe, preserve, protect, take care of; (Ni) be kept, be protected, be on one's guard (469)

שָׁנָה (Q) to change; (Pi) change, alter, pervert (15)

שָׁסָה (Q) to plunder, spoil (11)

שָׁעָה (Q) to gaze at, look at, look (regard) with favor, be concerned about (13)

שָׁעַן (Ni) to lean (on or against), support oneself on, depend on (22)

שָׁפַט (Q) to judge, make a judgment, decide (between), settle (a dispute or controversy); (Ni) go to court, plead, dispute (204)

שָׁפַךְ (Q) to pour (out), spill, shed (blood) (117)

שָׁפֵל (Q) to be(come) low, be(come) humble, humiliated or abased; (Hi) bring down, overthrow, abase, humiliate (30)

שָׁקַד (Q) to (keep) watch, be wakeful, be vigilant, watch over, be concerned about (12)

שָׁקָה (Hi) to give drink to, provide drink for, irrigate (62)

שָׁקַט (Q) to be quiet, be peaceful, be at peace, be at rest; (Hi) give (keep) peace (42)

שָׁקַל (Q) to weigh (out) (23)

שָׁקַף (Ni) to look down on (from above); (Hi) look down from above (22)

שָׁרַץ (Q) to swarm, teem (with), be innumerable (14)

שָׁרַק (Q) to hiss, whistle (12)

שָׁרַת (Pi) to minister, serve, attend to the service of God (98)

שָׁתָה (Q) to drink (217)

שָׁתַל (Q) to plant, transplant (10)

תּוּר (Q) to spy out, reconnoiter, explore, investigate (24)

תָּכַן (Q) to examine, consider, weigh; (Ni) be examined, be in order (18)

תָּלָה (Q) to hang (up) (29)

תָּמַךְ (Q) to grasp, take hold of, hold, support (21)

תָּמַם (Q) to be(come) complete or finished, come to an end, cease, be consumed, be spent, be burned out (64)

תָּעַב (Pi) to abhor, loathe, make an abomination (22)

תָּעָה (Q) to err, wander (about), stagger, go astray (animal); (Hi) lead astray, cause to err (51)

תָּפַשׂ (Q) to lay (take) hold of, seize, capture, grasp; (Ni) be seized, be caught, be captured, be conquered (65)

תָּקַע (Q) to drive or thrust (weapon into a person), pitch (tent), blow (trumpet), clap one's hands (70)

VERBAL ROOTS
IN THE DERIVED STEMS
LISTED BY FREQUENCY

The following lists contain those verbal roots that appear most frequently in each of the six major derived stems. Verbs are ordered by frequency of occurrence in the particular stem. Numbers denoting frequency of occurrence in the stem follow the numbers that indicate total occurrence.

NIPHAL. 444 verbal roots occur in the Niphal stem a total of 4,138 times. The 25 verbal roots that occur most frequently are listed below.

לָחַם   (Q, Ni) **to fight, do battle with** (rare in Q) (171; 167x in the Niphal)

שָׁבַע   **(Ni) to swear, swear (take) an oath, adjure**; (Hi) cause to take an oath, adjure, plead with someone (186; 154x in the Niphal)

מָצָא   (Q) to find (out), reach, obtain, achieve; **(Ni) be found, be found sufficient** (457; 142x in the Niphal)

רָאָה   (Q) to see, perceive, understand; (Ni) appear, become visible; (Pu) be seen; (Hi) let or cause someone to see (something), show someone (something) (1,311; 101x in the Niphal)

עָשָׂה   (Q) to do, make, create, acquire, prepare, carry out; **(Ni) be done, be made** (2,632; 99x in the Niphal)

שָׁאַר   **(Ni) to remain, be left over, survive**; (Hi) leave (something) remaining, spare (133; 94x in the Niphal)

נָבָא   **(Ni) to prophesy, be in a state of prophetic ecstasy**; (Hith) speak or behave as a prophet, be in a state of prophetic ecstasy (115; 87x in the Niphal)

נָתַן   (Q) to give, put, set; **(Ni) be given** (2,014; 83x in the Niphal)

אָסַף   (Q) to gather (in), take in, take away, destroy; **(Ni) be gathered, be assembled, be taken away** (200; 81x in the Niphal)

יָתַר   **(Ni) to be left over, remain**; (Hi) leave (over), have (something) left over or remaining (106; 81x in the Niphal)

כָּרַת   (Q) to cut off, cut down, make a covenant (with בְּרִית); **(Ni) be cut off (down)**; (Hi) cut off, eliminate, destroy, exterminate (289; 73x in the Niphal)

כּוּן   **(Ni) to be established, stand firm, be steadfast, be ready, be arranged**; (Hi) establish, set up, prepare, make ready, make firm; (Polel) set up, establish (219; 68x in the Niphal)

מָלַט   **(Ni) to escape, flee to safety, slip away**; (Pi) let someone escape, save someone, leave undisturbed (94; 63x in the Niphal)

קָרָא (Q) to call, summon, proclaim, announce, shout, read aloud, give a name to; **(Ni) be called, be summoned, be proclaimed** (739; 63x in the Niphal)

שָׁבַר (Q) to break (up), break in pieces, smash, shatter; **(Ni) be smashed, broken, shattered or destroyed;** (Pi) shatter, smash, break (148; 58x in the Niphal)

פָּלָא **(Ni) to be extraordinary, be wonderful, be too difficult;** (Hi) do something wonderful (71; 56x in the Niphal)

נָצַב **(Ni) to stand (firm), take one's stand, station oneself, be positioned;** (Hi) station, set (up), place, establish (74; 50x in the Niphal)

נָחַם **(Ni) to be sorry, regret, console oneself, comfort oneself, have compassion;** (Pi) comfort, console (108; 48x in the Niphal)

אָכַל (Q) to eat, consume; **(Ni) be eaten, be consumed;** (Hi) feed, cause to eat (820; 45x in the Niphal)

אָמַן **(Ni) to (prove to) be reliable, faithful or trustworthy;** (Hi) believe (in), trust, have trust in, put trust in (97; 45x in the Niphal)

יָרֵא (Q) to fear, be afraid, be in awe of, reverence, hold in deference; **(Ni) be feared, be held in honor** (317; 45x in the Niphal)

שָׁמַע (Q) to hear, listen to, understand, obey; **(Ni) be heard;** (Hi) cause to hear, proclaim (1,165; 43x in the Niphal)

יָדַע (Q) to know, have understanding, notice, observe, be(come) acquainted with, know sexually (have intercourse with); **(Ni) be(come) known, reveal oneself;** (Hi) make known (something to someone), inform (956; 41x in the Niphal)

קָבַר (Q) to bury; **(Ni) be buried** (133; 39x in the Niphal)

יָלַד (Q) to bear (children), give birth, bring forth, beget; **(Ni) be born;** (Pi) help at birth, serve as midwife; (Pu) be born; (Hi) beget, become the father of (499; 38x in the Niphal)

PIEL. 427 verbal roots occur in the Piel Stem a total of 6,473 times. The 25 verbal roots that occur most frequently are listed below.

דָּבַר   (Q) to speak (rare in Q); **(Pi) speak to, with or about (someone or something)** (1,136; 1,085x in the Piel)

צָוָה   **(Pi) to command, give an order, charge;** (Pu) be ordered, be told, receive a command (496; 487x in the Piel)

שָׁלַח   (Q) to send, stretch out; **(Pi) send, stretch out, send away, expel, let go free;** (Pu) be sent away (off) (847; 267x in the Piel)

בָּרַךְ   (Q Pass Ptc) blessed, praised, adored; **(Pi) bless, praise** (327; 233x in the Piel)

בָּקַשׁ   **(Pi) to seek, seek to find, seek to obtain, search for, look for, discover, demand, require;** (Pu) be sought (225; 222x in the Piel)

כָּלָה   (Q) to (be) complete, be finished, be at an end, come to an end, be accomplished, be spent, be exhausted; **(Pi) complete, finish, bring to an end** (207; 141x in the Piel)

כָּסָה   (Q) to cover, conceal, hide; **(Pi) cover (up), conceal, clothe** (153; 132x in the Piel)

הָלַל   **(Pi) to praise, sing hallelujah;** (Pu) be praised, be praiseworthy; (Hith) boast (146; 113x in the Piel)

מָלֵא   (Q) to be full, fill (up); (Ni) be filled (with); **(Pi) fill, perform, carry out, consecrate as priest** (252; 111x in the Piel)

שָׁרַת   **(Pi) to minister, serve, attend to the service of God** (98; 98x in the Piel)

כָּפַר   **(Pi) to cover (over), atone (for), make atonement** (102; 92x in the Piel)

שָׁלֵם   (Q) to be complete, be finished; **(Pi) complete, finish, make whole, restore, repay, requite, recompense, reward, perform (a vow);** (Hi) bring to completion, consummate, make peace (116; 89x in the Piel)

קָדַשׁ   (Q) to be holy, set apart or consecrated; (Ni) show oneself holy (of God), be honored or treated as holy; (Pi) set apart, consecrate or dedicate as holy, observe as holy; (Hi) consecrate, dedicate or declare as holy; (Hith) show or keep oneself holy (171; 75x in the Piel)

חָלַל   (Ni) to be defiled, be profaned, defile oneself; **(Pi) profane, pollute, defile, dishonor, violate;** (Hi) let something be profaned, begin (135; 67x in the Piel)

סָפַר   (Q) to count; **(Pi) count, recount, relate, make known, proclaim, report, tell** (107; 67x in the Piel)

חָזַק   (Q) to be(come) strong, grow firm, have courage; **(Pi) make firm, make strong, strengthen;** (Hi) strengthen, seize, grasp, take hold of; (Hith) strengthen oneself, show oneself as strong or courageous (290; 64x in the Piel)

נָצַח   **(Pi) to supervise, oversee or inspect works and activities related to the temple;** מְנַצֵּחַ **(Ptc) used as title (superscription) of 55 psalms** (65; 64x in the Piel)

מָהַר   **(Pi) to hasten, hurry, go or come quickly; Inf often used as an adverb with the sense of "hastily"** (81; 63x in the Piel)

לָמַד   (Q) to learn; **(Pi) teach** (87; 58x in the Piel)

חָיָה   (Q) to live, be alive, stay alive, revive, restore to life; **(Pi) preserve alive, let live, give life;** (Hi) preserve, keep alive, revive, restore to life (283; 57x in the Piel)

גָּלָה   (Q) to uncover, reveal, disclose; (Ni) uncover (reveal) oneself, be revealed; be exposed; **(Pi) uncover, reveal, disclose;** (Hi) take (carry away) into exile (187; 56x in the Piel)

עָנָה   (Q) to be afflicted, be humbled, become low; **(Pi) afflict, oppress, humiliate, violate** (79; 56x in the Piel)

נָחַם   (Ni) to be sorry, regret, console oneself, comfort oneself, have compassion; **(Pi) comfort, console** (108; 51x in the Piel)

טָמֵא (Q) to be(come) unclean; (Ni) defile oneself; **(Pi) defile, pronounce or declare unclean;** (Hith) defile oneself, become unclean (162; 50x in the Piel)

קָבַץ (Q) to collect, gather, assemble; (Ni) be gathered, be assembled; **(Pi) gather together, assemble** (127; 49x in the Piel)

PUAL. 186 verbal roots occur in the Pual Stem a total of 423 times. The 10 verbal roots that occur most frequently are listed below.

שָׁדַד (Q) to devastate, ruin, deal violently with, violently destroy; **(Pu) be devastated** (59; 20x in the Pual)

צָרַע (Q) to be afflicted with a skin disease (traditionally leprosy); **(Pu) be struck with a skin disease** (20; 15x in the Pual)

בָּרַךְ (Q Pass Ptc) blessed, praised, adored; (Pi) bless, praise; **(Pu) be blessed** (327; 13x in the Pual)

הָלַל (Pi) to praise, sing hallelujah; **(Pu) be praised, be praiseworthy;** (Hith) boast (146; 10x in the Pual)

שָׁלַח (Q) to send, stretch out; (Pi) send, stretch out, send away, expel, let go free; **(Pu) be sent away (off)** (847; 10x in the Pual)

צָוָה (Pi) to command, give an order, charge; **(Pu) be ordered, be told, receive a command** (496; 9x in the Pual)

יָדַע (Q) to know, have understanding, notice, observe, be(come) acquainted with, know sexually (have intercourse with); (Ni) be(come) known, reveal oneself; **(Pu Ptc) acquaintance, confidant;** (Hi) make known (something to someone), inform (956; 8x in the Pual)

אָדַם (Q) to be red; **(Pu) be reddened, be dyed red** (10; 7x in the Pual)

יָסַד (Q) to found, establish, appoint, destine, allocate; (Pi) found, appoint, establish; **(Pu) be founded** (41; 7x in the Pual)

כָּסָה (Q) to cover, conceal, hide; (Pi) cover (up), conceal, clothe; **(Pu) be covered** (153; 7x in the Pual)

HIPHIL. 521 verbal roots occur in the Hiphil Stem a total of 9,496 times. The 25 verbal roots that occur most frequently are listed below.

בּוֹא   (Q) to go in, enter, come to, come upon, arrive; **(Hi) bring (in), come (in)**; (Hoph) be brought (2,592; 557x in the Hiphil)

נָכָה   **(Hi) to strike, smite, beat, strike dead, destroy, injure**; (Hoph) be struck down dead, be beaten (501; 482x in the Hiphil)

שׁוּב   (Q) to turn back, return, go back, come back; **(Hi) cause to return, bring back, lead back, give back, restore**; (Polel) bring back, restore (1,075; 364x in the Hiphil)

נָגַד   **(Hi) to tell, announce, report, declare, inform**; (Hoph) be told, be announced, be reported (371; 336x in the Hiphil)

יָצָא   (Q) to go out, go forth, come out, come forth; **(Hi) cause to go out or come out, lead out, bring forth** (1,076; 282x in the Hiphil)

עָלָה   (Q) to go up, ascend; (Ni) be taken up; **(Hi) bring or lead up or out, offer up (sacrifice)**; (894; 260x in the Hiphil)

נָצַל   (Ni) to be rescued, be delivered, be saved, save oneself; **(Hi) tear from, snatch away, take away, deliver from** (213; 191x in the Hiphil)

יָשַׁע   (Ni) to be delivered, be victorious, receive help; **(Hi) help, save, deliver, rescue, come to the aid of** (205; 184x in the Hiphil)

קָרַב   (Q) to approach, draw near, come near, make a sexual advance; **(Hi) bring (near), present, offer a sacrifice or offering** (280; 177x in the Hiphil)

יָלַד   (Q) to bear (children), give birth, bring forth, beget; (Ni) be born; (Pi) help at birth, serve as midwife; (Pu) be born; **(Hi) beget, become the father of** (499; 176x in the Hiphil)

יָסַף   (Q) to add, continue (to do something more or again); **(Hi) add, increase, do again or more** (213; 174x in the Hiphil)

רָבָה   (Q) to be(come) numerous, be(come) great, increase; **(Hi) make many, make great, multiply, increase** (229; 166x in the Hiphil)

קוּם   (Q) to rise, arise, get up, stand (up); **(Hi) set up, erect, put up, cause to arise, establish** (627; 146x in the Hiphil)

מוּת   (Q) to die; **(Hi) kill, put to death**; (Hoph) be killed, suffer death (845; 138x in the Hiphil)

סוּר   (Q) to turn aside, turn off, leave (off), desist; **(Hi) remove, take away, get rid of** (298; 132x in the Hiphil)

חָזַק   (Q) to be(come) strong, grow firm, have courage; (Pi) make firm, make strong, strengthen; **(Hi) strengthen, seize, grasp, take hold of**; (Hith) strengthen oneself, show oneself as strong or courageous (290; 117x in the Hiphil)

שָׁלַךְ   **(Hi) to send, throw (down, into or away), cast**; (Hoph) be thrown, be cast (125; 112x in the Hiphil)

כּוּן   (Ni) to be established, stand firm, be steadfast, be ready, be arranged; **(Hi) establish, set up, prepare, make ready, make firm**; (Polel) set up, establish (219; 110x in the Hiphil)

שָׁחַת   **(Pi, Hi) to ruin, destroy, spoil, annihilate** (152; 105x in the Hiphil)

נוּחַ   (Q) to rest, settle down, repose; **(Hi) cause to rest, secure rest, set, lay, leave (behind, untouched)** (140; 104x in the Hiphil)

יָדָה   **(Hi) to thank, praise, confess**; (Hith) confess (111; 100x in the Hiphil)

רוּם   (Q) to be high, be exalted, rise, arise; **(Hi) raise, lift up, exalt, take away**; (Hoph) be exalted; (Polel) exalt, bring up, extol, raise (children) (197; 92x in the Hiphil)

עָמַד   (Q) to stand (up), take one's stand, stand still; **(Hi) station, set up, set in position, appoint, designate** (524; 86x in the Hiphil)

עָבַר   (Q) to pass over, pass through, pass by, cross; **(Hi) cause to pass over, bring over, cause or allow to pass (through), cause to pass through fire, sacrifice** (553; 81x in the Hiphil)

כָּרַת   (Q) to cut off, cut down, make a covenant (with בְּרִית); (Ni) be cut off (down); **(Hi) cut off, eliminate, destroy, exterminate** (289; 78x in the Hiphil)

HOPHAL. 100 verbal roots occur in the Hophal Stem a total of 396 times. The 10 verbal roots that occur most frequently are listed below.

מוּת   (Q) to die; (Hi) kill, put to death; **(Hoph) be killed, suffer death** (845; 69x in the Hophal)

נָגַד   (Hi) to tell, announce, report, declare, inform; **(Hoph) be told, be announced, be reported** (371; 35x in the Hophal)

בּוֹא   (Q) to go in, enter, come to, come upon, arrive; (Hi) bring (in), come (in); **(Hoph) be brought** (2,592; 24x in the Hophal)

שָׁזַר   **(Hoph Ptc) twisted; always spelled** מָשְׁזָר (21; 21x in the Hophal); all in Exod 26–39

נָכָה   (Hi) to strike, smite, beat, strike dead, destroy, injure; **(Hoph) be struck down dead, be beaten** (501; 16x in the Hophal)

שָׁלַךְ   (Hi) to send, throw (down, into or away), cast; **(Hoph) be thrown, be cast** (125; 13x in the Hophal)

יָבַל   (Hi) to bring (as gift or tribute), lead; **(Hoph) be brought, be led** (18; 11x in the Hophal)

יָצַק   (Q) to pour, pour out (liquid), cast (metal), flow (into); **(Hoph) be cast, be poured out, be emptied out** (53; 8x in the Hophal)

פָּקַד   (Q) to attend, attend to, pay attention to, take care of, miss (someone), muster, number, appoint, visit; (Ni) be missed, be visited, be appointed; (Hi) appoint, entrust; **(Hoph) be appointed, be commissioned** (304; 8x in the Hophal)

גָּלָה (Q) to uncover, reveal, disclose; (Ni) uncover (reveal) oneself, be revealed; be exposed; (Pi) uncover, reveal, disclose; (Hi) take (carry away) into exile; **(Hoph) be deported** (187; 7x in the Hophal)

HITHPAEL 171 verbal roots occur in the Hithpael Stem a total of 842 times. The 20 verbal roots that occur most frequently are listed below.

פָּלַל **(Hith) to pray, make intercession** (84; 80x in the Hithpael)

הָלַךְ (Q) to go, walk (metaphorically, behave), die, pass away; (Pi) go, walk; **(Hith) walk about, move to and fro** (1,554; 64x in the Hithpael)

יָצַב **(Hith) to take one's stand, stand firm, station oneself, present oneself before, resist** (48; 48x in the Hithpael)

נָבָא (Ni) to prophesy, be in a state of prophetic ecstasy; **(Hith) speak or behave as a prophet, be in a state of prophetic ecstasy** (115; 28x in the Hithpael)

חָזַק (Q) to be(come) strong, grow firm, have courage; (Pi) make firm, make strong, strengthen; (Hi) strengthen, seize, grasp, take hold of; **(Hith) strengthen oneself, show oneself as strong or courageous** (290; 27x in the Hithpael)

קָדַשׁ (Q) to be holy, set apart or consecrated; (Ni) show oneself holy (of God), be honored or treated as holy; (Pi) set apart, consecrate or dedicate as holy, observe as holy; (Hi) consecrate, dedicate or declare as holy; **(Hith) show or keep oneself holy** (171; 24x in the Hithpael)

הָלַל (Pi) to praise, sing hallelujah; (Pu) be praised, be praiseworthy; **(Hith) boast** (146; 23x in the Hithpael)

טָהֵר (Q) to be clean (ceremonially), be pure (morally); (Pi) cleanse, purify, pronounce clean; **(Hith) purify or cleanse oneself** (94; 20x in the Hithpael)

יָחַשׂ **(Hith) to have oneself (to be) registered in a genealogical table, be enrolled in a genealogical list; (Hith Inf as noun) genealogy, registration** (20; 20x in the Hithpael)

אָבַל (Q) to mourn, lament; **(Hith) observe mourning rites** (36; 19x in the Hithpael)

אָוָה (Pi) to wish, desire, want; **(Hith) crave, wish for, long for** (30; 19x in the Hithpael)

חָנַן (Q) to be gracious to, show favor to, favor; **(Hith) plead for grace, implore favor or compassion** (77; 17x in the Hithpael)

טָמֵא (Q) to be(come) unclean; (Ni) defile oneself; (Pi) defile, pronounce or declare unclean; **(Hith) defile oneself, become unclean** (162; 15x in the Hithpael)

נָדַב (Q) to incite, instigate; **(Hith) volunteer, make a voluntary decision, enlist as a volunteer, offer voluntarily, give a freewill offering** (17; 14x in the Hithpael)

גָּרָה **(Hith) to strive (against), oppose, battle** (15; 12x in the Hithpael)

חָתַן **(Hith) to intermarry with, become related by marriage, become a son-in-law** (11; 11x in the Hithpael)

יָדָה (Hi) to thank, praise, confess; **(Hith) confess** (111; 11x in the Hithpael)

חָבָא (Ni) to hide (oneself), be hidden; **(Hith) keep oneself hidden** (34; 10x in the Hithpael)

נָשָׂא (Q) to lift, carry, raise, bear (load or burden), take (away); (Ni) be carried, be lifted up, be exalted; (Pi) lift up, exalt; **(Hith) lift oneself up, exalt oneself** (659; 10x in the Hithpael)

חָטָא (Q) to miss (a goal or mark), sin, commit a sin; (Pi) make a sin offering; (Hi) induce or cause to sin; **(Hith) purify oneself, withdraw** (240; 9x in the Hithpael)

(1) WEAK VERBS: I-נ
LISTED ALPHABETICALLY

In the Hebrew Old Testament, there are 137 I-נ verbal roots with a total occurrence of 7,103 times. 64 of these verbs occur more than 10 times.

נָאַף (Q) to commit adultery; (metaphorically) commit idolatry; (Pi) commit adultery (31)

נָאַץ (Q) to spurn, despise; (Pi) treat disrespectfully or with irreverence (24)

נָבָא (Ni) to prophesy, be in a state of prophetic ecstasy; (Hith) speak or behave as a prophet, be in a state of prophetic ecstasy (115)

נָבַט (Hi) to look (at or out), gaze, behold (70)

נָבֵל (Q) to fade, wither, decay, crumble away, wear out (20)

נָבַע (Hi) to make (something) gush or bubble (forth), pour out or ferment (11)

נָגַד (Hi) to tell, announce, report, declare, inform; (Hoph) be told, be announced, be reported (371)

נָגַח (Q) to gore (ox); (Pi) push, butt, thrust, knock down (11)

נָגַן (Pi) to play a stringed instrument (15)

נָגַע (Q) to touch, strike, reach; (Hi) touch, reach, throw, arrive (150)

נָגַף (Q) to smite, strike, injure; (Ni) be smitten, be struck (with) (49)

נָגַר (Ni) to flow, gush forth, be poured (out), be spilled, be stretched out (hands); (Hi) pour (out, down) (10)

נָגַשׂ (Q) to oppress, press, force to work, be a slave driver or taskmaster, exact (contributions), collect (offerings) (23)

נָגַשׁ (Q) to draw near, come near, approach; (Ni) draw near; (Hi) bring (near), offer (sacrifice) (125)

נָדַב (Q) to incite, instigate; (Hith) volunteer, make a voluntary decision, enlist as a volunteer, offer voluntarily, give a freewill offering (17)

נָדַד (Q) to flee, wander (about), depart, move, flutter (of wings) (28)

נָדַח (Ni) to be scattered, be banished, be driven away, be thrust out; (Hi) scatter, drive away, disperse, thrust out, tempt, seduce (51)

נָדַר (Q) to make (perform) a vow, keep (make) a promise (31)

נָהַג (Q) to drive (flocks), lead, guide; (Pi) lead (people), lead away, drive away (30)

נָהַל (Pi) to lead, guide, escort, help along, give rest to, provide (with food), transport (10)

נוּד (Q) to move to and fro, sway, wander, be(come) aimless or homeless, express grief or sympathy (by shaking the head) (25)

נוּחַ (Q) to rest, settle down, repose; (Hi) cause to rest, secure rest, set, lay, leave (behind, untouched) (140)

נוּס (Q) to flee, escape (160)

נוּעַ (Q) to tremble, shake, totter, wave (of trees); (Hi) make unstable or unsteady, shake (up), disturb (42)

נוּף (Hi) to move back and forth, wave, brandish, wield (34)

נָזָה (Q) to spatter (blood); (Hi) sprinkle (24)

נָזַל (Q) to trickle, drip down, flow (16)

נָזַר (Ni) to devote, dedicate or consecrate oneself to (a deity), treat with awe, deal respectfully with, fast; (Hi) restrain from, abstain from, live as a Nazirite (10)

נָחָה (Q) to lead; (Hi) lead, guide, conduct (39)

נָחַל (Q) to take (as a) possession, obtain (receive) property, give as an inheritance; (Hi) give (leave) as an inheritance (59)

נָחַם (Ni) to be sorry, regret, console oneself, comfort oneself, have compassion; (Pi) comfort, console (108)

נָחַשׁ (Pi) to practice divination, seek and give omens, observe signs, foretell (11)

נָטָה (Q) to spread out, stretch out, extend, pitch (a tent), turn, bend; (Hi) turn, incline, stretch out, spread out (216)

נָטַע (Q) to plant (59)

נָטַף (Q) to drop, drip, secrete; (Hi) cause to drip, cause to flow (metaphorically, of prophetic speech), drivel (18)

נָטַשׁ (Q) to leave, forsake, abandon, give up (something); (Ni) be forsaken (40)

נָכָה (Hi) to strike, smite, beat, strike dead, destroy, injure; (Hoph) be struck down dead, be beaten (501)

נָכַר (Hi) to recognize, know, investigate, be acquainted with, acknowledge (50)

נָסָה (Pi) to test, put someone to the test, try, tempt (36)

נָסַךְ (Q) to pour out, pour (cast) a metal image or statue; (Hi) pour out libations, offer a drink offering (25)

נָסַע (Q) to pull (out or up), set out, start out, depart, journey, march (on) (146)

נָעַר (Q, Pi) to shake (out or off); (Ni) be shaken (out or off) (11)

נָפַח (Q) to breathe, blow, blow fire upon (set aflame), gasp, pant (12)

נָפַל (Q) to fall, fall prostrate, fall upon; (Hi) cause to fall, bring to ruin (435)

נָפַץ (Q) to shatter, smash to pieces; (Pi) smash (19)

נָצַב (Ni) to stand (firm), take one's stand, station oneself, be positioned; (Hi) station, set (up), place, establish (74)

נָצַח **(Pi) to supervise, oversee or inspect works and activities related to the temple; מְנַצֵּחַ (Ptc) used as title (superscription) of 55 psalms (65)**

נָצַל (Ni) to be rescued, be delivered, be saved, save oneself; (Hi) tear from, snatch away, take away, deliver from (213)

נָצַר   (Q) to keep watch, watch over, guard, protect, preserve (63)

נָקַב   (Q) to pierce, bore (through), stipulate, specify, designate, curse, slander (19)

נָקָה   (Ni) to be free (of), be without guilt (innocent), be exempt from (punishment), be emptied; (Pi) leave unpunished, hold innocent (44)

נָקַם   (Q) to avenge, take vengeance, take revenge; (Ni) avenge oneself, take revenge (35)

נָקַף   (Hi) to surround, go around, encircle, encompass, enclose, complete a circuit (17)

נָשָׂא   (Q) to lift, carry, raise, bear (load or burden), take (away); (Ni) be carried, be lifted up, be exalted; (Pi) lift up, exalt; (Hith) lift oneself up, exalt oneself (659)

נָשַׂג   (Hi) to reach, overtake (50)

נָשָׁא   (Hi) to deceive, cheat, trick (14)

נָשָׁה   (Q) to forget (18)

נָשַׁךְ   (Q, Pi) to bite (11)

נָשַׁק   (Q) to kiss (32)

נָתַךְ   (Q) to gush forth, pour out, be poured out; (Ni) gush forth, be poured (out or forth) (21)

נָתַן   (Q) to give, put, set; (Ni) be given (2,014)

נָתַץ   (Q) to tear down, pull down, break down, demolish (42)

נָתַק   (Q) to pull off, tear away; (Ni) be drawn out or away, be torn apart, be separated; (Pi) tear up (out), tear apart, tear to pieces (27)

נָתַשׁ   (Q) to uproot, pull out, extract, pull up, remove, drive out (nations) (21)

(2) WEAK VERBS: I-ʾ
LISTED ALPHABETICALLY

In the Hebrew Old Testament, there are 84 I-ʾ verbal roots with a total occurrence of 6,554 times. 40 of these verbs occur more than 10 times.

יָאַל   (Hi) to be intent (keen) on something, be determined, be resolved, show willingness (undertake) to do something, agree to (18)

יָבַל   (Hi) to bring (as gift or tribute), lead; (Hoph) be brought, be led (18)

יָבֵשׁ   (Q) to dry up, be(come) dry, wither; (Hi) make dry (up), make wither (59)

יָגַע   (Q) to toil, labor, struggle, grow or be weary (26)

יָדָה   (Hi) to thank, praise, confess; (Hith) confess (111)

יָדַע   (Q) to know, have understanding, notice, observe, be(come) acquainted with, know sexually (have intercourse with); (Ni) be(come) known, reveal oneself; (Hi) make known (something to someone), inform (956)

יָהַב   (Q) to give, come (33)

יָחַל   (Pi, Hi) to wait (for), hope for (42)

יָחַשׂ   (Hith) to have oneself (to be) registered in a genealogical table, be enrolled in a genealogical list; (Hith Inf as noun) genealogy, registration (20)

יָטַב   (Q) to be well with, go well with, be pleasing (to); (Hi) make things go well for, do good to, deal well with, treat kindly (117)

יָכַח   (Hi) to reprove, rebuke, reproach, chasten, punish, decide, mediate, arbitrate (59)

יָכֹל   (Q) to be able, be capable of, endure, prevail, be victorious (193)

יָלַד   (Q) to bear (children), give birth, bring forth, beget; (Ni) be born; (Pi) help at birth, serve as midwife; (Pu) be born; (Hi) beget, become the father of (499)

יָלַל   (Hi) to howl, lament, wail (31)

יָנָה   (Q, Hi) to oppress, mistreat (19)

יָנַק   (Q) to suck; (Hi) suckle, nurse (33)

יָסַד (Q) to found, establish, appoint, destine, allocate; (Pi) found, appoint, establish (41)

יָסַף (Q) to add, continue (to do something more or again); (Hi) add, increase, do again or more (213)

יָסַר (Pi) to teach, discipline, correct, chastise, rebuke (41)

יָעַד (Q) to designate, appoint; (Ni) make or have an appointment, meet by appointment, gather or assemble by appointment (29)

יָעַל (Hi) to profit, gain profit, benefit (23)

יָעַץ (Q) to advise, counsel, plan, decide; (Ni) consult (take counsel) together (80)

יָצָא (Q) to go out, go forth, come out, come forth; (Hi) cause to go out or come out, lead out, bring forth (1,076)

יָצַב (Hith) to take one's stand, stand firm, station oneself, present oneself before, resist (48)

יָצַג (Hi) to set, place, establish, take one's stand (17)

יָצַק (Q) to pour, pour out (liquid), cast (metal), flow (into); (Hoph) be cast, be poured out, be emptied out (53)

יָצַר (Q) to form, fashion, shape, create (63)

יָצַת (Q) to kindle, burn; (Hi) set on fire, set fire to (27)

יָקַץ (Q) to awake, wake up, become active (11)

יָקַר (Q) to be difficult, precious, prized, highly valued, esteemed, honored, costly or rare (11)

יָרֵא (Q) to fear, be afraid, be in awe of, reverence, hold in deference; (Ni) be feared, be held in honor (317)

יָרַד (Q) to go down, come down, descend; (Hi) bring down, lead down (382)

יָרָה (Q) to throw, shoot, cast (lots); (Hi) throw, shoot, cast (28)

יָרָה   (Hi) to instruct, teach (47)

יָרַשׁ   (Q) to inherit, take possession of, dispossess, take away someone's property; (Hi) cause to possess or inherit, dispossess, impoverish (232)

יָשַׁב   (Q) to sit (down), remain, dwell, inhabit; (Hi) cause to sit or dwell, settle (a city) (1,088)

יָשֵׁן   (Q) to sleep, go to sleep, be asleep (16)

יָשַׁע   (Ni) to be delivered, be victorious, receive help; (Hi) help, save, deliver, rescue, come to the aid of (205)

יָשַׁר   (Q) to be straight, be upright, be right, please, go straight (27)

יָתַר   (Ni) to be left over, remain; (Hi) leave (over), have (something) left over or remaining (106)

(3) WEAK VERBS: I-GUTTURAL
BUT NOT III-ה
LISTED ALPHABETICALLY

In the Hebrew Old Testament, there are 312 verbal roots of this type with a total occurrence of 14,719 times. 116 of these verbs occur more than 10 times.

אָבַד   (Q) to perish, vanish, be(come) lost, go astray; (Pi) cause to perish, destroy; (Hi) exterminate (185)

אָבַל   (Q) to mourn, lament; (Hith) observe mourning rites (36)

אָדַם   (Q) to be red; (Pu) be reddened, be dyed red (10)

אָהַב   (Q) to love (of human and divine love); (Pi Ptc) lover (217)

אוּץ   (Q) to urge, press, be in a hurry, be pressed (10)

אוֹר   (Hi) to give light, shine, illuminate, light up (44)

אָזַן   (Hi) to give ear (to), listen (to), hear, heed (41)

אָזַר   (Q) to gird (on), equip (16)

אָחַז   (Q) to seize, grasp, take hold (of), hold fast (63)

אָחַר   (Pi) to delay, cause one to delay, detain, hesitate, linger (18)

אָכַל   (Q) to eat, consume; (Ni) be eaten, be consumed; (Hi) feed, cause to eat (820)

אָמַל   (Pulal) to dry up, waste away, languish (15)

אָמַן   (Ni) to (prove to) be reliable, faithful or trustworthy; (Hi) believe (in), trust, have trust in, put trust in (97)

אָמֵץ   (Q) to be strong, be bold; (Pi) make firm, strengthen, harden someone's heart (41)

אָמַר   (Q) to say, mention, think; (Ni) be said, be called; (Hi) declare, proclaim (5,316)

אָנַח   (Ni) to sigh, groan (13)

אָנַף   (Q) to be angry (14)

אָסַף   (Q) to gather (in), take in, take away, destroy; (Ni) be gathered, assemble, be taken away (200)

אָסַר   (Q) to tie, bind, fetter, imprison (73)

אָרַב   (Q) to lie in ambush, lie in wait, ambush (41)

אָרַג   (Q) to weave; (Q Ptc) weaver (13)

אָרַךְ   (Hi) to make long, lengthen, extend (34)

אָרַר   (Q) to curse (63)

אָרַשׂ   (Pi) to become engaged to or betroth (a wife); (Pu) be(come) engaged or betrothed (11)

אָשֵׁם   (Q) to be(come) guilty, commit an offense, do a wrong (35)

אָשַׁר   (Pi) to call (consider) blessed, fortunate or happy; (Pu) be called blessed, fortunate or happy (10)

הָדַף   (Q) to thrust (away, out), push (away), drive away (out), shove (11)

הָלַךְ   (Q) to go, walk (metaphorically, behave), die, pass away; (Pi) go, walk; (Hith) walk about, move to and fro (1,554)

הָלַל   (Pi) to praise, sing hallelujah; (Pu) be praised, be praiseworthy; (Hith) boast (146)

הָלַל   (Q) to be infatuated, be deluded; (Hithpolel) be mad, act like a madman (15)

הָמַם   (Q) to make (a) noise, confuse, bring into motion and confusion (army), discomfit, disturb (13)

הָפַךְ   (Q) to turn, overturn, overthrow, destroy; (Ni) be destroyed, be turned into, be changed (95)

הָרַג   (Q) to kill, slay (167)

הָרַס   (Q) to tear down, demolish, destroy, throw down, overthrow, break through; (Ni) be ruined (43)

חָבָא   (Ni) to hide (oneself), be hidden; (Hith) keep oneself hidden (34)

חָבַל   (Q) to take, hold or seize (something) in pledge, exact a pledge from someone, bind by taking a pledge (13)

חָבַל   (Q) to act corruptly or ruinously; (Pi) ruin, destroy (11)

חָבַק   (Q) to embrace, fold the hands (in idleness); (Pi) embrace (13)

חָבַר (Q) to unite, ally oneself (with), be joined, join forces (28)

חָבַשׁ (Q) to saddle, bind, bind on (buckle on), bind up (wound), wrap, twist (rope), imprison (33)

חָגַג (Q) to stagger, reel, celebrate a pilgrimage festival (16)

חָגַר (Q) to gird (on), gird (oneself or someone), get ready (44)

חָדַל (Q) to cease, end, stop, refrain (from), desist, discontinue (55)

חָדַשׁ (Pi) to make new, renew, restore (10)

חוּל (Q) to go around, whirl (about), dance, writhe; also spelled חִיל (10)

חוּס (Q) to pity, look upon with compassion, spare (24)

חוּשׁ (Q) to hurry, make haste (18)

חָזַק (Q) to be(come) strong, grow firm, have courage; (Pi) make firm, make strong, strengthen; (Hi) strengthen, seize, grasp, take hold of; (Hith) strengthen oneself, show oneself as strong or courageous (290)

חָטָא (Q) to miss (a goal or mark), sin, commit a sin; (Pi) make a sin offering; (Hi) induce or cause to sin (240)

חִיל (Q) to writhe, travail, be in labor, tremble; also spelled חוּל (48)

חָכַם (Q) to be(come) wise, act wisely (28)

חָלַל (Ni) to be defiled, be profaned, defile oneself; (Pi) profane, pollute, defile, dishonor, violate; (Hi) let something be profaned, begin (135)

חָלַם (Q) to dream (29)

חָלַף (Q) to pass on or away (quickly), pass by, vanish; (Hi) change, replace, substitute (26)

חָלַץ   (Q) to draw (off), draw out, take off, withdraw, be girded (ready for battle); (Pi) rescue, deliver (44)

חָלַק   (Q) to divide, share (with), share (in), apportion, distribute; (Pi) divide (in pieces), apportion, scatter (55)

חָמַד   (Q) to desire, take pleasure (delight) in, crave, covet (21)

חָמַל   (Q) to have compassion (for), have pity (for), spare (41)

חָמַם   (Q) to be(come) warm, grow warm (23)

חָנַן   (Q) to be gracious to, show favor to, favor; (Hith) plead for grace, implore favor or compassion (77)

חָנֵף   (Q) to be godless (of a priest or prophet), be defiled (of land); (Hi) defile, pollute (11)

חָסֵר   (Q) to diminish, decrease, lack, be lacking (22)

חָפַז   (Q) to be in a hurry, hurry away (in alarm or fear), hasten in alarm; (Ni) run away in alarm (10)

חָפֵץ   (Q) to delight in, take pleasure in, desire, be willing (74)

חָפַר   (Q) to dig, track, search (for), scout out, spy out (23)

חָפֵר   (Q) to be ashamed (17)

חָפַשׂ   (Q) to search (out), examine; (Pi) search thoroughly, track down; (Hith) disguise oneself (23)

חָצַב   (Q) to quarry, hew (out), dig, dress (stones) (16)

חָקַק   (Q) to hew out or carve out (a grave), inscribe, engrave, enact, decree (19)

חָקַר   (Q) to explore, search, spy out (27)

חָרֵב   (Q) to dry up (intransitive), lie in ruins; (Hi) cause to dry up, lay waste, reduce to ruins, make desolate (36)

חָרַד   (Q) to tremble, do something with trembling, shudder, quake; (Hi) startle (39)

חָרַם   (Hi) to devote to the ban, dedicate for destruction, exterminate (50)

חָרַף   (Q) to taunt, reproach; (Pi) taunt, reproach, revile (38)

חָרַץ   (Q) to decide, cut (10)

חָרֵשׁ   (Q) to be silent, be deaf; (Hi) be(come) silent, be deaf, keep still (47)

חָרַשׁ   (Q) to plow, engrave, devise, plan (27)

חָשַׂךְ   (Q) to withhold, keep back, refrain, spare, save, restrain (28)

חָשַׂף   (Q) to strip, strip off, bare, skim (scoop) off (10)

חָשַׁב   (Q) to think, consider, devise, plan, value, esteem, reckon; (Ni) be reckoned, be accounted, be esteemed, be considered (as); (Pi) think, consider, devise, plan (124)

חָשַׁךְ   (Q) to be(come) dark, grow dim (eyes) (17)

חָשַׁק   (Q) to be attached to, cling to, love (11)

חָתַם   (Q) to seal (up), affix a seal (27)

חָתַן   (Hith) to intermarry with, become related by marriage, become a son-in-law (11)

חָתַת   (Q) to be shattered, be dismayed, be filled with terror (55)

עָבַד   (Q) to work, serve, toil, till, cultivate (289)

עָבַר   (Q) to pass over, pass through, pass by, cross; (Hi) cause to pass over, bring over, cause or allow to pass (through), cause to pass through fire, sacrifice (553)

עוּד   (Hi) to warn, admonish, witness, be a witness, call as witness, testify (40)

עוּף   (Q) to fly (27)

עוּר   (Q) to be awake, stir up; (Hi) arouse, rouse, wake up, stir up; (Polel) arouse, disturb, awaken (80)

עָוַת   (Q) to bend, make crooked, pervert (justice), falsify (balances), suppress (12)

עָזַב   (Q) to leave, leave behind, forsake, abandon, set free, let go (214)

עָזַז   (Q) to be strong, prevail (against), defy (11)

עָזַר   (Q) to help, assist, come to the aid of (82)

עָטַף   (Q) to be(come) weak, feeble or faint; (Hith) feel weak or faint (11)

עָכַר   (Q) to disturb, trouble, put into disorder, confuse, bring disaster (ruin); be stirred up, be ruined, be cut off (14)

עָלַז   (Q) to exult, triumph (17)

עָלַל   (Poel) to deal (act) severely with, treat violently, glean (19)

עָלַם   (Ni) to be concealed, be hidden; (Hi) conceal, hide, cover up; (Hith) hide oneself (28)

עָמַד   (Q) to stand (up), take one's stand, stand still; (Hi) station, set up, set in position, appoint, designate (524)

עָמַל   (Q) to labor, toil, exert oneself (12)

עָנַג   (Hith) to pamper oneself, take delight (pleasure) in, refresh oneself (10)

עָנַן   (Poel) to practice soothsaying, conjure up (spirits), interpret signs (11)

עָצַב   (Q) to hurt, pain, rebuke, grieve; (Ni) be pained for, be in grieving for, be worried, be distressed (15)

עָצַם   (Q) to be vast, mighty, powerful or numerous (17)

עָצַר   (Q) to hold back, restrain, hinder, imprison; (Ni) be restrained, be shut up, be brought to a halt, be detained (46)

עָרַב   (Q) to stand (as) surety for, pledge oneself (as surety for debts), be responsible for someone, conduct trade, barter (17)

עָרַךְ   (Q) to lay out, set in rows, arrange, set in order, stack (wood), draw up a battle formation (75)

עָרַץ   (Q) to tremble, be terrified, be in dread, be startled, be alarmed; (Hi) terrify, strike (inspire) with awe, be in terror (15)

עָשַׂר   (Q) to exact a tithe, take a tenth part of; (Pi) give, pay or receive a tenth, tithe (10)

עָשַׁק   (Q) to oppress, exploit, wrong (someone) (37)

עָשַׁר   (Q) to be(come) rich; (Hi) make rich, gain riches (17)

עָתַר   (Q) to pray, plead, entreat; (Ni) be pleaded with, be entreated; (Hi) pray, plead (20)

(4) Weak Verbs: I-Guttural and III-ה Listed Alphabetically

In the Hebrew Old Testament, there are 84 verbal roots of this type with a total occurrence of 8,787 times. 27 of these verbs occur more than 10 times.

אָבָה (Q) to be willing, consent, yield to, accede to, want something (54)

אָוָה (Pi) to wish, desire, want; (Hith) crave, wish for, long for (30)

אָפָה (Q) to bake (25)

אָתָה (Q) to come; (Hi) bring (21)

הָגָה (Q) to utter a sound, growl, moan, groan, coo (of a dove), speak, proclaim (25)

הָיָה (Q) to be, become, take place, happen, occur; (Ni) be done, be brought about, come to pass, occur (3,576)

הָמָה (Q) to make (a) noise, make a sound, roar, growl, moan, groan, be boisterous (34)

הָרָה (Q) to conceive, be(come) pregnant (43)

חָוָה (Hishtaphel) to bow down, worship (173)

חָזָה (Q) to see, behold, perceive (55)

חָיָה (Q) to live, be alive, stay alive, revive, restore to life; (Pi) preserve alive, let live, give life; (Hi) preserve, keep alive, revive, restore to life (283)

חָכָה (Pi) to wait (for), tarry, long for, be patient (14)

חָלָה (Q) to be(come) weak or tired, be(come) sick; (Ni) be exhausted, be made sick; (Pi) appease, flatter (75)

חָנָה (Q) to decline, camp, encamp, pitch camp, lay seige to (143)

חָסָה (Q) to seek or take refuge (37)

חָפָה (Q) to cover; (Pi) to overlay (with) (12)

חָצָה (Q) to divide (into) (15)

חָרָה (Q) to be(come) hot, burn with anger, become angry (93)

חָשָׁה (Q) to be silent; (Hi) be silent, order (someone) to be silent, hesitate, delay (16)

עָוָה   (Q) to do wrong; (Ni) be disturbed, be irritated; (Hi) twist, pervert, do wrong (17)

עָטָה   (Q) to wrap, cover or envelop (oneself) with (13)

עָלָה   (Q) to go up, ascend; (Ni) be taken up; (Hi) bring or lead up or out, offer up (sacrifice) (894)

עָנָה   (Q) to answer, respond, reply, testify; (Ni) be answered, receive answer (316)

עָנָה   (Q) to be afflicted, be humbled, become low; (Pi) afflict, oppress, humiliate, violate (79)

עָנָה   (Q) to sing (16)

עָרָה   (Pi) to uncover, reveal, expose, lay bare, empty; (Hi) uncover, make naked, expose, pour out (15)

עָשָׂה   (Q) to do, make, create, acquire, prepare, carry out; (Ni) be done, be made (2,632)

(5) WEAK VERBS: II-GUTTURAL LISTED ALPHABETICALLY

In the Hebrew Old Testament, there are 415 II-Guttural verbal roots with a total occurrence of 10,965 times. 154 of these verbs occur more than 10 times.

אָהֵב   (Q) to love (of human and divine love); (Pi Ptc) lover (217)

אָחַז   (Q) to seize, grasp, take hold (of), hold fast (63)

אָחַר   (Pi) to delay, cause one to delay, detain, hesitate, linger (18)

אָרַב   (Q) to lie in ambush, lie in wait, ambush (41)

אָרַג   (Q) to weave; (Q Ptc) weaver (13)

אָרַךְ   (Hi) to make long, lengthen, extend (34)

אָרַר   (Q) to curse (63)

אָרַשׂ   (Pi) to become engaged to or betroth (a wife); (Pu) be(come) engaged or betrothed (11)

בָּאַשׁ   (Q) to stink, have a bad smell; (Hi) make odious, become hated (18)

בָּהַל   (Ni) to be terrified, be horrified, be dismayed, be disturbed, make haste, be hasty; (Pi) terrify, make haste, act hastily (39)

בָּחַן   (Q) to test, put to the test, try, examine (29)

בָּחַר   (Q) to choose, test, examine (172)

בָּעַל   (Q) to rule over, be lord (husband), marry, own (take someone into possession as betrothed) (16)

בָּעַר   (Q) to burn (up), consume; (Pi) kindle, burn (60)

בָּעַר   (Pi) to graze, sweep away, remove, get rid of, purge (27)

בָּעַת   (Pi) to terrify, frighten, startle (16)

בָּרָא   (Q) to create (only of God); (Ni) be created (48)

בָּרַח   (Q) to run away, flee, go (pass) through (63)

בָּרַךְ   (Q Pass Ptc) blessed, praised, adored; (Pi) bless, praise (327)

בָּרַר   (Q) to purify, purge out, sort, choose, select (16)

גָּאַל   (Q) to redeem, deliver, act as kinsman (perform the responsibilities of the next-of-kin), avenge (104)

גָּאַל (Ni, Pu) to be defiled, become impure; (Hith) defile oneself (11)

גָּעַל (Q) to loathe, abhor, feel disgust (10)

גָּעַר (Q) to rebuke, reproach (14)

גָּעַשׁ (Q) to shake (10)

גָּרָה (Hith) to strive (against), oppose, battle (15)

גָּרַע (Q) to shave, trim (a beard), diminish, restrain, withdraw, take (away) (21)

גָּרַשׁ (Q) to drive out, banish; (Pi) drive out (away) (45)

דָּרַךְ (Q) to tread (also in the sense of pressing for wine or oil), march, bend (draw) the bow; (Hi) cause to tread, march or walk (63)

דָּרַשׁ (Q) to seek, inquire (of or about), investigate, ask for, require, demand (165)

הָרַג (Q) to kill, slay (167)

הָרָה (Q) to conceive, be(come) pregnant (43)

הָרַס (Q) to tear down, demolish, destroy, throw down, overthrow, break through; (Ni) be ruined (43)

זָהַר (Hi) to warn (about), admonish, caution (22)

זָעַם (Q) to curse, scold, denounce (12)

זָעַק (Q) to cry (out), call for help, summon (73)

זָרָה (Q) to scatter; (Pi) scatter, disperse, spread (38)

זָרַח (Q) to rise (sun), shine, come out (leprosy), appear, break out (18)

זָרַע (Q) to sow, scatter seed (56)

זָרַק (Q) to toss, throw, scatter, sprinkle (34)

חָרַב (Q) to dry up (intransitive), lie in ruins; (Hi) cause to dry up, lay waste, reduce to ruins, make desolate (36)

חָרַד (Q) to tremble, do something with trembling, shudder, quake; (Hi) startle (39)

חָרָה   (Q) to be(come) hot, burn with anger, become angry (93)

חָרַם   (Hi) to devote to the ban, dedicate for destruction, exterminate (50)

חָרַף   (Q) to taunt, reproach; (Pi) taunt, reproach, revile (38)

חָרַץ   (Q) to decide, cut (10)

חָרֵשׁ   (Q) to be silent, be deaf; (Hi) be(come) silent, be deaf, keep still (47)

חָרַשׁ   (Q) to plow, engrave, devise, plan (27)

טָהֵר   (Q) to be clean (ceremonially), be pure (morally); (Pi) cleanse, purify, pronounce clean; (Hith) purify or cleanse oneself (94)

טָעַם   (Q) to taste, eat, savor food, perceive (11)

טָרַף   (Q) to tear (in pieces), rend (25)

יָאַל   (Hi) to be intent (keen) on something, be determined, be resolved, show willingness (undertake) to do something, agree to (18)

יָהַב   (Q) to give, come (33)

יָחַל   (Pi, Hi) to wait (for), hope for (42)

יָחַשׂ   (Hith) to have oneself (to be) registered in a genealogical table, be enrolled in a genealogical list; (Hith Inf as noun) genealogy, registration (20)

יָעַד   (Q) to designate, appoint; (Ni) make or have an appointment, meet by appointment, gather or assemble by appointment (29)

יָעַל   (Hi) to profit, gain profit, benefit (23)

יָעַץ   (Q) to advise, counsel, plan, decide; (Ni) consult (take counsel) together (80)

יָרֵא   (Q) to fear, be afraid, be in awe of, reverence, hold in deference; (Ni) be feared, be held in honor (317)

יָרַד (Q) to go down, come down, descend; (Hi) bring down, lead down (382)

יָרָה (Q) to throw, shoot, cast (lots); (Hi) throw, shoot, cast (28)

יָרָה (Hi) to instruct, teach (47)

יָרַשׁ (Q) to inherit, take possession of, dispossess, take away someone's property; (Hi) cause to possess or inherit, dispossess, impoverish (232)

כָּהַן (Pi) to perform the duties of a priest, minister as a priest (23)

כָּחַד (Ni) to be hidden, effaced; (Pi) hide, conceal (32)

כָּחַשׁ (Pi) to deny, delude, deceive, lie, act deceptively, feign submission or obedience (22)

כָּעַס (Q) to be angry, be vexed; (Hi) vex, provoke, provoke to anger (God) (55)

כָּרָה (Q) to dig, excavate, hollow out (14)

כָּרַע (Q) to bow (down), kneel (down), fall to one's knees (36)

כָּרַת (Q) to cut off, cut down, make a covenant (with בְּרִית); (Ni) be cut off (down); (Hi) cut off, eliminate, destroy, exterminate (289)

לָאָה (Q) to be(come) tired or weary; (Ni) tire (oneself) out, weary oneself, be tired of something; (Hi) make weary (19)

לָהַט (Q) to blaze, burn; (Pi) set ablaze, devour (with fire or flame), scorch (10)

לָחַם (Q, Ni) to fight, do battle with (rare in Q) (171)

לָחַץ (Q) to squeeze, crowd, press, oppress, torment (19)

לָעַג (Q, Hi) to mock, ridicule, deride (18)

מָאֵן (Pi) to refuse (41)

מָאַס (Q) to refuse, reject, despise (74)

מָהַר   (Pi) to hasten, hurry, go or come quickly; Inf often used as an adverb with the sense of "hastily" (81)

מָחָה   (Q) to wipe, wipe out, destroy, annihilate (34)

מָחַץ   (Q) to smash, shatter, beat to pieces, smite (14)

מָעַט   (Q) to be(come) few, be too small; (Hi) make small or few, diminish, reduce, collect or gather little (22)

מָעַל   (Q) to be unfaithful, act unfaithfully or treacherously, act counter to one's duty or legal obligations (36)

מָרַד   (Q) to rebel, revolt (25)

מָרָה   (Q) to be rebellious, obstinate or contentious; (Hi) behave rebelliously or obstinately (44)

מָרַט   (Q) to make smooth (bare or bald), polish, scour, pull out (hair), sharpen (sword); (Pu) be polished, be smooth or bare (14)

מָרַר   (Q) to be bitter (of taste, experience or attitude), be desperate; (Hi) embitter, cause bitterness or grief (16)

נָאַף   (Q) to commit adultery; (metaphorically) commit idolatry; (Pi) commit adultery (31)

נָאַץ   (Q) to spurn, despise; (Pi) treat disrespectfully or with irreverence (24)

נָהַג   (Q) to drive (flocks), lead, guide; (Pi) lead (people), lead away, drive away (30)

נָהַל   (Pi) to lead, guide, escort, help along, give rest to, provide (with food), transport (10)

נָחָה   (Q) to lead; (Hi) lead, guide, conduct (39)

נָחַל   (Q) to take (as a) possession, obtain (receive) property, give as an inheritance; (Hi) give (leave) as an inheritance (59)

נָחַם   (Ni) to be sorry, regret, console oneself, comfort oneself, have compassion; (Pi) comfort, console (108)

נָחַשׁ   (Pi) to practice divination, seek and give omens, observe signs, foretell (11)

נָעַר   (Q, Pi) to shake (out or off); (Ni) be shaken (out or off) (11)

סָחַר   (Q) to pass through (of shepherds), travel about (conducting business); (Q Ptc) trader, merchant (21)

סָעַד   (Q) to support, sustain, strengthen (with food), uphold (12)

סָרַר   (Q) to be stubborn or rebellious (17)

עָרַב   (Q) to stand (as) surety for, pledge oneself (as surety for debts), be responsible for someone, conduct trade, barter (17)

עָרָה   (Pi) to uncover, reveal, expose, lay bare, empty; (Hi) uncover, make naked, expose, pour out (15)

עָרַךְ   (Q) to lay out, set in rows, arrange, set in order, stack (wood), draw up a battle formation (75)

עָרַץ   (Q) to tremble, be terrified, be in dread, be startled, be alarmed; (Hi) terrify, strike (inspire) with awe, be in terror (15)

פָּאַר   (Pi) to glorify, exalt, beautify; (Hith) show (manifest) one's glory, glorify oneself, be glorified, boast (13)

פָּחַד   (Q) to tremble, shiver, be startled, be in dread, be in awe (25)

פָּעַל   (Q) to do, make, perform, practice (58)

פָּרַד   (Ni) to divide, separate (intransitive), be scattered, be separated (26)

פָּרָה   (Q) to bear fruit, be fruitful (29)

פָּרַח   (Q) to bud, sprout, bloom, shoot, break out, break open (34)

פָּרַס   (Q) to break; (Hi) have a divided hoof (14)

פָּרַע   (Q) to let go, loose or free (i.e., remove restraint from), let the hair of the head hang loose, allow to run wild, leave unattended, neglect (16)

פָּרַץ   (Q) to break through, break (out or into), make a breach, burst open, spread out (46)

פָּרַק   (Q) to tear away, pull away, rescue; (Pi) pull or tear off; (Hith) pull or tear off from oneself, be pulled or torn off (10)

פָּרַר   (Hi) to break (out), destroy, put an end to, frustrate, make ineffectual (47)

פָּרַשׂ   (Q) to spread out (as with wings or hands in prayer), stretch (out or over) (67)

צָחַק   (Q) to laugh; (Pi) joke (with), play (with), amuse oneself, fondle (13)

צָעַק   (Q) to shout, cry (out), call for help; (Ni) be called together, be summoned (55)

צָרַע   (Q) to be afflicted with a skin disease (traditionally leprosy); (Pu) be struck with a skin disease (20)

צָרַף   (Q) to smelt (metal), refine (by smelting), test (34)

צָרַר   (Q: transitive) to wrap (up), tie up, bind, shut away; (Q: intransitive) be cramped, be restricted, be hampered, be depressed; (Hi) oppress, harass, afflict (47)

צָרַר   (Q) to be hostile (toward), treat with hostility, attack (26)

קָהַל   (Ni) to assemble (intransitive); (Hi) assemble (transitive), summon (39)

קָרָא   (Q) to call, summon, proclaim, announce, shout, read aloud, give a name to; (Ni) be called, be summoned, be proclaimed (739)

קָרָא   (Q) to meet, encounter, befall, happen; Inf Cstr with prep לְ (לִקְרַאת) toward, against, opposite (136)

קָרַב   (Q) to approach, draw near, come near, make a sexual advance; (Hi) bring (near), present, offer a sacrifice or offering (280)

קָרָה   (Q) to encounter, meet, befall, happen to (22)

קָרַע   (Q) to tear, rend, cut up, tear away (63)

רָאָה   (Q) to see, perceive, understand; (Ni) appear, become visible; (Pu) be seen; (Hi) let or cause someone to see (something), show someone (something) (1,311)

רָחַב   (Q) to open wide; (Hi) make wide (large), enlarge, extend (26)

רָחַם   (Pi) to show love for, have compassion, take pity on someone, greet (meet) someone with love (47)

רָחַץ   (Q) to wash (with water), wash (off or away), bathe, bathe oneself (72)

רָחַק   (Q) to be(come) far or distant, keep far from; (Hi) remove, put (keep) far away, keep at a distance (59)

רָעֵב   (Q) to be hungry, suffer famine (13)

רָעָה   (Q) to pasture, tend (flocks), graze, shepherd, feed (167)

רָעַם   (Q) to rage, roar (sea), thunder, storm; (Hi) thunder, storm (11)

רָעַע   (Q) to be bad, evil or displeasing; (Hi) do evil, do wickedly, do injury, harm, treat badly (98)

רָעַשׁ   (Q) to quake, shake (29)

שָׂחַק   (Q) to laugh, play; (Pi) play, entertain, amuse (37)

שָׂרַף   (Q) to burn (completely), destroy; (Ni) be burned (117)

שָׁאַב   (Q) to draw water (19)

שָׁאַג   (Q) to roar (21)

שָׁאַל   (Q) to ask (of), inquire (of), request, demand (176)

שָׁאַף   (Q) to gasp, pant (for or after), long for (14)

שָׁאַר   (Ni) to remain, be left over, survive; (Hi) leave (someone or something) remaining, spare (133)

שָׁחַח   (Q) to cower, crouch, bow down (18)

שָׁחַט   (Q) to slaughter (esp. animals for sacrifice) (81)

שָׁחַר   (Pi) to seek eagerly for, look diligently for, be intent on (12)

שָׁחַת   (Pi, Hi) to ruin, destroy, spoil, annihilate (152)

שָׁעָה   (Q) to gaze at, look at, look (regard) with favor, be concerned about (13)

שָׁעַן   (Ni) to lean (on or against), support oneself on, depend on (22)

שָׁרַץ   (Q) to swarm, teem (with), be innumerable (14)

שָׁרַק   (Q) to hiss, whistle (12)

שָׁרַת   (Pi) to minister, serve, attend to the service of God (98)

תָּעַב   (Pi) to abhor, loathe, make an abomination (22)

תָּעָה   (Q) to err, wander (about), stagger, go astray (animal); (Hi) lead astray, cause to err (51)

(6) WEAK VERBS: III-ה
LISTED ALPHABETICALLY

In the Hebrew Old Testament, there are 235 III-ה verbal roots with a total occurrence of 15,081 times. 89 of these verbs occur more than 10 times.

אָבָה   (Q) to be willing, consent, yield to, accede to, want something (54)

אָוָה   (Pi) to wish, desire, want; (Hith) crave, wish for, long for (30)

אָפָה   (Q) to bake (25)

אָתָה   (Q) to come; (Hi) bring (21)

בָּזָה   (Q) to despise, regard with contempt (42)

בָּכָה   (Q) to weep (in grief or joy), weep for (114)

בָּלָה   (Q) to be(come) worn out, used up or exhausted (16)

בָּנָה   (Q) to build (up), rebuild, build (establish) a family; (Ni) be built, get a child from (with מִן) (377)

גָּלָה   (Q) to uncover, reveal, disclose; (Ni) uncover (reveal) oneself, be revealed, be exposed; (Pi) uncover, reveal, disclose; (Hi) take (carry away) into exile (187)

גָּרָה   (Hith) to strive (against), oppose, battle (15)

דָּמָה   (Q) to be like, resemble; (Pi) liken, compare, imagine, ponder, devise (30)

דָּמָה   (Ni) to be destroyed, be ruined (12)

הָגָה   (Q) to utter a sound, growl, moan, groan, coo (of a dove), speak, proclaim (25)

הָיָה   (Q) to be, become, take place, happen, occur; (Ni) be done, be brought about, come to pass, occur (3,576)

הָמָה   (Q) to make (a) noise, make a sound, roar, growl, moan, groan, be boisterous (34)

הָרָה   (Q) to conceive, be(come) pregnant (43)

זָנָה   (Q) to commit fornication, be a harlot (prostitute), be unfaithful (60)

זָרָה   (Q) to scatter; (Pi) scatter, disperse, spread (38)

חָוָה   (Hishtaphel) to bow down, worship (173)

חָזָה   (Q) to see, behold, perceive (55)

חָיָה   (Q) to live, be alive, stay alive, revive, restore to life; (Pi) preserve alive, let live, give life; (Hi) preserve, keep alive, revive, restore to life (283)

חָכָה   (Pi) to wait (for), tarry, long for, be patient (14)

חָלָה   (Q) to be(come) weak or tired, be(come) sick; (Ni) be exhausted, be made sick; (Pi) appease, flatter (75)

חָנָה   (Q) to decline, camp, encamp, pitch camp, lay seige to (143)

חָסָה   (Q) to seek or take refuge (37)

חָפָה   (Q) to cover; (Pi) to overlay (with) (12)

חָצָה   (Q) to divide (into) (15)

חָרָה   (Q) to be(come) hot, burn with anger, become angry (93)

חָשָׁה   (Q) to be silent; (Hi) be silent, order (someone) to be silent, hesitate, delay (16)

יָדָה   (Hi) to thank, praise, confess; (Hith) confess (111)

יָנָה   (Q, Hi) to oppress, mistreat (19)

יָרָה   (Q) to throw, shoot, cast (lots); (Hi) throw, shoot, cast (28)

יָרָה   (Hi) to instruct, teach (47)

כָּבָה   (Q) to go out, be quenched, be extinguished; (Pi) to put out, quench, extinguish (24)

כָּלָה   (Q) to (be) complete, be finished, be at an end, come to an end, be accomplished, be spent, be exhausted; (Pi) complete, finish, bring to an end (207)

כָּסָה   (Q) to cover, conceal, hide; (Pi) cover (up), conceal, clothe (153)

כָּרָה   (Q) to dig, excavate, hollow out (14)

לָאָה   (Q) to be(come) tired or weary; (Ni) tire (oneself) out, weary oneself, be tired of something; (Hi) make weary (19)

לָוָה   (Q) to borrow; (Hi) lend to (14)

לָוָה   (Ni) to join oneself to (12)

מָחָה   (Q) to wipe, wipe out, destroy, annihilate (34)

מָנָה   (Q) to count, number, reckon, assign, appoint (28)

מָרָה   (Q) to be rebellious, obstinate or contentious; (Hi) behave rebelliously or obstinately (44)

נָזָה   (Q) to spatter (blood); (Hi) sprinkle (24)

נָחָה   (Q) to lead; (Hi) lead, guide, conduct (39)

נָטָה   (Q) to spread out, stretch out, extend, pitch (a tent), turn, bend; (Hi) turn, incline, stretch out, spread out (216)

נָכָה   (Hi) to strike, smite, beat, strike dead, destroy, injure; (Hoph) be struck down dead, be beaten (501)

נָסָה   (Pi) to test, put someone to the test, try, tempt (36)

נָקָה   (Ni) to be free (of), be without guilt (innocent), be exempt from (punishment), be emptied; (Pi) leave unpunished, hold innocent (44)

נָשָׁה   (Q) to forget (18)

סָפָה   (Q) to take, sweep, snatch or carry away; (Ni) be carried, swept or snatched away (19)

עָוָה   (Q) to do wrong; (Ni) be disturbed, be irritated; (Hi) twist, pervert, do wrong (17)

עָטָה   (Q) to wrap, cover or envelop (oneself) with (13)

עָלָה   (Q) to go up, ascend; (Ni) be taken up; (Hi) bring or lead up or out, offer up (sacrifice) (894)

עָנָה   (Q) to answer, respond, reply, testify; (Ni) be answered, receive answer (316)

עָנָה   (Q) to be afflicted, be humbled, become low; (Pi) afflict, oppress, humiliate, violate (79)

עָנָה   (Q) to sing (16)

עָרָה   (Pi) to uncover, reveal, expose, lay bare, empty; (Hi) uncover, make naked, expose, pour out (15)

עָשָׂה (Q) to do, make, create, acquire, prepare, carry out; (Ni) be done, be made (2,632)

פָּדָה (Q) to ransom, redeem, buy out (60)

פָּנָה (Q) to turn (toward, from, to the side, away) (134)

פָּצָה (Q) to open (the mouth), speak (15)

פָּרָה (Q) to bear fruit, be fruitful (29)

פָּשָׂה (Q) to spread (the symptoms of disease) (22)

פָּתָה (Q) to be simple, be inexperienced, be gullible; (Pi) fool, deceive, persuade, seduce (27)

צָוָה (Pi) to command, give an order, charge; (Pu) be ordered, be told, receive a command (496)

צָפָה (Q) to keep watch, watch attentively, spy (37)

צָפָה (Pi) to overlay, plate (with gold) (47)

קָוָה (Pi) to wait (for), wait with eagerness, hope (47)

קָנָה (Q) to get, acquire, buy (85)

קָרָה (Q) to encounter, meet, befall, happen to (22)

קָשָׁה (Q) to be heavy, hard or difficult; (Hi) make hard, harden, make stubborn or obstinate (28)

רָאָה (Q) to see, perceive, understand; (Ni) appear, become visible; (Pu) be seen; (Hi) let or cause someone to see (something), show someone (something) (1,311)

רָבָה (Q) to be(come) numerous, be(come) great, increase; (Hi) make many, make great, multiply, increase (229)

רָדָה (Q) to rule (over), have dominion over, govern (with the nuance of oppression), tread (in) the winepress (22)

רָוָה (Q) to drink one's fill; (Pi, Hi) drink abundantly, water thoroughly, drench, saturate (14)

רָעָה (Q) to pasture, tend (flocks), graze, shepherd, feed (167)

רָפָה   (Q) to sink, drop, relax, grow slack; (Hi) abandon, forsake, desert, leave (someone) alone (46)

רָצָה   (Q) to be pleased with, be favorable to, be well disposed toward, accept (with pleasure), become friends with (48)

שָׁבָה   (Q) to take captive, deport (47)

שָׁגָה   (Q) to stray (of sheep), go astray (morally), err, do or go wrong (unintentionally), stagger, reel (21)

שָׁוָה   (Q) to be(come) like (the same, the equal of), be equivalent to, resemble; (Pi) make like, make level (16)

שָׁנָה   (Q) to change; (Pi) change, alter, pervert (15)

שָׁסָה   (Q) to plunder, spoil (11)

שָׁעָה   (Q) to gaze at, look at, look (regard) with favor, be concerned about (13)

שָׁקָה   (Hi) to give drink to, provide drink for, irrigate (62)

שָׁתָה   (Q) to drink (217)

תָּלָה   (Q) to hang (up) (29)

תָּעָה   (Q) to err, wander (about), stagger, go astray (animal); (Hi) lead astray, cause to err (51)

(7) WEAK VERBS: III-ה/ע
LISTED ALPHABETICALLY

In the Hebrew Old Testament, there are 144 III-ה/ע verbal roots with a total occurrence of 7,207 times. 60 of these verbs occur more than 10 times.

אָנַח   (Ni) to sigh, groan (13)

בָּטַח   (Q) to trust, be confident, rely (upon) (118)

בָּלַע   (Q, Pi) to swallow (up), engulf (42)

בָּצַע   (Q) to cut off, sever, break off (away), make profit (16)

בָּקַע   (Q) to cleave, split, breach, break open; (Ni) be cleft, be split (open); (Pi) split, rip open (51)

בָּרַח   (Q) to run away, flee, go (pass) through (63)

גָּדַע   (Q) to cut off, cut down; (Ni) be cut off, be cut down, be cut into pieces; (Pi) cut down (through, off), cut to pieces (22)

גָּוַע   (Q) to die, expire, pass away, perish (24)

גָּלַח   (Pi) to shave (23)

גָּרַע   (Q) to shave, trim (a beard), diminish, restrain, withdraw, take (away) (21)

זָבַח   (Q) to slaughter (for sacrifice), sacrifice; (Pi) offer sacrifice, sacrifice (134)

זָנַח   (Q) to reject, spurn, exclude from (19)

זָרַח   (Q) to rise (sun), shine, come out (leprosy), appear, break out (18)

זָרַע   (Q) to sow, scatter seed (56)

טָבַח   (Q) to slaughter, butcher, slay (11)

טָבַע   (Q) to sink, penetrate; (Hoph) be sunk, be settled, be planted (10)

יָגַע   (Q) to toil, labor, struggle, grow or be weary (26)

יָדַע   (Q) to know, have understanding, notice, observe, be(come) acquainted with, know sexually (have intercourse with); (Ni) be(come) known, reveal oneself; (Hi) make known (something to someone), inform (956)

יָכַח   (Hi) to reprove, rebuke, reproach, chasten, punish, decide, mediate, arbitrate (59)

יָשַׁע   (Ni) to be delivered, be victorious, receive help; (Hi) help, save, deliver, rescue, come to the aid of (205)

כָּנַע   (Ni) be subdued, be humbled, humble oneself; (Hi) humble or subdue someone (36)

כָּרַע   (Q) to bow (down), kneel (down), fall to one's knees (36)

לָקַח   (Q) to take, grasp, capture, seize, lay hold of, accept, receive; (Ni) be captured, be taken away; (Pu) be taken (away) (967)

מָנַע   (Q) to withhold, hold back, retain, refuse, restrain (29)

מָשַׁח   (Q) to smear (with a liquid, oil or dye), anoint (70)

נָבַע   (Hi) to make (something) gush or bubble (forth), pour out or ferment (11)

נָגַח   (Q) to gore (ox); (Pi) push, butt, thrust, knock down (11)

נָגַע   (Q) to touch, strike, reach; (Hi) touch, reach, throw, arrive (150)

נָדַח   (Ni) to be scattered, be banished, be driven away, be thrust out; (Hi) scatter, drive away, disperse, thrust out, tempt, seduce (51)

נָטַע   (Q) to plant (59)

נָסַע   (Q) to pull (out or up), set out, start out, depart, journey, march (on) (146)

נָפַח   (Q) to breathe, blow, blow fire upon (set aflame), gasp, pant (12)

נָצַח   (Pi) to supervise, oversee or inspect works and activities related to the temple; מְנַצֵּחַ (Ptc) used as title (superscription) in 55 psalms (65)

סָלַח   (Q) to pardon, forgive; (Ni) be forgiven (47)

פָּגַע   (Q) to meet, encounter, fall upon, attack, assail, reach (46)

פָּרַח   (Q) to bud, sprout, bloom, shoot, break out, break open (34)

פָּרַע   (Q) to let go, loose or free (i.e., remove restraint from), let the hair of the head hang loose, allow to run wild, leave unattended, neglect (16)

פָּשַׁע   (Q) to revolt, rebel (against), transgress, break with, break away from, behave as a criminal (41)

פָּתַח   (Q) to open (up); (Ni) be opened, be loosened, be set free; (Pi) let loose, loosen, free, unsaddle (136)

צָלַח   (Q) to succeed, prosper, be successful; (Hi) be successful, succeed, cause to succeed or prosper (65)

צָמַח   (Q) to sprout, spring up, grow; (Hi) make grow or sprout (33)

צָרַע   (Q) to be afflicted with a skin disease (traditionally leprosy); (Pu) be struck with a skin disease (20)

קָרַע   (Q) to tear, rend, cut up, tear away (63)

רָבַע   (Q) to provide with four corners, make square (12)

רָגַע   (Q) to crust over or become hard (of skin), stir up (sea); (Hi) give rest to, come to rest, make peace, linger (13)

רָוַח   (Q) to get relief; (Pu) be wide or spacious; (Hi) smell (14)

רָעַע   (Q) to be bad, evil or displeasing; (Hi) do evil, do wickedly, do injury, harm, treat badly (98)

רָצַח   (Q) to kill, murder, slay (47)

רָקַע   (Q) to stamp (down or out), trample, spread out; (Pi) beat out, hammer out (11)

רָשַׁע   (Hi) to condemn, declare or pronounce guilty (35)

שָׂבַע   (Q) to be satisfied or satiated, have one's fill (of), eat or drink one's fill; (Hi) satisfy (97)

שָׂמַח   (Q) to rejoice, be joyful, be glad; (Pi) cause to rejoice, gladden, make someone happy (156)

שָׁבַע   (Ni) to swear, swear (take) an oath, adjure; (Hi) cause to take an oath, adjure, plead with someone (186)

שִׁוַּע   (Pi) to cry (call) for help (21)

שָׁחַח   (Q) to cower, crouch, bow down (18)

שָׁכַח   (Q) to forget; (Ni) be forgotten (102)

שָׁלַח   (Q) to send, stretch out; (Pi) send, stretch out, send away, expel, let go free; (Pu) be sent away (off) (847)

שָׁמַע   (Q) to hear, listen to, understand, obey; (Ni) be heard; (Hi) cause to hear, proclaim (1,165)

תָּקַע   (Q) to drive or thrust (weapon into a person), pitch (tent), blow (trumpet), clap one's hands (70)

(8) WEAK VERBS: III-א
LISTED ALPHABETICALLY

In the Hebrew Old Testament, there are 49 III-א verbal roots with a total occurrence of 4,696 times. 21 of these verbs occur more than 10 times.

בָּרָא   (Q) to create (only with God as subject); (Ni) be created (48)

דָּכָא   (Pi) to crush, beat to pieces (18)

חָבָא   (Ni) to hide (oneself), be hidden; (Hith) keep oneself hidden (34)

חָטָא   (Q) to miss (a goal or mark), sin, commit a sin; (Pi) make a sin offering; (Hi) induce or cause to sin (240)

טָמֵא   (Q) to be(come) unclean; (Ni) defile oneself; (Pi) defile, pronounce or declare unclean; (Hith) defile oneself, become unclean (162)

יָצָא   (Q) to go out, go forth, come out, come forth; (Hi) cause to go out or come out, lead out, bring forth (1,076)

יָרֵא   (Q) to fear, be afraid, be in awe of, reverence, hold in deference; (Ni) be feared, be held in honor (317)

כָּלָא   (Q) to shut up, restrain, withhold, keep back (17)

מָלֵא   (Q) to be full, fill (up); (Ni) be filled (with); (Pi) fill, perform, carry out, consecrate as priest (252)

מָצָא   (Q) to find (out), reach, obtain, achieve; (Ni) be found, be found sufficient (457)

נָבָא   (Ni) to prophesy, be in a state of prophetic ecstasy; (Hith) speak or behave as a prophet, be in a state of prophetic ecstasy (115)

נָשָׂא   (Q) to lift, carry, raise, bear (load or burden), take (away); (Ni) be carried, be lifted up, be exalted; (Pi) lift up, exalt; (Hith) lift oneself up, exalt oneself (659)

נָשָׁא   (Hi) to deceive, cheat, trick (14)

פָּלָא   (Ni) to be extraordinary, be wonderful, be too difficult; (Hi) do something wonderful (71)

צָבָא   (Q) to wage war, go to war, fight against, serve (in the cult) (14)

צָמֵא   (Q) to thirst, be thirsty (10)

קָנָא   (Pi) to envy, be envious of, be jealous, be zealous for (34)

קָרָא (Q) to call, summon, proclaim, announce, shout, read aloud, give a name to; (Ni) be called, be summoned, be proclaimed (739)

קָרָא (Q) to meet, encounter, befall, happen; Inf Cstr with prep לְ (לִקְרָאת) toward, against, opposite (136)

רָפָא (Q) to heal; (Ni) be healed, become whole; (Pi) heal, make healthy (69)

שָׂנֵא (Q) to hate; (Pi Ptc) enemy, (lit) the one who hates (148)

(9) WEAK VERBS: BICONSONANTAL LISTED ALPHABETICALLY

In the Hebrew Old Testament, there are approximately 180 Biconsonantal verbal roots with a total occurrence of approximately 9,000 times. 67 of these verbs occur more than 10 times.

אוּץ   (Q) to urge, press, be in a hurry, be pressed (10)

אוֹר   (Hi) to give light, shine, illuminate, light up (44)

בּוֹא   (Q) to go in, enter, come to, come upon, arrive; (Hi)
         bring (in), come (in); (Hoph) be brought (2,592)

בּוּז   (Q) to show contempt, despise (14)

בּוּס   (Q) to tread down, trample under foot (12)

בּוֹשׁ   (Q) to be ashamed; (Hi) put to shame, be ashamed
         (125)

בִּין   (Q) to understand, perceive, consider, give heed to;
         (Ni) be discerning, have understanding; (Hi)
         understand, make understand, teach; (Hith) show
         oneself perceptive, behave intelligently (171)

גּוּר   (Q) to sojourn, dwell (stay) as a foreigner or alien,
         dwell as a newcomer for a definite or indefinite time
         (82)

גּוּר   (Q) to be afraid, dread, stand in awe (10)

גִּיל   (Q) to shout with joy, rejoice (47)

דּוּשׁ   (Q) to tread on, trample down (out), thresh,
         exterminate, destroy; also spelled דִּישׁ (16)

דִּין   (Q) to judge, minister or execute judgment, plead
         one's cause, contend with (24)

זוּב   (Q) to flow (away), suffer a discharge (42)

זִיד   (Q) to act insolently; (Hi) boil or cook, become hot
         (with anger), behave arrogantly (10)

חוּל   (Q) to go around, whirl (about), dance, writhe; also
         spelled חִיל (10)

חוּס   (Q) to pity, look upon with compassion, spare (24)

חוּשׁ   (Q) to hurry, make haste (18)

חִיל   (Q) to writhe, travail, be in labor, tremble; also
         spelled חוּל (48)

טוֹב   (Q) to be good, be pleasing, be pleasant, be joyful, be well with (44)

טוּחַ   (Q) to plaster (wall of a house), coat, overlay (11)

טוּל   (Hi) to throw (far), cast, hurl; (Hoph) be thrown, be hurled (14)

כּוּל   (Q) to comprehend; (Pilpel) contain, sustain, provide, support; (Hi) contain, hold (in), sustain, endure (38)

כּוּן   (Ni) to be established, stand firm, be steadfast, be ready, be arranged; (Hi) establish, set up, prepare, make ready, make firm; (Polel) set up, establish (219)

לוּן   (Ni, Hi) to murmur (against), grumble (17)

לִין   (Q) to remain overnight, spend the night, stay, dwell (71)

לִיץ   (Q) to boast (28)

מוּג   (Q) to waver, melt; (Ni) wave, sway back and forth, undulate (17)

מוֹט   (Q) to totter, shake, waver, sway, stagger; (Ni) be made to stagger, stumble or totter (39)

מוּל   (Q) to circumcise; (Ni) be circumcised (32)

מוּר   (Hi) to change, alter, exchange (14)

מוּשׁ   (Q) to withdraw (from a place), cease from, leave off, depart (21)

מוּת   (Q) to die; (Hi) kill, put to death; (Hoph) be killed, suffer death (845)

נוּד   (Q) to move to and fro, sway, wander, be(come) aimless or homeless, express grief or sympathy (by shaking the head) (25)

נוּחַ   (Q) to rest, settle down, repose; (Hi) cause to rest, secure rest, set, lay, leave (behind, untouched) (140)

נוּס   (Q) to flee, escape (160)

נוּעַ   (Q) to tremble, shake, totter, wave (of trees); (Hi) make unstable or unsteady, shake (up), disturb (42)

נוּף　(Hi) to move back and forth, wave, brandish, wield (34)

סוּג　(Q) to backslide, be disloyal; (Ni) turn back, withdraw, become disloyal (24)

סוּךְ　(Q) to grease (oneself) with oil, anoint (10)

סוּר　(Q) to turn aside, turn off, leave (off), desist; (Hi) remove, take away, get rid of (298)

סוּת　(Hi) to incite (against), stir up, provoke, instigate, seduce, mislead, lead astray (18)

עוּד　(Hi) to warn, admonish, witness, be a witness, call as witness, testify (40)

עוּף　(Q) to fly (27)

עוּר　(Q) to be awake, stir up; (Hi) arouse, rouse, wake up, stir up; (Polel) arouse, disturb, awaken (80)

פוּחַ　(Hi) to testify (10)

פוּץ　(Q) to be spread, be dispersed, be scattered, overflow; (Ni) be scattered, be dispersed; (Hi) scatter, disperse (65)

צוּד　(Q) to hunt (for) (17)

צוּם　(Q) to fast, abstain from food and drink (21)

צוּק　(Hi) to oppress, press hard, harass, constrain (12)

צוּר　(Q) to tie up, bind, shut in, shut up, enclose, encircle, besiege (31)

קוּם　(Q) to rise, arise, get up, stand (up); (Hi) set up, erect, put up, cause to arise, establish (627)

קִיץ　(Hi) to awake, wake up (22)

רוּם　(Q) to be high, be exalted, rise, arise; (Hi) raise, lift up, exalt, take away; (Hoph) be exalted; (Polel) exalt, bring up, extol, raise (children) (197)

רוּעַ　(Hi) to shout, cry (out), shout a war cry (alarm of battle), sound a signal for war, cheer, shout in triumph (44)

רוּץ (Q) to run (104)

רוּשׁ (Q) to be poor (24)

רִיב (Q) to strive, contend, quarrel, dispute, conduct a legal case (72)

רִיק (Hi) to empty out, pour out (19)

שׂוּשׂ (Q) to rejoice; also spelled שִׂישׂ (27)

שִׂיחַ (Q) to consider, meditate, complain, lament, praise (20)

שִׂים (Q) to set (up), put, place, lay (upon), set in place, establish, confirm; also spelled שׂוּם (588)

שׁוּב (Q) to turn back, return, go back, come back, turn away from; (Hi) cause to return, bring back, lead back, give back, restore; (Polel) bring back, restore (1,075)

שׁוּט (Q) to roam (around), go (rove) about, row (across water); (Polel) roam about (around) (13)

שׁוּר (Q) to behold, regard, gaze on (15)

שִׁיר (Q) to sing (of); (Q and Polel Ptc) singer (88)

שִׁית (Q) to set, put, place, lay (hand upon), set one's mind to (86)

תוּר (Q) to spy out, reconnoiter, explore, investigate (24)

(10) WEAK VERBS: GEMINATE
LISTED ALPHABETICALLY

In the Hebrew Old Testament, there are 174 Geminate verbal roots with a total occurrence of 2,316 times. 50 of these verbs occur more than 10 times.

אָרַר   (Q) to curse (63)

בָּזַז   (Q) to plunder, spoil (43)

בָּלַל   (Q) to mix (up), confuse or confound (languages), mingle (44)

בָּרַר   (Q) to purify, purge out, sort, choose, select (16)

גָּזַז   (Q) to shear, cut (15)

גָּלַל   (Q) to roll (away) (18)

דָּמַם   (Q) to be silent, keep quiet, be still, be motionless, stand still, be (struck) dumb (19)

דָּקַק   (Q) to crush, become fine through grinding; (Hi) crush fine, pulverize; (Hoph) be crushed fine (12)

הָלַל   (Pi) to praise, sing hallelujah; (Pu) be praised, be praiseworthy; (Hith) boast (146)

הָלַל   (Q) to be infatuated, be deluded; (Hithpolel) be mad, act like a madman (15)

הָמַם   (Q) to make (a) noise, confuse, bring into motion and confusion (army), discomfit, disturb (13)

זָמַם   (Q) to consider, think, ponder, devise, plan (evil), purpose (13)

חָגַג   (Q) to stagger, reel, celebrate a pilgrimage festival (16)

חָלַל   (Ni) to be defiled, be profaned, defile oneself; (Pi) profane, pollute, defile, dishonor, violate; (Hi) let something be profaned, begin (135)

חָמַם   (Q) to be(come) warm, grow warm (23)

חָנַן   (Q) to be gracious to, show favor to, favor; (Hith) plead for grace, implore favor or compassion (77)

חָקַק   (Q) to hew out or carve out (a grave), inscribe, engrave, enact, decree (19)

חָתַת   (Q) to be shattered, be dismayed, be filled with terror (55)

יָלַל   (Hi) to howl, lament, wail (31)

כָּתַת (Q) to beat, crush fine, hammer (into pieces); (Pi) beat, hammer, crush to pieces (17)

מָדַד (Q) to measure, measure off (distance or expanse), measure out (grain) (52)

מָסַס (Ni) to melt (away), dissolve, become weak (21)

מָקַק (Ni) to rot (away), fester (wounds), dwindle or waste away, decay, melt, dissolve (10)

מָרַר (Q) to be bitter (of taste, experience or attitude), be desperate; (Hi) embitter, cause bitterness or grief (16)

מָשַׁשׁ (Q) to feel, touch; (Pi) feel (over, through), grope, search, rummage through (10)

נָדַד (Q) to flee, wander (about), depart, move, flutter (of wings) (28)

סָבַב (Q) to turn (about), go around, march around, surround; (Ni) to turn; (Hi) cause to go around, lead around; (Polel) encompass with protection (163)

סָכַךְ (Q) to overshadow, cover (protectively), protect (16)

סָלַל (Q) to pile up, heap up, lift up, exalt, praise (12)

סָרַר (Q) to be stubborn or rebellious (17)

עָזַז (Q) to be strong, prevail (against), defy (11)

עָלַל (Poel) to deal (act) severely with, treat violently, glean (19)

עָנַן (Poel) to practice soothsaying, conjure up (spirits), interpret signs (11)

פָּלַל (Hith) to pray, make intercession (84)

פָּרַר (Hi) to break (out), destroy, put an end to, frustrate, make ineffectual (47)

צָרַר (Q: transitive) to wrap (up), tie up, bind, shut away; (Q: intransitive) be cramped, be restricted, be hampered, be depressed; (Hi) oppress, harass, afflict (47)

צָרַר (Q) to be hostile (toward), treat with hostility, attack (26)

קָבַב (Q) to curse (14)

קָדַד (Q) to bow down, kneel down (15)

קָלַל (Q) to be small, be insignificant, be of little account, be swift; (Ni, Pi) declare cursed; (Hi) lighten, make lighter, treat with contempt (82)

קָצַץ (Q) to cut (chop) off, trim; (Pi) cut (chop) off, cut in pieces (14)

רָבַב (Q) to be(come) many, numerous or great (23)

רָנַן (Q) to call or cry aloud, shout with joy; (Pi) cry out (with joy), exult (53)

רָעַע (Q) to be bad, evil or displeasing; (Hi) do evil, do wickedly, do injury, harm, treat badly (98)

רָצַץ (Q) to crush, oppress, mistreat (19)

שָׁדַד (Q) to devastate, ruin, deal violently with, violently destroy; (Pu) be devastated (59)

שָׁחַח (Q) to cower, crouch, bow down (18)

שָׁלַל (Q) to plunder, spoil, capture, rob (14)

שָׁמֵם (Q) to be deserted, be uninhabited, be desolated, be appalled; (Ni) be made uninhabited, desolate or deserted; (Hi) cause to be deserted or desolated (92)

תָּמַם (Q) to be(come) complete or finished, come to an end, cease, be consumed, be spent, be burned out (64)

Identical Words
with Different Meanings
Listed Alphabetically

The following list contains Hebrew words that occur 10 times or more and are identical in spelling but differ in meaning and/or part of speech. We have selected 67 sets of identical forms with 137 total words. The most frequent of the identical forms is always listed first.

אוּלָם porch; also spelled אֵילָם (61)

אוּלָם but, however (19)

אוֹר (cs) light, daylight, sunshine (120)

אוֹר (Hi) to give light, shine, illuminate, light up (44)

אַיִל ram, ruler; (adj) mighty (171)

אַיִל pillar, doorpost; (ms cstr) אֵיל (22); 21x in Ezek

אַיִן (particle of nonexistence) is not, are not; most often spelled (747x) אֵין (790)

אַיִן where (from)? whence? (17)

אֶלֶף thousand; (md) אַלְפַּיִם two thousand (496)

אֶלֶף clan, tribe, region (11)

אַף nostril, nose; (metaphorically) anger; (md) אַפַּיִם (277)

אַף (conj) also, indeed, even (133)

אֵת (definite direct object marker) not translated; also spelled אֶת־; (with 3ms suff) אֹתוֹ (10,978)

אֵת (prep) with, beside; also spelled אֶת־; (with 3ms suff) אִתּוֹ (890)

בַּד carrying pole, gate bar; (mp) בַּדִּים (40)

בַּד linen cloth; (mp) בַּדִּים (23)

בּוּז (Q) to show contempt, despise (14)

בּוּז contempt (11)

בָּעַר (Q) to burn (up), consume; (Pi) kindle, burn (60)

בָּעַר (Pi) to graze, sweep away, remove, get rid of, purge (27)

בַּת daughter; (fp) בָּנוֹת (587)

בַּת (ms) liquid measurement, bath; (mp) בַּתִּים (13)

גָּאַל   (Q) to redeem, deliver, act as kinsman (perform the responsibilities of the next-of-kin), avenge (104)

גָּאַל   (Ni, Pu) to be defiled, become impure; (Hith) defile oneself (11)

גּוּר   (Q) to sojourn, dwell (stay) as a foreigner or alien, dwell as a newcomer for a definite or indefinite time (82)

גּוּר   (Q) to be afraid, dread, stand in awe (10)

גַּל   heap, pile; (mp) גַּלִּים (18)

גַּל   wave; (mp with 3ms suff) גַּלָּיו (16)

דִּין   (Q) to judge, minister or execute judgment, plead one's cause, contend with (24)

דִּין   judgment, legal claim (19)

דָּמָה   (Q) to be like, resemble; (Pi) liken, compare, imagine, ponder, devise (30)

דָּמָה   (Ni) to be destroyed, be ruined (12)

הָלַל   (Pi) to praise, sing hallelujah; (Pu) be praised, be praiseworthy; (Hith) boast (146)

הָלַל   (Q) to be infatuated, be deluded; (Hithpolel) be mad, act like a madman (15)

הֵנָּה   here (59)

הֵנָּה   (3fp pers pron) they; (fp dmstr pron and adj) those (29)

הָרָה   (Q) to conceive, be(come) pregnant (43)

הָרָה   (fs adj) pregnant (15)

זָקֵן   (Q) to be(come) old, grow old (26)

זָקֵן   (adj) old; (n) elder (180)

חָבַל   (Q) to take, hold or seize (something) in pledge, exact a pledge from someone, bind by taking a pledge (13)

חָבַל   (Q) to act corruptly (ruinously); (Pi) ruin, destroy (11)

חַיָּה   animal, beast; (fs cstr) חַיַּת (96)

חַיָּה   life; (with 3ms suff) חַיָּתוֹ (11)

חֹמֶר   mud, clay, mortar (17)

חֹמֶר   dry measurement, heap, pile, homer (13)

חָסֵר   (Q) to diminish, decrease, lack, be lacking (22)

חָסֵר   (adj) lacking, wanting; (ms cstr) חֲסַר (17)

חָפֵץ   (Q) to delight in, take pleasure in, desire, be willing (74)

חָפֵץ   (adj) delighting (in), desiring (13)

חָפַר   (Q) to dig, track, search (for), scout out, spy out (23)

חָפַר   (Q) to be ashamed (17)

חָרֵב   (Q) to dry up (intransitive), lie in ruins; (Hi) cause to dry up, lay waste, reduce to ruins, make desolate (36)

חָרֵב   (adj) dry, desolate, wasted; (fs) חֲרֵבָה (10)

חָרַשׁ   (Q) to be silent, be deaf; (Hi) be(come) silent, be deaf, keep still (47)

חָרַשׁ   (Q) to plow, engrave, devise, plan (27)

טוֹב   (adj) good, pleasant (530)

טוֹב   (Q) to be good, be pleasing, be pleasant, be joyful, be well with (44)

טָמֵא   (Q) to be(come) unclean; (Ni) defile oneself; (Pi) defile, pronounce or declare unclean; (Hith) defile oneself, become unclean (162)

טָמֵא   (adj) unclean; (fs) טְמֵאָה (88)

יָרֵא (Q) to fear, be afraid, be in awe of, reverence, hold in deference; (Ni) be feared, be held in honor (317)

יָרֵא (adj) fearful, afraid of (63)

יָרָה (Hi) to instruct, teach (47)

יָרָה (Q) to throw, shoot, cast (lots); (Hi) throw, shoot, cast (28)

כָּבֵד (Q) to be heavy, be weighty, be honored; (Ni) be honored; (Pi) make insensitive, honor; (Hi) make heavy, dull or insensitive, harden (heart), cause to be honored (114)

כָּבֵד (adj) heavy, severe (41)

כָּבֵד (fs) liver (14)

כָּלָה (Q) to (be) complete, be finished, be at an end, come to an end, be accomplished, be spent, be exhausted; (Pi) complete, finish, bring to an end (207)

כָּלָה complete destruction, annihilation (22)

כֵּן so, thus (741)

כֵּן (adj) honest, correct, right (24)

כֵּן base, stand; (with 3ms suff) כַּנּוֹ (11)

לָוָה (Q) to borrow; (Hi) lend to (14)

לָוָה (Ni) to join oneself to (12)

מוּל (prep) in front of, opposite (36)

מוּל (Q) to circumcise; (Ni) be circumcised (32)

מָלֵא (Q) to be full, fill (up); (Ni) be filled (with); (Pi) fill, perform, carry out, consecrate as priest (252)

מָלֵא (adj) full, filled (61)

מָנָה (Q) to count, number, reckon, assign, appoint (28)

מָנָה part, portion, share; (fp) מָנוֹת (12)

מַעַל   above, upward, on top of (140)

מַעַל   unfaithfulness, infidelity (29)

מַשָּׂא   load, burden (44)

מַשָּׂא   oracle, pronouncement (20)

מָשַׁל   (Q) to rule, reign, govern, have dominion (81)

מָשַׁל   (Q) to use a proverb, speak in parables or sentences of poetry; (Ni) be(come) like, similar or the same (17)

נֵבֶל   stringed instrument, harp; (mp) נְבָלִים (28)

נֵבֶל   jar, bottle (10)

עַד   (prep) until, as far as, during (1,263)

עַד   forever, eternal; spelled וְעַד with conjunction וְ (47)

עֹז   strength, power, might; (with 3ms suff) עֻזּוֹ (76)

עֹז   refuge, protection; (with 1cs suff) עֻזִּי (17)

עָנָה   (Q) to answer, respond, reply, testify; (Ni) be answered, receive answer (316)

עָנָה   (Q) to be afflicted, be humbled, become low; (Pi) afflict, oppress, humiliate, violate (79)

עָנָה   (Q) to sing (16)

פָּרָה   (Q) to bear fruit, be fruitful (29)

פָּרָה   cow; (fp) פָּרוֹת (26)

צָבָא   (cs) host, army, war, service; (cp) צְבָאוֹת (487); יְהוָה צְבָאוֹת "Lord of Hosts"

צָבָא   (Q) to wage war, go to war, fight against, serve (in the cult) (14)

צְבִי   ornament, something beautiful, splendor (18)

צְבִי   gazelle (12)

צוּר　rock, boulder (73)

צוּר　(Q) to tie up, bind, shut in, shut up, enclose, encircle, besiege (31)

צָפָה　(Pi) to overlay, plate (with gold) (47)

צָפָה　(Q) to keep watch, watch attentively, spy (37)

צַר　adversary, enemy; (mp cstr) צָרֵי (72)

צַר　(adj) narrow; (n) anxiety, distress (27)

צָרַר　(Q: transitive) to wrap (up), tie up, bind, shut away; (Q: intransitive) be cramped, be restricted, be depressed; (Hi) oppress, harass, afflict (47)

צָרַר　(Q) to be hostile (toward), treat with hostility, attack (26)

קָצַר　(Q) to gather in, reap, harvest (36)

קָצַר　(Q) to be short(ened), be(come) impatient (14)

קָרָא　(Q) to call, summon, proclaim, announce, shout, read aloud, give a name to; (Ni) be called, be summoned, be proclaimed (739)

קָרָא　(Q) to meet, encounter, befall, happen; Inf Cstr with prep לְ (לִקְרַאת) toward, against, opposite (136)

רֹאשׁ　head, top, chief; (mp) רָאשִׁים (600)

רֹאשׁ　poisonous herb, venom (12)

רַב　(adj) great, many; (mp) רַבִּים (419)

רַב　chief, captain, ruler (30)

רִיב　(Q) to strive, contend, quarrel, dispute, conduct a legal case (72)

רִיב　dispute, quarrel, lawsuit (62)

רִיק　(Hi) to empty out, pour out (19)

רִיק　emptiness, vanity (12)

רָעֵב   (adj) hungry; (mp) רְעֵבִים (20)

רָעֵב   (Q) to be hungry, suffer famine (13)

רָעָה   evil, wickedness, calamity, disaster (354)

רָעָה   (Q) to pasture, tend (flocks), graze, shepherd, feed (167)

שִׂיחַ   (Q) to consider, meditate, complain, lament (20)

שִׂיחַ   complaint, lament (14)

שָׁבַר   (Q) to break (up), break in pieces, smash, shatter; (Ni) be smashed, broken, shattered or destroyed; (Pi) shatter, smash, break (148)

שָׁבַר   (Q) to buy grain (for food) (21)

שִׁיר   (Q) to sing (of); (Q and Polel Ptc) singer (88)

שִׁיר   song (78)

שָׁלֵם   (Q) to be complete, be finished; (Pi) complete, finish, make whole, restore, repay, requite, recompense, reward, perform (a vow); (Hi) bring to completion, consummate, make peace (116)

שָׁלֵם   (adj) whole, complete, safe (28)

שָׁנָה   year; (fp) שָׁנִים (878)

שָׁנָה   (Q) to change; (Pi) change, alter, pervert (15)

שֵׁשׁ   six; (fs) שִׁשָּׁה; (fs cstr) שֵׁשֶׁת; (mp) שִׁשִּׁים sixty (274)

שֵׁשׁ   linen (39); 33x in Exod

	Pf	Impf	WC	Impv	Coh	Juss	Inf Cstr	Inf Abs	Ptc	Total
Qal	14051	8658	11540	2896	502	1270	4598	517	6512	**50544**
Niphal	1426	964	446	118	29	105	205	37	808	**4138**
Piel	2120	1085	979	436	123	136	708	84	679	**6473**
Pual	146	78	6	0	0	1	1	1	190	**423**
Hiphil	2684	1863	1761	740	131	308	951	223	835	**9496**
Hophal	109	129	31	2	1	2	8	6	108	**396**
Hithpael	137	210	158	64	10	42	95	3	123	**84**
Pilpel	14	13	5	1	0	0	7	1	9	**50**
Polel	40	47	13	9	5	4	9	0	52	**178**
Poel	15	26	4	1	2	1	2	3	30	**84**
Hithpolel	13	48	11	11	1	5	5	0	21	**114**
Hishtaphel	19	28	82	7	5	3	18	0	11	**173**
Other	**54**	**9**	**4**	**3**	**0**	**0**	**4**	**2**	**10**	**86**
Total	**20828**	**13158**	**15040**	**4288**	**809**	**1877**	**6610**	**876**	**8385**	**72997**

VERBAL ROOTS
IN THE DERIVED STEMS
LISTED ALPHABETICALLY

In the Hebrew Old Testament, few verbs will occur in each of the seven major verbal stems. In fact, only six verbs appear in all seven major stems. Only an additional ten verbs appear in six out of the seven major stems.

I. Hebrew verbal roots occurring in all seven major stems

בָּקַע   (Q) to cleave, split, breach, break open; (Ni) be cleft, be split (open); (Pi) split, rip open (51)

Qal	16
Niphal	15
Piel	12
Pual	3
Hiphil	2
Hophal	1
Hithpael	2

גָּלָה   (Q) to uncover, reveal, disclose; (Ni) uncover (reveal) oneself, be revealed; be exposed; (Pi) uncover, reveal, disclose; (Hi) take (carry away) into exile (187)

Qal	50
Niphal	32
Piel	56
Pual	2
Hiphil	38
Hophal	7
Hithpael	2

חָלָה   (Q) to be(come) weak or tired, be(come) sick; (Ni) be exhausted, be made sick; (Pi) appease, flatter (75)

Qal	36
Niphal	10
Piel	18
Pual	1
Hiphil	4
Hophal	3
Hithpael	3

יָדַע (Q) to know, have understanding, notice, observe, be(come) acquainted with, know sexually (have intercourse with); (Ni) be(come) known, reveal oneself; (Hi) make known (something to someone), inform (956)

Qal	828
Niphal	42
Piel	3
Pual	8
Hiphil	71
Hophal	3
Hithpael	2

יָלַד (Q) to bear (children), give birth, bring forth, beget; (Ni) be born; (Pi) help at birth, serve as midwife; (Pu) be born; (Hi) beget, become the father of (499)

Qal	271
Niphal	38
Piel	10
Pual	1
Hiphil	176
Hophal	2
Hithpael	1

פָּקַד (Q) to attend, attend to, pay attention to, take care of, miss (someone), muster, number, appoint, visit; (Ni) be missed, be visited, be appointed; (Hi) appoint, entrust (304)

Qal	235
Niphal	21
Piel	1
Pual	2
Hiphil	29
Hophal	8
Hithpael	8

II. Hebrew verbal roots occurring in six of the seven major stems

אָסַף (Q) to gather (in), take in, take away, destroy; (Ni) be
gathered, assemble, be taken away (200)

Qal	104
Niphal	81
Piel	8
Pual	5
Hiphil	1
Hithpael	1

חִיל (Q) to writhe, travail, be in labor, tremble; also spelled
חוּל (48)

Qal	28
Piel	7
Pual	5
Hiphil	4
Hophal	1
Hithpael	3

חָלַק (Q) to divide, share (with), share (in), apportion,
distribute; (Pi) divide (in pieces), apportion, scatter (55)

Qal	17
Niphal	6
Piel	27
Pual	3
Hiphil	1
Hithpael	1

כָּבֵד   (Q) to be heavy, be weighty, be honored; (Ni) be
honored; (Pi) make insensitive, honor; (Hi) make heavy,
dull or insensitive, harden (heart), cause to be honored
(114)

Qal	22
Niphal	31
Piel	38
Pual	3
Hiphil	17
Hithpael	3

עָנָה   (Q) to be afflicted, be humbled, become low; (Pi) afflict,
oppress, humiliate, violate (79)

Qal	8
Niphal	4
Piel	55
Pual	4
Hiphil	2
Hithpael	6

פָּרַד   (Ni) to divide, separate (intransitive), be scattered, be
separated (26)

Qal	1
Niphal	12
Piel	1
Pual	1
Hiphil	7
Hithpael	4

קָדַשׁ   (Q) to be holy, set apart or consecrated; (Ni) show oneself
         holy (of God), be honored or treated as holy; (Pi) set
         apart, consecrate or dedicate as holy, observe as holy;
         (Hi) consecrate, dedicate or declare as holy; (Hith) show
         or keep oneself holy (171)

         Qal   11
         Niphal   11
         Piel   75
         Pual   5
         Hiphil   45
         Hithpael   24

קָלַל   (Q) to be small, be insignificant, be of little account, be
         swift; (Ni, Pi) declare cursed; (Hi) lighten, make lighter,
         treat with contempt (82)

         Qal   12
         Niphal   11
         Piel   42
         Pual   3
         Hiphil   13
         Hithpael   1

רוּם   (Q) to be high, be exalted, rise, arise; (Hi) raise, lift up,
         exalt, take away; (Hoph) be exalted; (Polel) exalt, bring
         up, extol, raise (children) (197)

         Qal   73
         Piel   25
         Pual   3
         Hiphil   91
         Hophal   3
         Hithpael   2

שָׁמֵם (Q) to be deserted, be uninhabited, be desolated, be appalled; (Ni) be made uninhabited, desolate or deserted; (Hi) cause to be deserted or desolated (92)

Qal	37
Niphal	25
Piel	4
Hiphil	17
Hophal	4
Hithpael	5

INDEX OF HEBREW WORDS

The following index contains an alphabetical listing of the Hebrew words found throughout this volume. This index does not include inflected forms listed within entries or proper nouns, which are listed alphabetically in word list 3a (pp. 138-146). Identical words are distinguished by their entry number in the first list (*Hebrew Words Arranged by Frequency*).

Basics of Biblical Hebrew Grammar

Gary D. Pratico and Miles V. Van Pelt

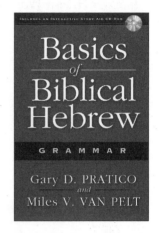

Basics of Biblical Hebrew takes the ground-breaking integrative approach of William Mounce's widely used *Basics of Biblical Greek* and applies it to learning and teaching biblical Hebrew. This book makes learning Hebrew a natural process and shows from the very beginning how understanding Hebrew helps in understanding the Old Testament.

Includes a CD-ROM featuring the full answer key to the accompanying workbook; and full-color, printable charts and diagnostics. Includes Acrobat Reader. (Windows® 95, 98, 2000, ME, NT4 and Mac® OS 8.1 or later.) With an Internet connection, you can also access additional resources including FlashWorks™, a fun and effective vocabulary-drilling program from Teknia Language Tools.

Hardcover: 0-310-23760-2

Basics of Biblical Hebrew Workbook

Gary D. Pratico and Miles V. Van Pelt

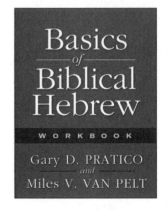

This workbook is designed for use with *Basics of Biblical Hebrew Grammar,* which presents a new, integrated method for teaching and learning Old Testament Hebrew. Field-tested in actual classroom settings, *Basics of Biblical Hebrew* combines the best of inductive and deductive approaches to make learning Hebrew a natural process and to show students from the very beginning how understanding Hebrew helps them understand the Old Testament.

Softcover: 0-310-23701-7

Basics of Biblical Hebrew
FlashCards for Palm™ OS

Introducing a study tool that will allow PDA users (Palm™, Handspring™, Sony, etc.) to quickly and easily learn biblical Hebrew words via the flash card method. The program is coordinated with and makes an excellent companion to the popular, widely used text *Basics of Biblical Hebrew Grammar* (Pratico and Van Pelt), from which vocabulary words are derived.

These fun and easy-to-use electronic learning aids offer many exciting benefits:
- PDAs have a small, convenient size compared with large stacks of traditional flash cards.
- Automatic randomization of vocabulary words avoids manual shuffling of cards.
- Backlit screens of PDAs allow for study even in the dark.
- "Quiz mode" keeps track of right and wrong guesses and repeats words until learned, automatically removing memorized words.
- "Review mode" flips cards manually or automatically at specified time intervals.
- "Quick Lex" rapidly searches for words—Hebrew to English, or English to Hebrew.
- Verb charts allow choice of verb type, stem, tense/aspect.
- Select vocabulary words by textbook chapters, frequency of appearance, or patterns (e.g., all words starting with Nun letter).
- Filter verbs, nouns, adjectives, prepositions, and others.

Textbook Use: Beginning Hebrew
ebook
ISBN 0-310-24822-1

Pick up a copy today at your favorite bookstore!

GRAND RAPIDS, MICHIGAN 49530 USA
WWW.ZONDERVAN.COM

STUDY TOOLS AS IN-DEPTH AS
THE DEMANDS OF YOUR PROFESSION

Zondervan
Bible Study Library
–Professional Edition 5.0

PACKED WITH RESOURCES
YOU'LL FIND NOWHERE ELSE.

Only the Zondervan Bible Study Library is built on today's most used, most trusted Bible translation, the *New International Version* (NIV). This is the only software that is a completely NIV-based reference system. It gives you the exact relationship of the NIV word to the Greek or Hebrew, allowing you to conduct thorough original language studies. But don't think its powerful advantages are only available to NIV users. You'll find a broad selection of Bible translations and classic study resources—all in an intuitive format that's designed to make you feel instantly at home, so you can spend your time studying God's Word, not the owner's manual.

When your professional needs require a far-reaching grasp of the Bible, turn to the *Zondervan Bible Study Library Professional Edition*. All the help and information you need and more is right here at your fingertips. Whether you're preparing a sermon, writing a term paper, or researching for a book, this powerful software takes your work as seriously as you do.

- Gain essential insights on Christian doctrines and creeds, Bible difficulties, and cults and religions.
- Conduct topical studies and obtain verse-by-verse commentary —25 volumes worth.
- Acquire an essential grasp of biblical Greek and Hebrew/Aramaic grammar and vocabulary.
- Bookmark any verse or topic to recall instantly when you need it.
- Print any verse, chapter, topic, image, or search result.

Contains:
- 9 Bible Translations
- 20 Study Resources
- 5 Dictionaries & Encyclopedias
- 8 Commentaries

- 9 Specialty Bibles
- 2 Devotionals
- 8 Biblical Languages
- 8 Bible Introduction & Creeds

CD-ROM: 0-310-23068-3

NIV-BASED.
MULTI-TRANSLATIONAL.
INTUITIVE.

Zondervan Bible Study Library —Scholar's Edition 5.0

PACKED WITH RESOURCES
YOU'LL FIND NOWHERE ELSE.

Only the Zondervan Bible Study Library is built on today's most used, most trusted Bible translation, the *New International Version* (NIV). This is the only software that is a completely NIV-based reference system. It gives you the exact relationship of the NIV word to the Greek or Hebrew, allowing you to conduct thorough original language studies. But don't think its powerful advantages are only available to NIV users. You'll find a broad selection of Bible translations and classic study resources—all in an intuitive format that's designed to make you feel instantly at home, so you can spend your time studying God's Word, not the owner's manual.

This is material you'll actually use, resources you already know, trust, and reach for consistently!

- Conduct penetrating Greek and Hebrew/ Aramaic language studies with ease.
- Search out word meanings and etymologies.
- Access archaeological and historical information and in-depth commentary faster, with a fraction of the effort.
- Obtain a seminary-level education on your computer with language and reference resources that stand up to the exacting rigors of Bible scholarship.
- Print any verse, chapter, topic, image, or search results.

Contains:
- 9 Bible Translations
- 20 Study Resources
- 8 Dictionaries & Encyclopedias
- 10 Commentaries

- 9 Specialty Bibles
- 2 Devotionals
- 17 Biblical Languages
- 10 Bible Introduction & Creeds

CD-ROM: 0-310-23054-3

The Interlinear NIV Hebrew-English Old Testament

John R. Kohlenberger III

This one-volume work includes the standard Hebrew text *Biblia Hebraica Stuttgartensia,* the NIV (North American version) as the English parallel text, a word-for-word translation for renderings of specific Hebrew words, and an introduction on how to use the Interlinear text.

Features:

- The standard Hebrew text, *Biblia Hebraica Stuttgartensia,* with all necessary variant readings and major textual conjectures in footnotes.
- The *New International Version* (North American Edition) as the English parallel text, complete with special indentation and paragraphing, section headings, and footnotes.
- A grammatically literal, word-for-word translation with English phrases reading in normal left-to-right order for renderings of specific Hebrew words.
- A complete introduction explaining translation techniques and characteristics of the Hebrew and English texts.
- A special introduction for the general reader on how to use an interlinear for word studies and learning Hebrew.

Hardcover: 0-310-40200-X

Pick up a copy today at your favorite bookstore!

ZONDERVAN™

GRAND RAPIDS, MICHIGAN 49530 USA

WWW.ZONDERVAN.COM

The Hebrew-English Concordance to the Old Testament

John R. Kohlenberger III
and James A. Swanson

The Hebrew-English Concordance to the Old Testament is the exhaustive index to the *Biblia Hebraica Stuttgartensia*, 4th edition, and the Hebrew text underlying the *New International Version* of the Bible. It replaces the venerable *Englishman's Hebrew and Chaldee Concordance of the Old Testament* by George Wigram, published over 150 years ago.

Features:
- Lists all occurrences of a given Hebrew word (even when there is no direct English equivalent) in Hebrew alphabetical order.
- Shows the interrelationship between the English and Hebrew texts, including redundant cognates and repeated Hebrew words, as well as multiple-word translations.
- Uses the Goodrick-Kohlenberger numbering system (with cross-reference to Strong's numbers), allowing for accurate identification of Hebrew words and use with *The NIV Exhaustive Concordance.*
- Keyed to Brown, Driver, and Briggs' *Hebrew and English Lexicon*, Koehler and Baumgartner's *Hebrew and Aramaic Lexicon*, and Holladay's *Concise Hebrew and Aramaic Lexicon*.
- Contains a complete NIV-to-Hebrew index.

Hardcover: 0-310-20839-4

Pick up a copy today at your favorite bookstore!

ZONDERVAN™

GRAND RAPIDS, MICHIGAN 49530 USA

WWW.ZONDERVAN.COM

A Reader's
Hebrew-English Lexicon
of the Old Testament

Terry A. Armstrong,
Douglas L. Busby, and Cyril F. Carr

Few pastors continue to read their Hebrew Old Testament after semi-nary. One reason is that it is too time-consuming, since many words have to be looked up in the dictionary. *The Reader's Hebrew-English Lexicon of the Old Testament,* complete in one volume, enables the pastor and the student to read the Hebrew Old Testament with relative ease. Listed in sequence by chapter and verse are all words that occur fewer than fifty times in the Old Testament, complete with translation (based on Brown, Driver, and Briggs' *Lexicon*) and numbers indicating how often the word occurs in the particular book and in the Old Testament as a whole. At the end of each entry is the page number in Brown, Driver, and Briggs' *Lexicon* where a discussion of the word can be found. Appendixes list all Hebrew words occurring more than fifty times in the Old Testament and all Aramaic words occurring more than ten times.

Hardcover: 0-310-36980-0

Pick up a copy today at your favorite bookstore!

GRAND RAPIDS, MICHIGAN 49530 USA

WWW.ZONDERVAN.COM

We want to hear from you. Please send your comments about this
book to us in care of zreview@zondervan.com. Thank you.

GRAND RAPIDS, MICHIGAN 49530 USA

WWW.ZONDERVAN.COM

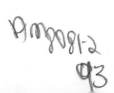